BESTSELLING
BOOK SERIES

Law For Dummies,®
2nd Edition

SO-AUP-304

Cheat Sheet

Important Organizations and Government Agencies

If you're having trouble paying your bills and want help negotiating lower monthly debt payments, contact a nonprofit credit counseling office (most of them are known as Consumer Credit Counseling Service) that is affiliated with the nonprofit National Foundation for Credit Counseling (NFCC). To find a NFCC-affiliated office near you, go to the organization's Web site at www.nfcc.org or call 1-800-388-2227.

If you've been denied credit, employment, housing, or insurance because of information in your credit record, request a free copy of your credit report from whichever national credit reporting agency reported the information that caused the denial. The three national credit reporting agencies are

✔ Equifax
Disclosure Department
P.O. Box 740241
Atlanta, GA 30374
www.equifax.com

✔ Experian
National Consumer Assistance Center
P.O. Box 2002
Allen, TX 75013-2104
www.experian.com/consumer/index.html

✔ TransUnion
Consumer Disclosure Center
P.O. Box 1000
Chester, PA 19022
800-888-4213
www.transunion.com

If a mortgage lender denies you a loan or a seller refuses to sell you a home and you believe that you're being discriminated against, file a complaint with the Department of Housing and Urban Development (HUD) by going to the department's Web site, www.hud.gov/complaints/house discrim.cfm or by calling 800-669-9777. Be sure to file your complaint within one year of the incident.

Is there an unsafe or unhealthy situation at your workplace? Bring it to the attention of your employer or contact the federal Occupational Safety and Health Administration (OSHA) at 1-800-321-6742.

When you want to apply for Social Security benefits — retirement, survivor, or disability benefits — call 800-772-1213 or go to the Web site of the Social Security Administration at www.ssa.gov.

If a telemarketer contacts you with an offer that sounds too good to be true, or if you receive such an offer via the Internet, check out the offer by contacting the National Fraud Information Center/International Internet Watch Center at 1-800-876-7060. You can file a complaint if you are a fraud victim at the Center's Web site, www.fraud.org/welset.

The Auto Safety Hotline maintained by the National Highway Traffic Safety Administration provides information about auto safety and new and used vehicle recalls. Call the hotline at 1-888-327-4236. Also, visit the Administration's Web site at www.nhtsa.gov/hotline to find out about safety recalls, to file a defect report, and much more.

For a fill-in-the-blanks living will that is legally valid in your state, contact Partnership for Caring at www.partnershipforcaring.org.

If you are a small business owner, take advantage of the Small Business Advisor Web site, www.business.gov, a collaborative effort among various federal agencies and managed by the Small Business Administration. The site provides information to help you start and grow a business and to make it easier to weave your way through the maze of federal rules and regulations.

The Federal Trade Commission (FTC) Consumer Response Center offers a wide variety of informative publications and fact sheets about the laws that the FTC administers. Read them online or order hard copies at www.ftc.gov. You can also order them by calling 1-877-382-4357.

Law For Dummies, 2nd Edition

Cheat Sheet

Free or Almost Free Sources of Legal Information

Need legal advice but don't have the means to pay for it? These resources may be of service:

- **An attorney who practices in the area of law that you need information about:** Find an attorney who will give you a free initial consultation about your legal problem (most do). Come to that meeting well prepared and you may learn all you need to know to resolve your legal problem yourself, assuming it's relatively simple and straightforward.

- **Bankrate.com:** Give yourself a financial education by spending time at www.bankrate.com. You'll find information about a wide variety of topics, including credit cards, debt consolidation, mortgage and home equity loans, and much more.

- **The Federal Citizen Information Center:** Click your mouse on www.pueblo.gsa.gov to access a wealth of information, including helpful brochures on such topics as housing, autos, money, health, employment, small business, scams, and federal government programs. While there you can also connect to more than 26 million state and local government Web sites and get your questions about a federal government program or service answered by the federal National Contact Center.

- **The Consumers Action Handbook:** Every home in America needs a copy of this publication, which provides practical information for being a smart consumer. It includes reviews of some of the most important consumer laws, suggestions for handling your own legal problems and a sample complaint letter, the addresses and phone numbers of offices to contact for help resolving consumer problems, including national consumer organizations, corporate consumer contacts, trade associations, government agencies, and dispute resolution programs. To order a copy, write to Handbook, Federal Citizen Information Center, Pueblo, CO 81009 or call 1-888-878-3256. You can also read the handbook online at www.pueblo.gsa.gov.

- **Your Federal Elected Officials:** Contact the offices of your U.S. senator and representative for help dealing with a problem you are having with a government agency or program, updates on pending legislation, and more. Hey, they are your public servants! To connect with your U.S. elected officials, call 202-225-3121 or e-mail them. For their e-mail and street addresses go to THOMAS, the Web site of the Library of Congress, www.thomas.loc.gov.

- **Business Veterans:** If you're an entrepreneur or aspiring entrepreneur, check out what SCORE (Service Corps of Retired Executives) has to offer. A national nonprofit organization that is a "resource partner" with the federal Small Business Administration, SCORE harnesses the know-how and experience of retired business owners to help you establish a business or grow an existing one. Get online advice and counseling from SCORE volunteers by going to www.score.org, or visit the SCORE office closest to you. To locate that office, go to the SCORE Web site or call 1-800-634-0245.

For Dummies: Bestselling Book Series for Beginners

Law
FOR
DUMMIES®
2ND EDITION

by John Ventura, JD

WILEY

Wiley Publishing, Inc.

Law For Dummies®, 2nd Edition

Published by
Wiley Publishing, Inc.
111 River St.
Hoboken, NJ 07030-5774
www.wiley.com

Copyright © 2005 by Wiley Publishing, Inc., Indianapolis, Indiana

Published by Wiley Publishing, Inc., Indianapolis, Indiana

Published simultaneously in Canada

For general information on our other products and services, please contact our Customer Care Department within the U.S. at 800-762-2974, outside the U.S. at 317-572-3993, or fax 317-572-4002.

For technical support, please visit www.wiley.com/techsupport.

Wiley also publishes its books in a variety of electronic formats. Some content that appears in print may not be available in electronic books.

Library of Congress Control Number is available from the publisher.

ISBN: 0-7645-5830-7

Manufactured in the United States of America

10 9 8 7 6 5 4 3

2O/RQ/QS/QV/IN

WILEY

About the Author

John Ventura is a small-business owner, best-selling author, and attorney. He is also a national authority on consumer and small business financial and legal problems.

John earned an undergraduate degree in journalism and a law degree from the University of Houston. He envisioned providing ordinary people with affordable, caring legal services, and he hoped to educate people on how to use the law to protect their rights.

He and a partner established a law firm in Texas, building it into one of the most successful consumer bankruptcy firms in the state. When the partnership ended, John established the Law Offices of John Ventura in the Rio Grande Valley of Texas where he now has three busy offices. He also has a fourth office in Corpus Christi. His firm offers legal advice and assistance in the areas of bankruptcy and personal injury. John estimates that during his 27 years as an attorney, his firm has helped more than 12,000 consumers and small-business owners.

Today, John is a frequent guest on radio programs across the country. He has been interviewed by such publications as *The Wall Street Journal, Newsweek, Inc. Magazine, Money Magazine, Kiplinger's Personal Finance Magazine, Playboy, The New York Times,* and *The Chicago Tribune*. He has also been a guest on National Public Radio, CNNfn, CNBC, and Bloomberg Television and Radio.

John writes about small business and consumer legal issues for a number of local publications in Texas. In addition, he is the author of 12 books for consumers and small-business owners.

Dedication

To my brother Frank, who is always there for me, and his wife, "Cool Janet."

Author's Acknowledgments

Thank you to Mary Reed, whose vision matches my own and whose hard work on our projects far exceeds mine. I also want to thank her for the sound of the wind chimes I often hear when we talk by phone. They remind me that life can be simple and sweet.

Also, a heartfelt thank you to the people I work with every day: my friends and associates at the Law Offices of John Ventura, P.C. They guarded my time when I needed to work on this book, and they share my pleasure in helping people resolve their legal problems.

Thank you to Tim Gallan, my project editor for this book, and Elizabeth Rea, my copy editor. I truly appreciated their invaluable questions and comments during the editing process. They helped make this book better. Finally, a special thanks to my agent, Carol Mann.

Publisher's Acknowledgments

We're proud of this book; please send us your comments through our Dummies online registration form located at www.dummies.com/register/.

Some of the people who helped bring this book to market include the following:

Acquisitions, Editorial, and Media Development

Senior Project Editor: Tim Gallan

Acquisitions Editor: Mikal Belicove

Copy Editor: Elizabeth Rea

Editorial Program Assistant: Courtney Allen

Technical Editor: Moises Salas

Editorial Manager: Christine Meloy Beck

Editorial Assistants: Hanna Scott, Melissa S. Bennett, Nadine Bell

Cover Photos: © Getty Images/Photodisc Blue

Cartoons: Rich Tennant, www.the5thwave.com

Composition Services

Project Coordinator: Adrienne Martinez

Layout and Graphics: Andrea Dahl, Barry Offringa, Jacque Roth, Heather Ryan

Proofreaders: Leeann Harney, Jessica Kramer, TECHBOOKS Production Services

Indexer: TECHBOOKS Production Services

Publishing and Editorial for Consumer Dummies

Diane Graves Steele, Vice President and Publisher, Consumer Dummies

Joyce Pepple, Acquisitions Director, Consumer Dummies

Kristin A. Cocks, Product Development Director, Consumer Dummies

Michael Spring, Vice President and Publisher, Travel

Brice Gosnell, Associate Publisher, Travel

Kelly Regan, Editorial Director, Travel

Publishing for Technology Dummies

Andy Cummings, Vice President and Publisher, Dummies Technology/General User

Composition Services

Gerry Fahey, Vice President of Production Services

Debbie Stailey, Director of Composition Services

Contents at a Glance

Table of Contents

Introduction

I've been a practicing attorney for nearly 30 years, and during that time, I've counseled many, many consumers and small business owners. Through my work, I've come to realize that most people are woefully ignorant of the laws that affect their lives, and they often pay a steep price for their ignorance.

Ignorance causes many people to be denied important loans due to credit bureau errors that they don't know how to correct. It gets some people in trouble with the IRS because they don't understand their obligations as business owners. Others have their legal rights violated by unscrupulous employers or end up in needless and expensive lawsuits because they don't understand their legal rights and obligations or their options for addressing legal problems without lawsuits. Still other consumers are taken advantage of by telemarketers, credit repair firms, and debt counseling firms that are out to make a buck off of someone else's financial troubles, or they can't get their landlords to make much-needed apartment repairs.

Therefore, eight years ago, I decided to write a book that would explain the law to everyday people in simple, straightforward language, not in legal mumbo-jumbo. I wanted to cover many of the laws that affect our lives: workplace and employment laws; laws relating to personal finances, retirement, and health care; and laws relating to families, housing, divorce, and even privacy.

I wanted my book to help readers "take the law into their own hands," so to speak. I don't mean that I wanted them to become vigilantes; rather, I wanted to provide them with reliable, easy-to-understand information about their legal rights, responsibilities, and obligations so that they could make the laws in their lives work *for* them, not against them. I wanted readers to have the information they needed to avoid legal problems and, when problems did develop, resolve them as quickly as possible with a minimum amount of cost and hassle. My book would also give readers a better understanding of when to call an attorney and how to find a good one they can afford.

The book I dreamed of is this book, *Law For Dummies*.

And now, I've written the second edition of that book — the new and improved version. I've updated all the information in the first edition to include details about the trends in our society that are changing our laws as well as information about new laws you should know about that were passed after the first edition was published. For example, I expanded the chapter on privacy because protecting our personal, medical, and financial information has become harder to do, especially because the crime of identity theft now threatens each of us every day. Also, I've updated the chapter on credit to reflect major changes that Congress has made to the federal Fair Credit Reporting Act, the law that gives you certain rights when it comes to credit reporting agencies and your credit records. I've also expanded the discussion on credit scores.

About This Book

If you're like many Americans today, you probably feel overwhelmed by the rules, regulations, and red tape that seem to govern and complicate every aspect of your daily life. Every time you turn around, another law is telling you what to do and how to do it, or what not to do and what will happen if you do! As Anatole France once said about us, "America, where thanks to Congress, there are 40 million laws to enforce 10 commandments!"

As our laws and our society have become more complicated, many of us have responded by becoming dependent on attorneys to tell us our rights and help us resolve our problems — often by filing lawsuits. In fact, we've become the most litigious country in the world! If you're a consumer, you're paying higher prices because of our nation's litigiousness. If you're a business owner, your bottom line is being hurt.

So, what can we do? I say this: Get smart. Become informed about the law. Understand how to avoid legal problems and how to resolve them yourself when you can. Knowledge is power!

But where do you get the knowledge? You probably didn't get much legal education in high school or college. I know I didn't, and neither did my kids. And most people aren't going to teach themselves about the law unless they want a sure cure for insomnia. Traditionally, the unfortunate reality has been that most of us don't get a legal education until we have a legal problem — that's an expensive way to learn, both emotionally and financially!

This new edition of *Law For Dummies* helps you become more informed about your legal rights, responsibilities, and obligations in a wide range of subject areas. It also improves your understanding of how to use laws without resorting to attorneys. Here are just a few of the legal problems that this book addresses:

- You've been denied an important loan because of incorrect information in your credit report, and you don't know how to get the erroneous information removed.

- You're thinking about working with a debt or credit counseling firm but you've heard a lot of negative things about those sorts of firms, and you don't know how to tell a good one from a rip-off.

✔ Your ex-spouse, who lives in another state, has suddenly stopped making his or her child support payments. You depend on that income to help meet your children's needs, but you don't know your rights or who can help you.

✔ Credit accounts that you don't recognize show up in your credit reports. You're afraid that you may be the victim of identity theft, but you don't know how to get your identity back and undo any damage the thief may have done to your finances.

✔ You run a small business and frequently use independent contractors to help you accomplish your work. Recently, you were talking with another business owner who told you that she's in hot water with the IRS because two workers she treated as independent contractors were actually employees according to the IRS. She's worried about how to come up with the back taxes that the agency claims she owes for the misclassified workers. Now you're concerned that you may also be misclassifying workers, and you're wondering what your options are if you end up in the same situation as your friend.

✔ Your strong-willed, elderly father is in a nursing home and doesn't want to be there. He's also refusing the medical treatment that his doctor has ordered. Is there anything you can do?

✔ Your next-door neighbor isn't maintaining his property. Not only has it become an eyesore, but also you're worried that the collecting garbage may be a danger to the children in your neighborhood. What can you do to get your neighbor to clean up his act? Can you get your local government to help, or do you need to take legal action?

Conventions Used in This Book

If you've ever seen an episode of *Law & Order,* you probably know that the law is full of all kinds of technical jargon. When explaining legal terms in this book, I use *italics* to highlight the defined words.

Sometimes I go off on a tangent and present an interesting anecdote or explain a concept that may or may not be of interest to most readers. In these instances, I place the text in *sidebars,* which are the gray boxes you'll see from time to time throughout the book.

How This Book Is Organized

Law For Dummies, 2nd Edition, starts out with the general in Part I and then moves on to cover the specifics in the remaining parts. The following sections briefly describe what you'll find in each part:

Part I: Basic Legal Stuff

The first three chapters introduce you to this country's legal system, including its philosophical underpinnings; explain the jurisdictions of the various courts in our country, from small claims to the Supreme Court; and discuss alternatives to lawsuits, specifically things you can do to resolve your own legal problems. And if an attorney's help is necessary, these early chapters provide practical information about how to find and work with a good one.

Part II: Laws That Affect Your Daily Life

This part covers a whole range of seemingly unrelated topics — everything from family law and your job to driving and privacy. The common thread among these chapters is that they discuss laws that affect some of the most important aspects of your everyday life: your family, your job, driving from here to there and back, and maintaining the privacy of your personal, medical, and financial information.

Part III: The Law and Your Money

The information in the first chapter in this part is for those of you who own your own business or aspire to someday. The next two chapters cover everyday money matters, from using credit wisely and rebuilding your financial life after serious money troubles to spotting a scam and buying a used car. The last chapter is all about buying and selling your home.

Part IV: Tough Stuff: Being Sick, Getting Older, Dying

Getting sick, growing old, and dying happen to the best of us. Yet, these facts of life can be troubling to deal with, not to mention frightening sometimes. How are we going to pay for the health care we or a loved one may need? How are we ever going to fund our retirement? What can we do to make sure that our loved ones are well cared for after we die? What resources can help us? The chapters in this part will help you understand the laws governing things like medical care, pensions, and estate planning.

Part V: Crime and Punishment

In this part, I cover two topics everyone hopes they won't have to become experts about — criminal law and juvenile law.

Part VI: The Part of Tens

Every *For Dummies* book ends with some top-ten lists, and this one is no different. In this part, I present the following topics:

- ✔ Easy ways to avoid legal problems
- ✔ Common mistakes consumers make when hiring an attorney

Icons Used in This Book

What do those funny little pictures in the margins mean? Read on.

This arrow and dartboard targets information that will help you solve problems or simply get things done in an efficient manner.

This icon flags particularly noteworthy information — stuff you shouldn't forget.

You don't have to read the information next to this nerdy guy because it relates to more technical aspects of the law. If, however, you're faced with a legal problem and want to learn as much as possible about the law involved, the technical stuff can be helpful. And if you want to impress ("bore" may be a more appropriate word) your friends and family members with your grasp of the law, the technical stuff is just what you need!

This icon flags all kinds of dangers and scams you should avoid. Heed the advice next to this icon to avoid headache, heartache, hair loss, and financial ruin.

This icon calls your attention to the location of additional information available on the Internet. For example, if you want to learn all about the many aspects of running your own business, go to Business Owners' IdeaCafé at www.businessownersideacafe.com. And if you want to download a living will that's legally valid in your state, go to www.partnershipforcaring.org.

The law can get pretty dry and boring, so occasionally this book uses real-life stories to illustrate legal problems. If you want to read about everyday people and the law, look for this icon.

Where to Go from Here

If you have a specific question about the law as it relates to a particular area of your life, just turn to the chapter that talks about that area. (Peruse the table of contents or look up the topic in the index.) For example, if you're fired from your job and you want to know your rights, refer to Chapter 6. If you and your spouse are buying a home — the single biggest financial transaction you've ever made — and you want to be sure that you do everything right, read Chapter 12. And if you're a small business owner with a home-based business and you want to avoid problems with the IRS, Chapter 9 is the one for you.

If you want, you can read the book cover to cover to gain a more comprehensive understanding of the American legal system. That way, if you encounter legal problems later in life, you'll already be aware of a law that can help you.

Part I
Basic Legal Stuff

The 5th Wave · By Rich Tennant

"I'm glad your second year in law school has you thinking like an attorney, but you've got to stop submitting a bill with your homework."

In this part . . .

It's difficult to understand the law if you don't first know how this country's legal system works. The first chapter in this section discusses the court system, civil trials, and contracts. The next chapter presents ways that you can solve basic legal problems without the help of an attorney, and I wrap up this part by helping you discern when you need an attorney and how to find the right one for you.

Chapter 1

All About Our Legal System

*W*hat do you think of when you hear the words *legal system?* If you're like many Americans, you probably think of a courtroom where lawyers, using language you can't understand, argue with one another, and where a jury of people you don't know, or a judge in a black robe behind an imposingly high desk, makes decisions about your life using laws you know little or nothing about. That's an intimidating image, but it's only a very small part of the picture! Our legal system is much more than just courtroom action.

This chapter expands your definition of what our legal system is by providing you with information you probably never got in high school — or don't remember learning, anyway. Maybe you slept through class the day these things were covered! With a more complete understanding of our legal system, you're better able to avoid getting into legal hot water, and you feel more confident about exercising your legal rights when you do.

And now for your remedial crash course on our legal system. . . .

What Are Laws and Where Do They Come From?

Our laws reflect society's standards, values, and expectations. They establish "the rules of the game" in our personal interactions and in our business dealings, helping to ensure that we're treated fairly and that we treat others fairly, too. Laws establish our responsibilities and our rights and help us both avoid problems and resolve problems.

The laws that govern our lives come from six basic sources: the U.S. Constitution, the Bill of Rights, statute law, administrative law, common law, and case law.

The Constitution

The Constitution is the granddaddy of all U.S. law, the supreme law of the land, and the standard against which all other laws are measured. It established this country as a republic and determined the structure of our Congressional system. The Constitution applies to all Americans.

The Constitution is a "living" document because our lawmakers can amend it to respond to changes in our country's needs, concerns, and values. Presently, the Constitution consists of 7 articles, 10 amendments that make up the Bill of Rights, and 17 other amendments that have been adopted over the years.

The Bill of Rights

The Bill of Rights defines the fundamental rights of all Americans. It places limits on how much control the federal government can exercise over our lives by guaranteeing certain freedoms, which include the following:

- The right to free speech
- The right to freedom of religion
- The right to freedom of the press
- The right to a speedy and public trial
- The right to bear arms
- The right to protection against unreasonable searches and seizures

State law

In addition to the U.S. Constitution, each of the 50 states has its own constitution, which provides the basis for the states' own laws. States can make their own laws as long as those laws don't conflict with federal laws and don't violate the tenets of the U.S. Constitution. In fact, state laws frequently expand or enhance federal laws. For example, the federal Fair Credit Reporting Act says that consumers have the right to receive a free copy of their credit report if they apply for credit, employment, or insurance and are denied it due to information in their report. Some states have passed their own laws related to credit bureaus; such laws specify that consumers are entitled to a free copy of their credit report every year, whether or not they're turned down for credit, insurance, or employment.

When a federal law applies to a legal problem you're faced with, check with your state attorney general's office to find out if your state has an additional law that can help you.

Statute law

Another basic kind of law is *statute* law — laws adopted by the U.S. Congress and by state and local elected officials. These laws most affect our daily lives, which is why we really should be familiar with them. They apply to such things as our credit rights, our rights when we're contacted by a debt collector, the right to leave our property to others, our rights and responsibilities as married couples or parents, the rules of the road, and so on. Many of these laws are covered in this book.

Administrative law

Administrative law is perhaps better described as rules and regulations created and enforced by regulatory agencies. For example, the Internal Revenue Service has the power to tell us what we can and can't deduct on our tax returns and can fine us when we violate its rules; the Federal Trade Commission can establish rules governing what telemarketers and debt collectors can and can't do when they contact us, and it can take legal action against businesses that ignore its rules; and the Environmental Protection Agency has the power to control the kinds and levels of emissions that businesses may release into the environment and to impose penalties and other sanctions on companies that endanger our water supply and clean air.

Common law

We can trace the origins of common law all the way back to 12th century England, when there were no legal precedents to guide the decisions of judges. These early judges used the customs of the time and their own common sense to help them decide how to resolve legal controversies. Their decisions created legal precedents that guide our judges even today.

Case law

When a judge interprets and applies the law to a particular case, he or she creates a legal precedent. That precedent is expected to guide other judges in that same court and all lower courts within the same jurisdiction when they are deciding similar cases in the future.

The FindLaw Web site at `www.findlaw.com` is a good resource for more information on all aspects of the law, including federal and state law. You can also obtain information about a wide variety of legal topics and download sample legal forms, among other things.

Civil Law versus Criminal Law

The American legal system has two major categories of law: civil and criminal law. Each has its own court systems and procedures.

The vast majority of legal problems in the United States involve civil law: consumer problems, spats between neighbors, family problems, and so on. In fact, family problems such as divorce, child custody, and child support represent the majority of civil law cases.

You can file a civil lawsuit yourself, or your attorney can do it for you. When you initiate a lawsuit, you become the *plaintiff* and whomever you sue becomes the *defendant.* You may file a civil lawsuit because you want to receive monetary compensation for a perceived wrong or because you want to force someone to do or not do something. By the way, when you try to force someone not to do something, you're seeking *injunctive relief.*

Criminal law, on the other hand, deals with crimes against society: murder, theft, assault, embezzlement, abuse, arson, and much more. You can't initiate a criminal lawsuit yourself; only a federal or state prosecutor can do that. Defendants found guilty in criminal cases face monetary penalties, public service, prison time, or even death, depending on the defendant's past criminal history, the seriousness of the crime, and the state in which the trial takes place.

Because the potential penalty in a criminal case is so much more serious than what a defendant faces in a civil case, the burden of proof in a criminal case is much higher than in a civil case. In criminal court, the prosecuting attorney must prove "beyond a reasonable doubt" that a defendant is guilty. In a civil case, however, a defendant is guilty if the "preponderance of the evidence" points to guilt.

Our Court Systems

Our court system is actually made up of many court systems — a federal system and 50 state systems. Each system has its own structures and procedures, and all systems are multi-tiered. Legal cases begin in a lower court and sometimes work their way up to a higher court. In fact, some cases initiated in a state court system ultimately end up in the federal court system.

State courts

Most legal issues are resolved in state trial courts, which are the courts at the lowest tier in a state's court system. For example, O.J. Simpson's infamous criminal and civil trials were both conducted in California trial courts. Depending on how your state court system is structured, the trial courts may be city or municipal courts, justice of the peace (or *jp*) courts, county or circuit courts, superior courts, district courts, or even regional trial courts.

Most states have two levels of trial courts: trial courts with *limited jurisdiction* and trial courts with *general jurisdiction. Jurisdiction* simply refers to the types of cases a court can hear. For example, trial courts of limited jurisdiction — which can include municipal courts, magistrate courts, county courts, and justice of the peace courts — hear some types of civil cases, juvenile cases, minor criminal cases, and cases relating to traffic violations. Most legal problems are resolved in trial courts of limited jurisdiction.

Some trial courts with limited jurisdiction also hold pretrial hearings for more serious criminal cases.

Courts of general jurisdiction include circuit courts, superior courts, district courts, or courts of common pleas, depending on your state. Courts of this jurisdiction hear lawsuits that involve greater amounts of money or more serious types of crimes than the cases heard in trial courts of limited jurisdiction.

Many states also have specialized trial courts that hear cases related to a very specific area of the law. These courts can include probate courts, family law courts, juvenile courts, and small claims courts.

On the next tier up in the typical state court system are the appellate courts. These courts don't hold trials but instead review the decisions and procedures of the trial courts in their systems and either uphold or reverse their decisions or modify the amount of a monetary reward. Sometimes appellate courts order retrials.

Lower court decisions aren't automatically appealed. You must initiate an appeal and provide a legal basis for appealing. Thinking that you "got a raw deal" is not enough.

Every state has a court of last resort, generally called the "supreme court." Although supreme court decisions are final within a state court system, sometimes they can be appealed to the U.S. Supreme Court. Like appellate courts, supreme courts review the decisions and the procedures of lower courts; they don't hold trials.

Federal courts

Most of the federal court system is divided into districts and circuits. Every state has at least one federal district, but populous states can have multiple districts. For example, Texas has a northern, western, southern, and eastern district.

Generally, federal lawsuits begin at the district level in a federal court. Most are civil, not criminal, cases involving legal issues that fall within the jurisdiction of the federal, not state, government. A lawsuit dealing with certain types of federal law is heard in a special federal court. Tax court, bankruptcy court, court of federal claims, and court of veteran appeals are all examples of special federal courts.

Each federal circuit includes more than one district and is home to a Federal Court of Appeal. This court plays a role analogous to a state appellate court.

At the very top of the federal court system is the U.S. Supreme Court. Its legal interpretations are the final word on the law in this country. The nine justices who sit on the Supreme Court are nominated by the President and approved by the U.S. Senate. They remain on the court until their death or until they resign.

Only a very small number of cases are ever heard by the U.S. Supreme Court. To get to that level, a case must usually work its way up through the lower tiers of a state court system and/or the federal system. The justices choose the cases they hear every year based on a case's implications for Americans in general or for a certain group within society, not just on the impact on the parties actually involved in the lawsuit itself. What follows are some of the more famous Supreme Court cases that meet these criteria.

- ✔ *Brown vs. The Board of Education of Topeka:* This ruling was the beginning of the end of racial segregation in America's public schools.

- ✔ *Roe vs. Wade:* This ruling gave all American women the right to decide for themselves, in consultation with their doctors, whether or not to have an abortion.

- ✔ *Miranda vs. Arizona:* This ruling gave persons who are arrested the right to be informed of their legal rights at the time of their arrest: "You have the right to remain silent. . . ."

The Constitution only allows certain kinds of cases to be heard by the federal courts. In general, these courts are limited to cases that involve the following:

- ✔ Issues of Constitutional law

- ✔ Certain issues between residents of different states

- ✔ Issues between U.S. citizens and foreigners

- ✔ Issues that involve both federal and state law

Our legal system is based on the *adversarial process,* which means that fundamental to all court procedures, regardless of the court, is the belief that all parties in a legal dispute must have an equal opportunity to state their case to a neutral jury or judge and to poke holes in what the other side says. Attorneys usually do most of the case-stating and hole-poking.

So that everyone has an equal chance to win in a lawsuit, both sides are required to play by the same set of rules. This requirement helps level the playing field, ensuring that everyone is treated fairly. Attorneys learn these rules in law school.

For a humorously irreverent but fact-filled tour of the legal system and many of the important laws that affect our lives as consumers or businesspeople, check out Inter-Law's 'Lectric Law Library at www.lectlaw.com. From this location, you can download legal software and sample legal forms, learn about court rules and state and federal laws affecting many of the topics covered in this book, refer to a legal encyclopedia and dictionary, read the transcripts of actual legal cases, and even get a few laughs at the expense of the legal establishment by reading lawyer jokes!

All about Contracts

Written and unwritten contracts are essential parts of our legal system and form the basis of many of our personal and business transactions. To protect yourself, especially when money is involved, and to avoid legal entanglements, a basic understanding of contracts is essential.

Contracts are voluntary, legally binding agreements between two or more people to do or not do something. Whether you realize it or not, you enter into contracts all the time: when you borrow money from a bank, enroll in a health club, get married or divorced, sign for a home loan, lease office equipment, buy a car, hire a roofer, sign a credit card agreement, and so on.

Legally binding contracts have certain characteristics. At the risk of losing you with too much legalese, here they are:

- ✔ All parties to a contract must be mentally capable of understanding what they're agreeing to. So if your 4-year-old son or your senile Uncle Al agrees to a contract, the contract is not legal and won't stand up in court. Although there are exceptions, all parties to a contract must be legal adults — 18 or 21 years of age depending on your state.

- ✔ The contract can't involve doing or selling anything illegal. So for example, if you sign a contract to invest in your friend's marijuana field and don't get the return on investment you were promised, you're out of luck because your contract isn't legal.

✔ You must be able to prove that a contract exists. Doing so shouldn't be difficult if you have a written contract and you've kept a copy (as you always should, for this very reason). If the contract is oral or "understood," however, proving its existence may be a challenge and may require the help of an attorney.

✔ The contract must involve an offer, an acceptance, and consideration. Here's where the legalese begins to get tough. Keep reading for an explanation.

You have an *offer* if you clearly indicate to someone else (the *offeree*) your intention to enter into a contract. Suggesting to someone that you want to talk about a transaction or negotiate something is not an offer. You have to "put an offer on the table" so that someone else can respond by accepting or rejecting it.

If your offer is accepted voluntarily, then you've got an *acceptance.*

If both you and the other party to a contract voluntarily give, exchange, perform, or promise one another something of value, then you've got *consideration.*

Here's a real-life example of the offer-acceptance-consideration process. Over dinner one night, you and a friend casually discuss the possibility of your buying your friend's sailboat, but you don't make an offer. So far, no contract. Later, after talking with your spouse, you decide to make your friend an offer, and after some back and forth negotiating, you and your friend agree on a purchase price and the terms of the purchase. You agree to buy the boat for $6,000 and to pay that amount over six months. So far, you've got an offer and an acceptance. To clinch the deal, you give your friend a check as a deposit on the cost of the boat and make arrangements to pick up the boat the following week. With that, you now have a consideration and a legally binding contract. So if the following week you go out to get the boat only to find it gone because your friend sold it to someone else for more money, or if you take the boat but after two months stop making payments on it, then each of you in your own way has broken your contract, and you have grounds for taking legal action against one another. (By the way, even though you were dealing with a friend, this transaction really needed a written contract, not an oral one.)

Although legally valid contracts are most often thought of as written, they can also be oral or "implied."

By the way, if you behave as though you have accepted an offer but you don't actually say that you accept it, then from the law's point of view, you have legally accepted it.

Written contracts

The best contract is always a written one in which all the things that have been agreed to — the *terms* of the contract — are spelled out, right there in black and white. Terms usually include the following:

✔ Who's obligated to do what and for how much

✔ Applicable deadlines

✔ Answers to questions such as "What happens if . . .?"

As important and helpful as written contracts are, they're not necessary for every single agreement or transaction you make in life. But if money is involved, or if you have a lot at stake emotionally, a written contract is essential. That's true even if you're dealing with a close friend or relative.

The story of small business owner Mike helps illustrate why written contracts are so important. Mike sold his business to his brother for $20,000 and a handshake — no contract. After all, if he couldn't trust his brother, whom could he trust? During the first couple months of their agreement, Mike's brother had some health problems that prevented him from paying Mike the monthly installments they'd agreed on. Six months came and went, and Mike still hadn't received one red cent from his brother. Then his brother sold the business and recouped his investment. Mike felt certain that finally he'd get his money. Yet two months later, he was still waiting to get paid. His brother claimed he needed every dollar he made from the sale. Mike was left with a difficult dilemma: Take his brother to court or forget about his $20,000? If he went to court, it would be his word against his brother's because they had not put the terms of the sale in writing. No matter what Mike decided to do, his relationship with his brother would never be the same.

In some states, certain kinds of contracts must be in writing to be legally enforceable. They usually involve promises to

✔ Guarantee someone else's debt. For example, you might sign a contract to help a close relative secure a bank loan.

✔ Sell real property.

✔ Buy or sell goods worth more than $500 or lease goods worth more than $1,000.

✔ Do something that can't be completed in a year.

✔ Give someone certain property after your death (which is why you write a will or set up a living trust).

Implied contracts: How can I be held to something I didn't agree to?

When you do something under an unstated expectation that you will follow your initial action with another action, you've entered into a special, legally enforceable contract called an *implied* or *understood* contract. For example, if you go to a grocery store and fill up your cart with chicken and vegetables, you've implied that you'll pay for your groceries at the cash register. In other words, you and the store have an implied contract. If you break that contract by shoplifting, the store can take legal action against you because this kind of contract is legally enforceable.

Form contracts

Fill-in-the-blanks contracts are only appropriate for very straightforward agreements; they're not a good idea if your agreement must address unusual or special situations or concerns.

Now you can e-sign on the dotted line

With 2001's passage of the federal Electronic Signatures in Global and National Commerce Act (ESGNCA), entering into legally binding contracts can be as easy as a click of a mouse on your computer screen. Rather than signing a hard copy of a contract related to the purchase of an insurance policy, a new car, your mortgage closing, or a stock purchase, for example, some Web sites allow you to click on a hyperlink or button that says "I agree" or "I accept," and voila!, you've signed a contract. However, the law also gives you the right to sign an old-fashioned paper contract with the company you're doing business with if you prefer. In addition, the law requires the use of paper contracts for certain types of contracts and legal documents, including:

- ✔ Wills and testamentary trusts
- ✔ Court orders and other court documents
- ✔ Family law-related documents, including paperwork related to divorces and adoptions
- ✔ Notices regarding the cancellation of residential utility service
- ✔ Notices regarding a repossession or foreclosure

- Eviction notices
- Notices about the recall of products that affect consumer health and safety

Your state may have its own electronic signature law or it may have adopted the federal Uniform Electronic Actions Act, which also makes electronic signatures legally binding. If your state has its own law, the ESGNCA can't preempt or override that law as long as there are no major differences between your state's law and the federal law.

The federal law also requires businesses to

- Inform you before you sign an e-contract of the kind of software and hardware you need to read and save the contracts.
- Let you know if a paper contract is available.
- Let you know what fees or penalties may apply if you don't want to use an electronic contract.
- Notify you that you can ask for a paper contract if you use an e-contract and later decide that you would prefer a paper one.

What if I want out?

The fact that a legal contract is binding on everyone who signs it provides society with an important benefit. To understand that benefit, stop and think for a moment what life would be like if contracts could be canceled willy-nilly just because someone decided that an agreement was inconvenient or because a better deal came along. Imagine the chaos! Banks could begin changing the terms of our loans whenever they wanted; we could no longer be assured that the price we were quoted for something would be what we'd actually have to pay; marital and divorce agreements "wouldn't be worth the paper they're written on." Talk about lack of trust!

Notwithstanding its binding nature, however, a contract can be broken under certain conditions, which include the following:

- You're defrauded by another party to the contract. For example, you sign a contract to buy a majority interest in a Texas oil well with promises that you'll soon be making barrels of money. You, however, are never told one critical detail — the well hasn't produced in years, and geologists don't expect it to produce anytime soon.
- One party to the contract *breaches* the contract — a fancy phrase for not living up to the terms of the agreement. If the company you hire to put a new roof on your house never completes the job, it has breached your contract.

If a contract you sign is breached, you may have the right to sue for monetary damages and/or to sue to compel the other party to meet the terms of the contract.

✔ You sign the contract because you're being threatened. For example, if you sign a contract because someone holds a gun to your head, the contract isn't legally binding.

✔ You and the other parties to the contract agree to cancel it.

Contract dos and don'ts

Here's some general information that can help you when drafting or getting ready to sign a contract.

✔ If you don't want to agree to something in a contract, before you sign it, cross out what you don't like and initial what you're deleting. If you want to add something, write it in and initial it. Although the other party to the contract may not want to go through with the deal after seeing your changes, at least you aren't agreeing to something you're not comfortable with.

Whether you're adding or deleting, be sure your changes appear on every copy of the contract before you sign it. The same goes for contract changes made by someone else. Don't trust someone who says, "Just sign here, and I'll make those changes on the other copies later" because the changes may never get made. Even so, if you sign the contract, you're obligated to meet its terms.

✔ If you don't feel comfortable negotiating a contract or even discussing its details, ask someone you trust implicitly to do it for you.

For contracts that involve a lot of money or that obligate you to do something really important, it's a good idea to hire an attorney to help with the negotiations.

✔ Don't (that means NEVER, EVER!) sign a contact without reading it completely.

✔ Don't be pressured into signing a contract. Take the time you need to think about it.

✔ Never sign a contract that you're not happy with or don't understand. If you ask for an explanation of something in a contract and the answer you get is unsatisfactory, don't be embarrassed to say, "You didn't answer my question" or "I still don't understand." Remember, after you've signed on the dotted line, it's usually too late to back out.

✔ If the contract is important and you want to minimize the potential for problems with it later, ask an attorney to review the contract before you sign it. The attorney can point out any weaknesses in the contract and suggest changes to give you more legal protection.

What to Expect If You're Involved in a Lawsuit

Most litigation stems from allegations relating to breaches of contracts. No matter whether you sue over a contract problem or you're the defendant in such a lawsuit, knowing what to expect, if nothing more, makes the process less stressful for you.

Incidentally, because most legal problems are matters of civil, not criminal, law (thank goodness), this chapter focuses on describing a civil lawsuit. If you want to know about criminal lawsuits, just flip ahead to Chapter 17.

In the beginning . . .

To initiate a lawsuit, you must file a *complaint* with the court that has jurisdiction over your particular legal problem — within a certain period of time. That period of time is called the *statute of limitation,* and it's a different length for different kinds of legal problems. If you wait until after the statute of limitation has run out, you're out of luck no matter how serious the legal problem.

You can file a complaint yourself as you would if you were using small claims court, or your attorney can file one for you. The complaint explains the reason for your lawsuit, cites the relevant law, and states what you want the court to do for you.

After a complaint is filed, the defendant in your lawsuit receives a *summons,* which is an official notification of the lawsuit. Usually, a summons is *served,* or personally delivered, by a sheriff or marshal, although it may be sent via certified or registered mail.

The plot thickens . . .

The defendant must file an *answer,* or formal response, to the charges in your complaint by a deadline specified in the complaint. If the defendant doesn't meet the deadline or ignores the complaint, your attorney files a motion for a default judgment against the defendant, which means that you win your case without any more time or expense (if the motion is not opposed).

Before filing an answer, however, the defendant's attorney may try to end the lawsuit by filing a *motion to dismiss.* If the court denies the motion, the lawsuit moves forward, and the defendant must file an *answer.* The defendant can also respond by filing a counterclaim against you. The defendant may take this action in order to pressure you into dropping your lawsuit or to get you to settle quickly knowing that dealing with one lawsuit is expensive but having to deal with a counterclaim as well can be a bank breaker.

Compromise, compromise

The court may encourage, if not require, you and the defendant to try to resolve your differences outside of court through *mediation.* Mediation is an opportunity for you to talk things over with the help of a trained mediator in an effort to identify a solution both you and the defendant can accept. (I talk more about mediation in the next chapter.)

Just the facts! Nothing but the facts!

If mediation doesn't work, your case moves into the *discovery* phase, a potentially time-consuming and expensive part of a lawsuit. In fact, when your attorney's bills from this phase start coming in, you may think back on your mediation session and regret that you hadn't been more willing to compromise! Take heart, however, because at this stage in the lawsuit you can still settle. In fact, you or the defendant can propose a settlement at any time during the lawsuit. Often, a settlement is proposed during discovery, when both sides have begun laying their cards on the table and it has become obvious to one side or the other that the cards are stacked against them. The judge may also encourage you to settle by scheduling a pretrial conference to talk things over. Ninety percent of all civil lawsuits are settled before going to trial.

Either you or the defendant can also end the lawsuit early by filing a *motion for summary judgment* before or during discovery. This action is appropriate when there's no disagreement over the facts of your case, so there's no need for witnesses to be called or evidence to be introduced. If the court grants the motion, the lawsuit is decided based on the facts of the case and relevant law.

Discovery is when the lawyers for each side in your lawsuit do much of the formal information gathering that they need in order to develop their case and prepare for trial. They may collect their information by

- ✔ **Taking depositions:** Potential witnesses are asked to answer oral or written questions under oath.

- ✔ **Filing interrogatories:** You and/or the defendant respond under oath to a set of written questions from the opposing side.

- ✔ **Filing motions to produce documents:** Each side asks the other to produce documents related to the case.

- ✔ **Filing *requests to admit:*** Each side asks the other to admit or deny certain facts about the case so that those facts won't have to be proved during the trial. Doing so saves time and money.

It's show time!

If your case has gone through the discovery phase and you still haven't reached a settlement, a trial date is set. The trial can either be a *bench trial,* heard and decided by a judge, or a *jury trial.* A bench trial is usually cheaper, but your attorney may feel that a jury is more apt to decide in your favor.

Some states prohibit jury trials for certain kinds of cases, such as divorce and probate.

Usually, to have a bench trial, both parties in a lawsuit must waive their constitutional rights to a trial by jury.

If you opt for a jury trial, the judge plays an important role in the trial by deciding questions of law, making decisions regarding what is and isn't admissible in court (evidence that an attorney can or cannot introduce for the jury's consideration), advising the jury about the law, and providing the jury with guidelines that they must use to help them arrive at a verdict.

Winning isn't everything

If you're a lawsuit novice, you may be surprised to find out that even if you win your case and you're awarded money by the court, you may never see a dime of it. No, you don't get to leave the court with a check for the amount of the judgment!

It's up to you and your attorney to make sure that you get paid. If the defendant doesn't write you a check for the full amount, you can try to negotiate an installment payment plan with the defendant. But if the defendant won't agree to the plan or can't afford to pay you anything, your attorney must ask the court to help enforce the judgment by allowing you to do one of the following:

- ✔ Garnish the defendant's wages. A percentage of the defendant's paycheck automatically goes to you. Only some states allow this form of collection.

- ✔ Seize and sell assets that the defendant owns, and apply the proceeds toward your award.

- ✔ Place a lien on an asset that the defendants owns so that it can't be sold or used as loan collateral without you being paid first.

- ✔ Levy against the defendant's bank accounts. You get access to the money in those accounts up to the amount of your award.

If your attorney feels that the defendant is trying to hide money or assets that may be used to satisfy the judgment in your favor, your attorney can ask the court to issue a subpoena requiring the defendant to appear in court to answer certain questions under oath. If the subpoena is issued and the defendant fails to show up, your attorney can ask the court to find him or her in contempt of court. If the defendant is found in contempt, he or she is fined or sent to jail.

Be careful that you don't get so carried away with collecting your judgment that when you do finally collect your money, you have little to show for your efforts after paying filing fees, attorney fees, and other legal expenses.

If justice wasn't done

If either you or the defendant are unhappy with the outcome of the lawsuit, and if there are sufficient grounds, either of you can appeal the final verdict. Grounds for appeal must be based on errors in courtroom procedure that caused the trial to be unfair to one party or the other or on questions regarding the judge's interpretation of the law. No, you can't appeal just because you don't like a trial's outcome!

You have only a limited period of time to file your appeal — as little as ten days after a judgment is entered depending on your case and the court you're dealing with.

Chapter 2

Do It Yourself: Solving Your Own Legal Problems

In This Chapter

▶ Accepting problem-solving advice

▶ Conducting dispute resolution: Mediation and arbitration

▶ Taking it to small claims court

I have some good news and some bad news. First, the bad news: There are no guarantees in life. Even if you follow my basic rules for avoiding legal entanglements, legal problems may still develop no matter how careful you are in your dealings with others.

Now the good news: You can resolve most everyday legal problems yourself. Most of them aren't complicated — at least not at their outset; most aren't the result of someone else's deliberate negligence or dishonesty; and most don't happen because someone is "out to get you."

Easy Ways to Solve Legal Problems

More often than not, everyday legal problems are the result of miscommunication and honest mistakes; therefore, whether your problem is with a neighbor, employer, business, friend, ex-spouse, or whomever, save your money, don't hire an attorney right away, and follow my legal problem-solving advice first.

Communicate

Contact the person or business you're having the problem with. If you're dealing with a small business, start with the manager or owner; if the business is medium to large, you probably need to contact a customer relations or consumer affairs representative. If you get nowhere with the first person you contact at a business, talk with his or her superior. This person may be more open to working things out or may have more decision-making authority.

Nip it in the bud

Don't delay when it comes to dealing with a problem. Procrastination usually makes it worse. Also, some laws include deadlines by which you must take a certain action in order to preserve your right to request specific information from a business or take a particular action, such as filing a lawsuit. If you miss the deadline, you're out of luck.

Offer a reasonable solution

Before you contact someone about a problem, think about how you'd like it to be resolved. If appropriate, propose a compromise solution that makes everyone a winner.

Be polite

Yelling, accusing, and using insulting language won't encourage anyone to work with you to resolve a problem. In fact, these behaviors usually do just the opposite. A non-accusatory, "I'm sure we can work things out" attitude can work wonders.

Prove it

Pull together any documents or records you have that help explain or prove your problem and that may support the resolution you're seeking. Documentation can include correspondence, contracts, warranties, repair records, receipts, bills, canceled checks, photos that illustrate the problem, and so on.

Keep a record of any unpaid time you have to take off from work to deal with your legal problem, as well as a record of other expenses related to the problem — the mental health counseling you may receive, for example. If you end up suing to resolve your legal problem and you win your lawsuit, the court may order the defendant to reimburse you for your lost wages and out-of-pocket expenses.

Keep records

Every time you communicate about the problem, whether in person or by phone, keep a record of whom you speak with and the date of your conversation, and note any promises or agreements made. If you communicate via letter, keep a copy for your files. And if you send supporting documentation with your letter, send copies, not originals. Also, if the individual or business with whom you're having a problem sends you a letter, file it away, too. Good record keeping that documents what you do to try to resolve your problem can be invaluable if you have to take legal action later.

If you take unpaid time off from work or spend any money trying to resolve your problem, include that information in your records. If you end up having to file a lawsuit and you win, the court may order the defendant to reimburse you for your lost wages and out-of-pocket expenses.

Get it down in black and white

If you're able to resolve your problem and especially if the resolution involves money, put your agreement in writing and have everyone involved sign it. You may want an attorney to review your agreement or even draft one for you. Keep a copy of the agreement for your files.

I know we're still at the let's-try-to-avoid-an-attorney stage of problem solving, but sometimes, a "better settle, or here's what will happen" letter from an attorney can signal to the other party that you mean business and can help resolve a problem quicker than if the letter comes from you.

Dispute Resolution: Burying the Hatchet

If my problem-solving advice gets you nowhere, don't despair! You still have options — dispute resolution, for example.

Dispute resolution is an increasingly popular means of settling legal disagreements outside of court. In fact, many courts now require or encourage the parties to a lawsuit to try dispute resolution before the court will schedule a trial. *Mediation* and *arbitration* are two types of dispute resolution. People most often use arbitration to settle business and contractual problems. In fact, many contracts include an arbitration clause that says that arbitration must be used to resolve contract-related problems.

Mediation: Let's talk

You can use mediation to settle just about any problem that involves civil law, including disagreements between neighbors or employer and employee, marital problems that don't involve abuse (including divorce-related property settlement negotiations), landlord-tenant problems, consumer-business disputes, and even problems between you and your children.

Mediation is all about communication. If you and the others involved in a problem agree to try mediation, during a mediation session, you all have an opportunity to explain your sides of the problem, and you're expected to listen to one another with open minds. A trained mediator, sometimes an attorney, acts as a neutral party, helping everyone stay calm and focused on the issue. The mediator doesn't decide who is right or wrong and doesn't resolve the problem — that's your job and the job of the other session participants.

If you're able to resolve your problem, formalize your agreement in writing and get it signed by everyone involved. The mediator may require you to put it in writing. The mediator may draft the agreement, or you may need to hire an attorney to do so. After it's written and signed, you've got a legally binding contract.

Mediation has many advantages. It's a lot cheaper than hiring an attorney (sometimes even free!), and it's quicker than going to court. No waiting months for a court date or spending hours, maybe days, away from work in a stuffy courtroom. The non-confrontational nature of mediation is another advantage; it's less stressful than resolving your problem in court. Most importantly, when you participate in a mediation session, you and the other participants are in control: You, not a judge or jury, decide together on a solution to your problem. If the session is successful, mediation makes everyone a winner — unlike a trial, which has clear winners and losers. And if mediation is unsuccessful, you can still hire an attorney.

Arbitration: Let's get someone else to fix things

Arbitration is a more formal method of voluntary dispute resolution. The arbitration process is similar to a trial. Participants in an arbitration session, or the attorneys who represent them, each present their side of the issue, sometimes even bringing witnesses in to testify. An arbitrator runs the session and acts much like a judge, including deciding how a problem will be resolved. Generally, the arbitrator's decision is legally binding on all participants, like it or not.

Many communities have dispute resolution centers. Contact your local or state bar association to learn about the one closest to you. Also, some Better Business Bureaus offer dispute resolution services.

The Federal Trade Commission

Perhaps no other regulatory body is as important to consumers and businesses than the Federal Trade Commission, or FTC. Originally established by Congress to help ensure a competitive marketplace for consumers and businesses, the FTC's authority has expanded over the years. Today, it has the power to enforce a wide variety of important consumer protection laws enacted by Congress as well as the trade regulations written by the FTC. Here are just a few of the legal areas that the FTC oversees.

✔ **Protecting consumers from deceptive or unsubstantiated advertising:** Among other things, FTC activities in this area focus on tobacco and alcohol advertising and advertising claims for food and over-the-counter drugs.

✔ **Enforcing a wide variety of laws that relate to consumer credit:** Examples of the laws enforced by the FTC are the Equal Credit Opportunity Act, the Fair Credit Reporting Act, the Truth in Lending Act, the Fair Debt Collection Practices Act, the Credit Repair Organizations Act, and the Identity Theft and Assumption Deterrence Act.

✔ **Regulating business marketing and warranty practices:** Among other things, the FTC takes action against fraudulent telemarketing schemes; helps enforce the provisions of the Magnuson-Moss Act, which requires that warranty information be available to consumers before they make a purchase; and enforces the Franchise and Business Opportunities Rule, which requires sellers of franchises and business opportunities to provide potential buyers certain information.

✔ **Protecting consumers from consumer frauds and market failures that impose substantial costs on consumers:** The FTC's activities in this area focus on consumer fraud in investments such as art, precious metals, and oil leases, and also certain types of lotteries.

✔ **Enforcing laws and trade regulation rules:** The FTC enforces the Mail Order Rule, the Care Labeling Rule, the Used Car Rule, the Cooling-Off Rule, and others. This book covers many of the laws and rules enforced by the FTC.

The FTC's Office of Consumer and Business Education, located in Washington, publishes a wide variety of informative materials to educate consumers and businesses about their rights and responsibilities related to the laws administered by the FTC. To get your hands on those materials, contact the Office of Consumer and Business Education; FTC, 600 Pennsylvania Avenue, NW, Washington, DC, 20580; phone 202-326-2222. You can also visit the office's Web site at www.ftc.gov. You can find the text of more than 140 consumer and business publications here.

If you have a consumer problem or complaint, inform the FTC by contacting Consumer Response Center FTC, 600 Pennsylvania Avenue, NW, Washington, DC, 20580; phone 1-877-382-4357. You can also file a complaint online at www.ftc.gov.

If you want to be placed on the FTC's mailing list for regular updates on FTC rulings and actions that may affect you, contact its Office of Public Affairs, FTC, Washington, DC, 20580; phone 202-326-2180.

For more information about the subject or for help resolving a problem using a dispute resolution professional in your area, you may want to contact one of the following:

- Association for Conflict Resolution: www.acresolution.org
- American Arbitration Association: www.adr.org
- American Bar Association: www.abanet.org/dispute

Organizations and agencies you should know about

If your legal problem involves a business, then resources like the media, non-profit groups, associations, and government agencies may be able to help you. Although none of them can solve your problem for you, they can often pressure a business into settling with you.

Better Business Bureau (BBB)

This nonprofit business organization has local offices throughout the country. Although the BBB in your area can't resolve problems for you, if you're having problems with a local business, the BBB may have a dispute resolution program that can help you and the business reach a resolution. The BBB's consumer/business dispute resolution program is one of the country's largest with 100 local BBB offices participating in it.

The media

Public exposure by the media can be embarrassing for a business and sometimes can even affect its bottom line. So, if your problem is especially poignant or dramatic, you may want to contact your local television stations and newspapers to see if they can give you some attention. You may be amazed by what a little negative publicity can accomplish!

Call for Action is a national nonprofit network of consumer hotlines that works with local media to help resolve consumer problems. To find out if there's a Call for Action hotline in your community, contact the organization at 5272 River Road, Suite 300, Bethesda, MD, 20816; phone 301-657-7490; Web site www.callforaction.org.

Industry trade associations

In the interest of maintaining a positive image for their members, some trade associations assist consumers who are having problems with one of the association's members. Their assistance may include mediation and arbitration. Use the *Encyclopedia of Trade Associations* at your local library to get the name, address, and phone number of the appropriate association to contact. Another resource is the Trade and Professionals section of the federal *Consumer Action Handbook.* You can access the information in this handbook online at `www.consumeraction.gov,` or you can order a copy by writing to Handbook, Federal Citizen Information Center, Pueblo, CO, 81009 or calling 888-878-3256. This handbook also provides contact information for businesses and car manufacturers with dispute resolution programs.

Your state attorney general's office or the consumer protection office of your local, county, or state government

These offices can explain your rights under the law and suggest additional steps you may take to resolve your problem, but they won't take legal action on your behalf. If, however, you and enough other citizens file complaints against a particular business or category of business and establish a pattern of abuse or law breaking, these offices will take action to ensure that other citizens are not victimized in the future.

State or federal regulatory agencies

The business practices and activities of many types of businesses (from banks, insurance companies, and brokers to utilities, phone companies, telemarketers, and licensed trades such as plumbers and electricians) are regulated by government regulatory agencies. You can get information from these agencies about your rights if you're having problems with a business they regulate. You can also file a formal complaint with them against a regulated business. Like state and local consumer assistance offices, these regulatory agencies don't act on behalf of a single consumer but will take legal action against a business if the volume of consumer complaints they receive about the business establishes a pattern of disregard for the law.

The People's Court

Small claims court is a do-it-yourself court where ordinary people, including businesses, can act as their own attorneys and where paperwork and legal mumbo jumbo are kept to a minimum. The court is a quick and inexpensive way to resolve relatively simple, non-criminal matters. Cases heard in small claims court commonly involve problems relating to car repair, property damage, small business issues, and landlord-tenant disputes. In the vast majority of states, a judge, not a jury, hears your case.

Contact the small claims court in your area to find out the specifics for bringing a lawsuit in that court. The court should have printed information to send to you and people with whom you can discuss your case.

Ordinarily, you can only sue for monetary damages in small claims court. If you want to sue someone to force him to do or not do something (live up to the terms of a contract, for example), then small claims court is not the court for you. Also, as its name implies, suits brought in small claims court involve relatively small amounts of money. In most states, the maximum you can sue for in small claims court is between $3,000 and $5,000. However, at the time this book was researched, the maximum in Kentucky was just $1,500, and in Delaware and Georgia you could sue for as much as $15,000.

You can reduce the amount you sue for so that it meets your state's maximum. Doing so is called "waiving the excess."

Going to trial

All the things a lawyer may do to initiate a civil lawsuit and prepare for a trial are your responsibilities when you sue in small claims court. It's up to you to file the appropriate paperwork, meet deadlines, and arrange to have each of the defendants in your case served with a notice of your lawsuit. You're also responsible for deciding

- ✔ What evidence is important to your case
- ✔ Whether or not to call witnesses
- ✔ Which witnesses may be most convincing to a judge
- ✔ How to present your evidence so that you increase your chance of winning your lawsuit

If you call witnesses, talk with them ahead of time about your lawsuit, about the defendant's position, and about what you need them to say. Doing so is perfectly legal as long as you're not asking a witness to lie. This pretrial preparation can help ensure that you don't lose your case because a witness inadvertently sabotages it.

If the defendant doesn't appear in court on the date of your trial, you will probably win your lawsuit by default; otherwise, you learn the judge's decision by mail.

A growing number of judges are announcing their decisions while the plaintiff and defendant are still in the courtroom, which gives the judge an opportunity to explain the decision.

If the court rules in your favor, the judge has the discretion to award you the full amount of money you ask for in your lawsuit or something less. The judge can also order the defendant to pay your award in a single payment or in a series of payments.

Depending on your state, if you're the plaintiff in a small claims case, you may not be able to appeal the judge's verdict. If you're the defendant and lose, you can usually appeal.

Getting your money

Winning in small claims court is only the beginning — you still have to collect your money. The court won't do it for you, and hiring an attorney to collect the money for you may not be cost-effective if the court awards you a small amount of money.

If the defendant in your case is a good loser and readily pays up, lucky you! But if your lawsuit is like most in small claims court, you have to take the initiative to collect from the defendant. Start by writing a polite letter that references the lawsuit and the judge's decision and that asks for payment. Send it certified mail. If that doesn't work, another letter may be in order. Or you may want to ask the court's permission to use another collection method, such as

- ✔ Placing a lien on the defendant's property.

    In some situations, you can execute on the judgment. When this happens, the property is seized and sold in a public distress sale, probably at below market value. Depending on the amount of any outstanding loans on the property, and depending on whether any government agency or creditors already have liens on the property, you may see little money from the sale because others get their money first.

- ✔ Levying on the defendant's bank account.

    You get whatever is in the account at the time of the levy, up to the amount of the judgment. Of course, you need to know where the defendant banks. It's likely that after you levy on the account, the defendant will change banks, so if you don't get the amount of your full judgment with the first levy, a second levy is probably not a real possibility. Bank levies also face restrictions.

- ✔ Garnishing the defendant's wages.

    If the court gives you permission to do this, the defendant's employer must take a percentage of the defendant's wages and send them to the court. The court in turn sends the money to you. The defendant's wages are garnished until the judgment has been paid. Obviously, for this collection method to succeed, you have to know where the defendant works. Some states prohibit wage garnishment.

- ✔ Levying on a business defendant's assets, including its available cash.

Representing yourself in small claims court

Here are some tips that may help your cause when you go to small claims court.

✔ Dress neatly.

✔ Be polite.

✔ Be organized. Know what you're going to say and be as specific as possible. To bolster your case, when possible, provide receipts, contracts, warranties, invoices, canceled checks, letters, and so on. When appropriate, illustrate your problem with used car parts, shoddy merchandise, and photos of damage.

✔ Be as brief as possible when presenting your case to the court, and don't get carried away! If you go on too long, introduce too many witnesses, or start acting like you think you're an attorney, you risk alienating the judge and losing your case.

✔ Be certain that before you end your presentation, the judge knows that you want to be reimbursed for your court costs if you win.

Other possible options for collecting your money include levying on stocks and bonds and motor vehicles (including boats, recreational vehicles, and planes), and any other property owned by the defendant that is not exempt from collections according to your state's property exemption law.

Using any of these collection options costs you money, some of which you can recover from the defendant — assuming you're ever able to get access to funds.

Given the potential collection problems you face when you use small claims court, before filing a lawsuit in that court, be realistic about your chances for collecting if you win and about how much of your time and money the collecting may take. If the defendant has no significant assets — land or real estate, office equipment, or bank accounts — small claims court may not be worth your time or money.

Judgments are only good for a limited number of years (usually from five to ten). If you're unable to collect your money from a defendant within the judgment period set by your state, you can renew the judgment if you do so before its expiration date. Call your small claims court to learn how. You can also renew any existing liens related to your collection efforts.

Chapter 3

Solving Legal Problems with an Attorney

*I*n today's litigious society, not using an attorney when you have a legal problem may sound like a wild, radical idea. But in fact, it's really an old-fashioned concept that has withstood the test of time!

Not so long ago, hiring an attorney was a serious step, and most people resolved their legal problems themselves with a friendly letter, a polite phone call, or a calm, face-to-face conversation. Today, these simple, no-cost/low-cost problem-solving tools seem to have gone the way of the penny postcard and payphones. As a result, "I'll see you in court!" has become an all too familiar refrain, and we've come to view legal problem solving as something only lawyers can do for us. As a result, our hard-earned money is helping many lawyers earn very comfortable livings, something you're not going to hear them complaining about!

At the same time, paradoxically, many of us fail to use attorneys when we should — when they can give us the up-front advice and guidance we need to avoid expensive legal troubles, or when they can help us resolve a problem before it gets really serious. We may not get their help because we don't know how to find a good one, because we don't want to spend the money, or even because we don't understand when an attorney's help is a good idea.

Obviously, we need to strike a balance between using attorneys too much and not using them enough. This chapter explains when you need an attorney and when you don't (and helps you save an immeasurable amount of money and hassle in the process!). For practical advice and information about how to resolve everyday legal problems yourself, see Chapter 2.

When You Need an Attorney

Let's start with when and why to hire an attorney. Get an attorney's help if

- ✔ You're faced with complicated or emotionally difficult business or personal decisions that have important financial implications for you or your loved ones. Up-front advice about your legal rights, the legal risks involved, and ways to minimize them can help you avoid costly mistakes, not to mention headaches and heartaches. An ounce of prevention is truly worth a pound of cure when it comes to lawyers and legal help.
- ✔ You've tried unsuccessfully to resolve an important legal problem yourself.
- ✔ You've been sued.

Here are some common, real-life examples of when you need an attorney:

- ✔ You're getting married for the second time and want a prenuptial agreement.
- ✔ Your spouse is battling you for custody of your kids.
- ✔ You're starting a business and want to make sure that you do what you can to protect it from potential legal pitfalls.
- ✔ You want to provide for your spouse and children after you die by writing a will or preparing and funding a living trust.
- ✔ Your business is failing, and despite your efforts to negotiate with your creditors and slash expenses, you think it's bankruptcy time.
- ✔ You paid a contractor a substantial amount of money to remodel your home, and he refuses to finish the job to your satisfaction.

Why You Need an Attorney

Attorneys don't attend law school for three grueling years for nothing. As a result of their education and training, they know a thing or two that you probably don't. Their knowledge and skills can make the difference between your being able to protect your rights and resolve your legal problems successfully and your getting your rights trampled on and losing your legal battle. Specifically, a good attorney knows how to

✔ Prepare and evaluate contracts and other legal documents so that your interests are protected and you prevail in court

✔ Resolve complicated legal problems outside of court

✔ Prepare a legal case for trial

✔ Persuasively present your case court

✔ Use legal procedures and courtroom techniques to your advantage

What to Look For in an Attorney

Now that you understand when to hire an attorney, you're probably thinking, "What should I look for in an attorney, and how do I find a good one?" The answer is this: Define your needs, establish your budget, and comparison shop — just like you would for any other important purchase. This section helps you understand what to look for when you're shopping for an attorney.

Things you should know when you hire an attorney

An attorney's help doesn't come cheap, so it pays to be aware of the following points when you hire one.

✔ Before handing over any money, be sure that you and the attorney sign a fee agreement. This binding contract spells out the work the attorney will perform and the costs involved.

✔ Unless the fee agreement says otherwise, attorneys are free to change their fee arrangement with you at any time if the scope of the work that they're doing for you changes.

✔ If you're being charged by the hour, your lawyer's clock is usually ticking every time you meet or whenever you talk by phone, even if it's just to talk about the status of your case. So know what you're going to ask before you call, and be as concise as possible.

✔ Retainers may not be refundable. For example, if you fire your attorney, you may lose the retainer. Before paying a retainer, find out whether you can get it back and under what circumstances. This information should be spelled out in the fee agreement. See the section "Talking Dollars and Cents" later in this chapter for more on retainers.

✔ You have the right to detailed, itemized, monthly invoices, if you request them. They're a good idea if you're paying your attorney on an hourly basis or if you're liable for all or a portion of the expenses that your attorney runs up related to your legal problem.

✔ If you ignore your attorney's invoice and your case is still active, your attorney can ask the court's permission to stop representing you. If your case is over, you can be sued for nonpayment.

The right qualifications and experience

Remember the old adage about "horses for courses"? The same holds true for attorneys. Not all are equally skilled and experienced, and some lawyers are better than others for certain kinds of legal problems. If your problem is relatively simple, an attorney with a general practice will probably fit the bill. This kind of attorney handles a wide variety of relatively simple legal problems, including drawing up straightforward contracts, helping collect on past due bills, and writing simple wills.

But if your problem is legally complicated or involves a very specific area of the law, you probably need a specialist. For example, if you're getting divorced or heading for a child custody battle, look for a family law attorney. If you're contemplating bankruptcy, hire a bankruptcy attorney. If your child is in legal trouble, find an attorney who specializes in juvenile law. If you've been seriously injured in an accident, you need a personal injury lawyer. You get the point.

Twenty states offer lawyers the opportunity to become certified in a specific area of the law, usually by passing a special exam. States that certify lawyers are Alabama, Arizona, California, Connecticut, Florida, Georgia, Idaho, Indiana, Louisiana, Maine, Minnesota, New Jersey, New Mexico, North Carolina, Ohio, Pennsylvania, South Carolina, Tennessee, Texas, and Utah. Also, national organizations accredit attorneys in specific practice areas. These organizations include: National Board of Trial Advocacy, National Board of Professional Liability Attorneys, National Association of Estate Planners and Councils, and National Elder Law Foundation. Although certification doesn't guarantee an attorney's skills or effectiveness, it does tell you that the attorney has a special interest in a certain area of the law and has pursued advanced education in that area.

Other important factors

You need to look for an attorney who talks to you in plain English, not in legalese; who answers your questions without acting like they're an imposition; and who returns your phone calls within a reasonable period of time. These aren't unrealistic expectations. After all, you're paying the bill!

You want an attorney who demonstrates interest in your case and who provides you with the information you need to make good decisions regarding your legal problem.

You'll feel more comfortable if you have an attorney you can trust. You may have to share highly personal and even embarrassing information about your life with this person.

Last but certainly not least, you need an attorney you can afford. This subject is covered in more detail later in this chapter.

Where to Find an Attorney

With 896,140 lawyers practicing in the United States and about two-thirds of them in private practice, the kind of lawyer I describe in "What to Look for in an Attorney" does exist. To find a good attorney, consult

- ✔ Trusted friends, family members, or business associates who have had legal problems like yours and were satisfied with the help they received.

- ✔ Your local or state bar association. They usually maintain a list of attorneys, organized by specialty. Keep in mind that just being on the list is not a bar association endorsement.

- ✔ Lawyer ads. They won't give you any information about an attorney's abilities, but they can help you identify lawyers with a specific specialty.

- ✔ Court personnel. The people who work in the courts on a daily basis know who the good lawyers are. Although officially, they're not supposed to refer you to a specific attorney, the truth is, many will do so if you ask.

- ✔ Legal Web sites. Many of these Web sites can refer you to an attorney in your area who may be able to help you with your legal problem. However, depending on the Web site, the attorney may have paid to get the referral.

If money is tight . . .

If you're unable to afford the expense of an attorney, don't despair. You may find resources in your community that you can use.

- ✔ The Legal Services Corporation is a federal organization that helps fund Legal Aid offices across the country. Presently, it funds 179 local Legal Aid programs around the country. These programs provide a limited variety of free or low-cost legal services to people who qualify on the basis of income. Although each program decides on the kinds of cases it handles, Legal Aid tends to focus on legal issues such as landlord-tenant problems, consumer issues, family issues (divorce, adoption, and so on), government benefits, and unemployment. To find a Legal Aid office near you, look in your local phone book, call your local or state bar association, or contact the Legal Services Corporation at 3333 K Street, NW, 3rd Floor, Washington, DC, 20007-3522; phone 202-295-1500; Web site www.lsc.gov.

- ✔ Some law schools run low-cost/no-cost legal clinics for consumers. Sometimes they're associated with Legal Aid. Many local bar associations also sponsor legal clinics. Low-cost/no-cost legal clinics can help with relatively simple, routine legal problems like traffic violations, uncomplicated divorces, simple wills, and more.

If you're accused of a crime and can't afford an attorney, the U.S. Constitution guarantees you the right to a lawyer who will defend you. If you request legal help, the court either appoints a public defender or a private attorney to work with you. In either case, the legal help is free.

No matter how you obtain an attorney's name, it's up to you to determine whether or not the attorney is qualified to help you.

Getting to Know You, Getting to Know All About You

To find the best lawyer for you, schedule a "get-acquainted" meeting with a couple attorneys. You may be charged a reduced fee or perhaps nothing for an initial meeting. The following are good questions to take to such a meeting. Don't hesitate to bring a pen and paper so that you can make notes about each lawyer's answers.

- ✔ How many years have you been practicing law?

- ✔ Are you board certified in any areas of the law? Which areas?

- ✔ What kind of cases do you handle most often?

- ✔ Approximately what percentage of the cases you've handled has been like mine? Of these, what percentage did you win?

- ✔ Based on the information you have, what do you see as the strengths and weaknesses of my case? How strong is it?

- ✔ How do you charge for your services? Will you put that in writing?

- ✔ How much should I be prepared to pay from start to finish if you take my case?

- ✔ Will I be consulted before you make any important decisions regarding my case? (You should be.)

- ✔ How long do you think it will take to resolve my legal problem? (If it's going to take longer than a month, ask if the attorney will provide you with a monthly written progress report.)

- ✔ Can I get an itemized bill? (You have the right to specify exactly what details you want included on your bill.)

- ✔ Who is actually going to be working on my case — you, another attorney, a paralegal? (If another attorney or a paralegal will be doing most of the work, find out about that person's experience and success rate in handling cases like yours.)

Expect straightforward answers — the preceding aren't tough questions! Don't consider an attorney who seems irritated by the questions or reluctant to answer them.

Talking Dollars and Cents

Exactly how much you have to pay for an attorney's help depends on any number of factors:

- Whether an attorney practices in an urban or rural area: Urban attorneys tend to charge more than rural lawyers.

- The size and reputation of the law firm an attorney practices with: An attorney with a big firm is apt to cost more than one with a small firm or a solo practitioner.

- The number of years an attorney has been practicing and the attorney's reputation: Experienced, well-regarded attorneys tend to cost more than ones who are relatively new to law.

How much you pay for legal help is also affected by

- The complexity of your legal problem.

- The amount of work your case will require and how much time the lawyer will have to spend in the courtroom rather than in the law library. Courtroom time is more expensive than research.

- Your relationship with the attorney. If you have an on-going business relationship with an attorney or law firm, you may be charged less than a one-time or infrequent client.

- The method used to calculate your legal fee.

- How much of the expenses associated with your case you have to pay.

On average, an attorney's hourly rate can range from about $100 per hour in a smaller community to $500 per hour or even more in a large, metropolitan area or in a very affluent community.

Most lawyers charge by the hour; however, an attorney may charge you a flat fee if your legal need is very straightforward, with a clear beginning and end. For example, you want a lawyer to draft a simple will or contract for you.

Prepaid legal plans

Prepaid legal plans are a source of legal help that many people don't know about. Some employers, unions, and credit unions offer membership in these plans as a benefit to their employees or members, but you can also find plans that individuals can join by themselves. A good idea if you have many ongoing legal needs, prepaid legal plans operate much like prepaid health organizations: In exchange for paying a monthly fee, you get legal advice or representation from one of the plan's member attorneys.

Know exactly what you are and aren't getting for your money before enrolling in a prepaid legal plan because the quality and type of lawyers and the types and costs of services offered can vary from plan to plan. All plans, however, usually entitle you to a limited number of services and/or a limited number of hours of legal assistance each month. Anything over the limit costs extra.

For additional information about prepaid legal plans, contact American Prepaid Legal Services Institute (APLSI), 321 North Clark Street, Chicago, IL 60601; phone 312-988-5751; Web site www.aplsi.org. APLSI is affiliated with the American Bar Association.

Most attorneys expect you to pay them a *retainer,* especially if your legal problem is going to take months to resolve and will cost a lot of money. A retainer is an amount of money paid to an attorney to begin work on a case. It's a down payment on the total cost of the attorney's services.

If you want to sue a business or individual to be compensated for the harm done to you as a result of violating your legal rights, an attorney may take your case *on contingency,* which means the attorney gets a percentage of the winnings (usually a third) if he or she wins your lawsuit. And if the attorney loses, you may have to pay nothing but the expenses associated with your case. Personal injury and medical malpractice lawsuits are commonly billed this way. Criminal cases are never handled on contingency, and many states forbid lawyers from taking domestic cases on a contingency basis. The legal term for the money you sue for is *damages.*

It's to your advantage if your attorney's share of the winnings is based on the net, not the gross award. If the attorney is adamant about using the gross monetary award as the basis, ask him or her to take a smaller percentage.

Some attorneys may not want to take your case on a 100-percent contingency basis and instead may want to receive some guaranteed money with the balance paid on contingency. Attorneys who charge this way should be willing to take a smaller than usual percentage of the winnings.

Some states limit the amount of expenses a client has to pay in a contingency fee case.

A lawyer's fees are rarely etched in stone. So, during a get-acquainted meeting with an attorney, don't hesitate to ask whether he or she is willing to accept something less than what's proposed. You may also be able to negotiate the amount of legal expenses you have to pay. The worst that can happen is that the attorney says "no."

Some attorneys may let you pay for their services on an installment basis, and some may let you do some of the work on your case yourself — research, phone calls, and errands, for example — in order to help minimize your legal costs.

Don't propose to help work on your case unless you're certain you have the time to help; otherwise, you could slow the progress of your case and possibly run up its costs in the end.

The Attorney-Client Relationship

Attorneys are expected to act in accordance with various codes of ethics. These codes control how they treat their clients, the quality of their work, their fees, and what they can tell others about a case. If an attorney violates an ethical standard, he can be fined, censured, or even lose his license to practice law. For example, your attorney may not share with anyone information about your case that you've shared with him or her (unless you reveal that you're going to commit a crime or fraud). That's *privileged* information, which not even a court can force your attorney to reveal.

Information that your attorney may learn from others about your case is considered *confidential,* however. With some exceptions, your lawyer may only share confidential information with others if doing so will help you. Exceptions apply if the court issues an order to share the information with it, or if confidential information causes your attorney to believe that you may be going to commit a criminal act, especially a violent one.

If you file a formal grievance against your attorney for misconduct, or if you sue your attorney for malpractice, the attorney can use both confidential and privileged information related to your case in his or her defense. The same holds true if you and your attorney become involved in a fee dispute.

It takes two to tango, and that idea applies to working with an attorney. Being a cooperative client can help resolve your legal problem more quickly, save you money, and help ensure that your attorney achieves the results you want. Here are some suggestions for how you can be a good client:

- Be honest with your attorney and forthcoming with the facts. No attorney wants to be blindsided by a client.

- Return phone calls.

- Meet any deadlines your attorney sets for you.

- Obey court orders.

- Show up for all appointments related to your case.

- Let your attorney know about any changes that may affect your case.

- Follow your attorney's advice regarding who and who not to talk with regarding your case.

- Be open to your attorney's suggestions for ways to settle your legal problem short of going to trial.

- Be on time with your payments.

Legal-related expenses you may have to pay

Although every legal case is different and may involve different legal expenses, here are some of the more common expenses:

- Photocopying

- Long-distance calls

- Postage

- Overnight delivery and courier services

- Court fees

- Facsimiles

- Travel

- Court reporter and process server fees

Some attorneys mark up expenses, which means you're billed for more than the actual amount of an expense. Ask the attorneys you talk to if this is their policy. If it is, view it as negotiable.

If You're Unhappy with Your Attorney

Your attorney works for you. So if you have a question about an invoice or about something your attorney does or doesn't do, or if you're not satisfied with the quality of your attorney's work, don't stay silent and stew. Ask for an explanation and express your concerns. You can even fire your attorney and hire a new one. What follows are some common client-attorney problems and how to deal with them.

You get what you think is an excessive invoice

Ask for an explanation and for an adjustment if necessary. If you're unhappy with the explanation, or if your attorney refuses to adjust the bill, contact your local or state bar association to find out what you can do. Arbitration or mediation may be a possibility.

You're unhappy with the quality of your attorney's work

Talk with your attorney about your concerns. If you don't get a satisfactory explanation, or if things don't improve, you can fire the attorney. Fire an attorney in writing, and when you do, request that your case file be returned to you. Be prepared to lose any retainer you may have already paid. Also, you may have to pay the attorney for work already performed before you can get him to hand over your case file.

Don't discuss the details of your case with your new attorney or ask him or her to do anything for you until you've fired your old one. Working on a case while another attorney is still officially handling it is a violation of an attorney's code of ethics.

If you feel that your attorney failed to do what was promised or failed to act in a professionally responsible manner, file a formal complaint against the attorney. Every jurisdiction has its own set of ethical standards for lawyers and a disciplinary review process for those accused of violating them. Call your state's bar association to learn about the complaint process in your state. Suing your attorney for malpractice may be another option depending on the circumstances.

Why Didn't I Think of That First?

After you understand when you should hire an attorney, how to find one, and what to expect when you work with one, it's time to discover what you can do to avoid attorneys. Although it should be clear to you by now that there are times when an attorney's help is advisable if not downright essential, in truth, most legal problems can be prevented, and when they do develop, most can be resolved without an attorney's help. Some simple rules of thumb are:

- Know the laws that affect your life and understand your legal rights. Reading this book is a great first step to following this rule.

- Approach your business and personal transactions with a spirit of fairness and honesty. That means "Do unto others as you would have them do to you." It may be trite, but living by this Golden Rule can help keep you out of legal hot water.

- Bring a healthy dose of skepticism to any opportunities you may be offered, especially if they involve money. If something sounds too good to be true, it probably is!

- Get things down in black and white before you pay any money or agree to pay any money. I'm talking contracts (which are discussed in Chapter 1).

- Thoroughly read any contract you're asked to sign, and get all your questions answered before signing.

For more info on solving everyday legal problems without an attorney, see Chapter 2.

Can't I Act as My Own Attorney?

Sure you can; no law says that you can't. But if you're in the middle of a legal crisis — you've been sued; you're in jeopardy of losing your business; you're in a messy divorce — then acting as your own attorney is not a good idea, especially if the other party has one. You're immediately at a serious disadvantage: You don't know the nuances of the laws involved; you don't know how to make the law work for you; and you aren't familiar with legal processes and procedures and how to use them to your advantage. Are you convinced yet?

Bottom line: If you want a fair shot at resolving a legal problem, and especially if the other side has an attorney, get a lawyer. In the end, hiring one can be a lot cheaper than the consequences of not hiring one.

Part II
Laws That Affect Your Daily Life

The 5th Wave   By Rich Tennant

What's the chance of settling this without getting attorneys involved?

HARVARD LAW SCHOOL ALUMNI PICNIC

ANTS, GNATS AND BEES

In this part . . .

This part covers several different but important legal topics. I start out with a couple of chapters on family law, which address issues related to both heterosexual and same-sex families. I then discuss legal issues that relate to being on the job and driving a car. This part rounds out with a new chapter about privacy and the law and how to protect yourself in today's high-tech world.

Chapter 4

Relationships, Marriage, and Divorce

*I*n this day and age, we can no longer even pretend that families on TV shows such as *Leave it to Beaver* and *The Brady Bunch* represent the American norm. Many couples live together without being married; gay and lesbian couples are increasingly open about their relationships and have begun to demand the same legal rights as straight married couples. Some same-sex couples have formalized their relationships in civil unions or domestic partnerships or even by getting legally married where such unions are legal, while others have flouted the law and gotten married in civil ceremonies. According to the 2000 U.S. Census, unmarried couples — heterosexual and same-sex — now represent 11 million households, an increase of more than 72 percent since 1990!

Although family law — the kind of law that deals with marriage, divorce, and parent-children relationships — is still largely based on a traditional definition of family, the societal changes we're experiencing are forcing our legal system at all levels to rethink its assumptions about the rights and obligations that come with certain personal relationships. For example, our legal system has to answer hard questions about what's fair when it comes to divorce, whether unmarried heterosexual couples should have the same rights and responsibilities as married couples, and what rights and responsibilities gay and lesbian couples should be given. Should they be allowed to enter into domestic partnerships or civil unions? Should they be allowed to marry just like heterosexual couples? Because of these and many other issues, family law is in great flux.

As many of us know from personal experience, you can never guarantee that close personal relationships will be trouble free, or that, if there's trouble in paradise, the people involved will be able to resolve their differences with a minimum amount of angst and damage to their pocket books. If, however, you understand how family law affects your legal rights and responsibilities before you get married, file for divorce, start a family, take a live-in lover, and so on, you'll have a greater appreciation for the legal implications of what you're about to do. You'll also have a better understanding of the steps you can take to minimize the potential for legal and financial problems down the road.

Love No Longer Equals Marriage

Remember the popular old song about how love and marriage go together like a horse and carriage? That pretty picture isn't necessarily true anymore. Although couples who are in love and who want to be together are still most likely to get formally married, many opt just to live together. Others become informally married in states where common law marriages are legally recognized. (For more on common law marriages, see the sidebar "We're married because we say we are," later in this chapter.)

How you structure your relationship affects your legal and financial obligations both while you're together and (heaven forbid) after you split up. Given that marriage is a time-honored tradition that the law continues to view as a relationship to be promoted and supported, the rights and responsibilities that married couples have to one another during and after marriage are very well defined. The law is much less clear when it comes to other kinds of live-in relationships; therefore, when you're madly in love with someone and are certain that you'll live "happily ever after," it's important that you understand the implications of getting married versus just living together. Unfortunately, many of us don't gain a true appreciation for the legal pros and cons of each option until our relationships fall apart.

Living Together

Although some changes are being made, in most states, if you live in an unmarried relationship with someone, neither of you has any automatic legal rights or responsibilities to the other while you're together or after you split up.

You and your partner can, however, voluntarily give yourselves rights and responsibilities, including many of the ones that automatically come with marriage, in a legally binding *cohabitation agreement*. Get an attorney's help in drafting such an agreement if you want to be sure that it's legally binding. A lawyer's help is particularly important if your agreement involves a significant amount of money or property, such as a home.

Same sex relationships

The legal status of same sex couples is in a state of almost constant change, both nationally and within individual states. Questions about how to define marriage and whether the relationship between committed same sex couples should be legally recognized and if so, what rights and responsibilities should go hand in hand with that status will probably be hot button issues for the foreseeable future. Presently, when it comes to formalizing the legal relationship between same sex couples, states represent a patchwork quilt of laws and constitutional amendments. What follows are some of the laws, constitutional amendments, legislative initiatives, and court rulings that are in place as of this book's revision.

✔ The federal Defense of Marriage Act was adopted in 1996. The law defines marriage as being between a man and a woman and declares that one state doesn't have to recognize a same sex marriage performed in another state.

✔ To date, efforts by some members of Congress to prohibit same sex marriages by amending the U.S. Constitution have been defeated. However, some members want to introduce an amendment to the U.S. Constitution prohibiting same sex marriages.

✔ Twenty-three states have laws banning same sex marriage, thirteen states have laws as well as constitutional amendments outlawing same sex marriages, and three states have constitutional amendments only banning such marriages. Only four states — New Mexico, New York, Wisconsin, and Wyoming — have not banned same sex

marriages through either a constitutional amendment or legislation. It's anticipated that constitutional amendments outlawing same sex marriages may be introduced in as many as 20 additional states in the next couple of years.

✔ Massachusetts is the only state that legally recognizes same sex marriages, while Vermont recognizes civil unions for gays and lesbians. Couples who enter into a civil union in that state are entitled to the same state-granted rights and benefit as heterosexual couples in Vermont.

✔ California, Delaware, Maine, New Jersey, and Hawaii as well as the District of Columbia allow same sex partners to enter in *domestic partnerships,* a legal arrangement that gives partners some but not all of the rights of a civil union. Although the particular rights that couples in these states get by legally formalizing their relationships one way or another short of marriage varies from state to state, at a minimum, the rights usually include the right to apply for some state-offered benefits.

✔ About 40 states have "defense of marriage" laws on their books.

✔ A judge in Washington State has ruled that prohibiting same sex couples from marrying would violate their rights.

✔ The California Supreme Court has declared null and void the 4,000 same sex marriages conducted in San Francisco between February 11 and March 11, 2004.

Here are some of the topics your cohabitation agreement should cover:

- ✔ How you will own any property you acquire during your relationship. For example, you may agree that when you purchase a home, you will own it jointly with right of survivorship. That way, when one of you dies, the other one automatically owns the property.

- ✔ Whether either of you has any legal right to the assets you bring into the relationship.

- ✔ How you want to deal with any money or other assets one of you may inherit during your relationship.

- ✔ How you will divide your property if you decide to end your relationship. Although you'll probably agree that each of you will exit the relationship with the individual property you brought into it, you should spell out how you'll divide the property you acquired together.

- ✔ What happens to your individual property if and when one of you dies. It's important to address this issue because unmarried partners don't have an automatic right to the other's assets when one partner dies. Clearly spell out your individual intentions in the agreement, but also prepare individual estate plans. At a minimum, each plan should include a legally binding will as well as a living will and durable powers of attorney for health and finances. You may also want to include a living trust in your estate plan.

Some states don't enforce cohabitation agreements, but most do.

Cohabitation agreements are particularly good ideas for gay and lesbian couples who consider themselves married and who want to provide themselves with some of the same rights and obligations that heterosexual couples automatically get through marriage.

Although formalizing your relationship in a cohabitation agreement can help eliminate some of the important drawbacks to living together, legally, in most states, your relationship still has some important drawbacks or limitations that you should know about. For example:

- ✔ You may not be able to add your partner to your health insurance plan.

- ✔ You aren't entitled to visit your partner in intensive care.

- ✔ You don't have automatic rights to inherit from your partner.

- ✔ You aren't entitled to receive alimony.

- ✔ You can't take advantage of employment-related family leave benefits.

- ✔ You can't file joint tax returns.

✔ You don't have the right to use laws related to divorce, child custody, child support, alimony, and so on.

✔ You have no right to spouse-related Social Security and Medicare benefits.

✔ You can't claim one another as an exemption on your federal taxes.

Presently, some states as well as many local governments and employers offer domestic partnership benefits to same sex couples as well as unmarried heterosexual couples. At a minimum, the benefits usually mean that one partner can put the other on his or her health insurance policy.

To address some of the drawbacks and limitations of simply living together, gay and straight couples should consider taking some additional steps to provide their partners with some of the other rights and benefits associated with heterosexual married couples.

✔ Make your bank accounts and other important property *joint property.* The classification makes you both equal owners.

✔ Make your partner the beneficiary of your life insurance policy, employee benefit plan, retirement account, and so on.

✔ Remember your partner in your will, or make your partner the beneficiary of a living trust.

✔ Give your partner a durable power of attorney for finances so that he or she can make business and financial decisions and transactions on your behalf should you become mentally or physically incapacitated. (This kind of durable power of attorney is covered in Chapter 15.)

✔ Give your partner a durable power of attorney for health care. This document helps ensure that if you become critically ill and can't make medical decisions for yourself, your partner can make them for you. You can also give your partner the right to push to get your living will enforced. A living will is a legal document that spells out the kinds of medical care and treatment you do and do not want when you're close to death and have no hope of recovery. (For more on this topic, see Chapter 16.)

Owning key assets as *joint owners with the right of survivorship* legally guarantees that when one partner dies, the other assumes 100 percent control of the property, and the assets don't have to go through probate.

If you have children with a live-in partner, both of you may not automatically assume the legal obligations and rights of parents. Parental responsibility in these types of situations depends on your state's laws and the specifics of your relationship. See Chapter 5 for information on parental responsibility.

We're married because we say we are

Some states allow heterosexual couples to enter into informal marriages simply by living together and acting as if they're married. This arrangement is called a *common law marriage*. These couples are legally married with all the same rights and responsibilities as couples who are formally married by a judge, minister, priest, rabbi, and so on. In fact, to end a common law marriage, you have to get legally divorced, just like any other married couple.

If you have a common law marriage and move to a state that doesn't allow common law marriages, your new state will recognize your marriage as legal.

The following states, plus the District of Columbia, recognize common law marriages:

- Alabama
- Colorado
- Georgia (assuming the common law marriage was created prior to January 1, 1997)

- Idaho (assuming the common law marriage was created prior to January 1, 1996)
- Iowa
- Kansas
- Montana
- New Hampshire (recognized for inheritance purposes only)
- Ohio (assuming the common law marriage was created prior to October 10, 1991)
- Oklahoma
- Pennsylvania
- Rhode Island
- South Carolina
- Texas
- Utah

Getting Married

If you're like most married couples, you tied the knot in a formal civil or religious ceremony and were married by a justice of the peace, a judge, a minister, a priest, or a rabbi — someone legally authorized to perform the ceremony. When you recited your marriage vows, you probably promised to love, honor, and cherish one another — the romantic side of marriage. But when you married, you also entered into a legally binding contract with your spouse. The contract gives both of you legal obligations and rights that are defined, recognized, regulated, and enforced by your state. For example, your marriage contract obligates each of you to support the other, although the law leaves it up to you to decide how you will provide that support. Both you and your spouse can work outside the home, or your marriage can be more traditional with one spouse earning the income and the other caring for your home and any children you may have.

Unless you both signed a prenuptial agreement to the contrary, you also agreed to share the property you acquire and the income you earn while you're together, as well as many of your debts. Exactly how you share depends on the property laws of your state, and usually, this issue isn't a concern unless you decide to get divorced. I get into property law and divorce later in this chapter.

When your spouse dies, marriage also entitles you to a share of the deceased's estate, regardless of whether or not your spouse prepared an estate plan. (The share you receive depends on the laws of your state.) Among other things, marriage also gives you the right to file joint tax returns and the right to visit your spouse in intensive care.

Getting a marriage license

Before you can become legally married in a formal ceremony, you have to apply to your state for a marriage license; you can usually do this at your county courthouse. To get the license, you have to meet certain basic requirements. Although they vary somewhat from state to state, here are the most typical requirements:

- ✔ **Age matters.** You can't marry unless you're at least 18 years old or unless you have the permission of your parents or guardian.

- ✔ **Health counts.** You may have to prove that both you and your spouse-to-be have been vaccinated for certain diseases or that you've each had a recent physical exam, and in a few states, you have to get a blood test for measles, certain genetic diseases, or venereal disease. If either you or your partner tests positive for a venereal disease, your state may not issue you a marriage license, or it may only do so if both of you are aware of the test results. If you test positive for measles or a genetic disease, you'll be issued a marriage license, but your future spouse will be informed of the results because they could affect whether or not you're able to begin a family together. When you receive your license, you may also be given printed information about HIV and AIDS.

- ✔ **No close relatives.** You can't marry your parent, grandparent, sibling, aunt, or uncle. Some states also prohibit marriages between stepparents and stepchildren, and you may not be able to marry a first cousin either.

- ✔ **Only one spouse at a time.** If you're already married, you can't get married again, even if your religion recognizes multiple marriages. In fact, bigamy is a crime in most states.

- ✔ **Understand the significance of marriage.** Your state won't grant you a marriage license if the state has reason to believe that you can't or don't understand the significance of marriage due to mental illness, mental incapacitation, or drug or alcohol abuse.

Most marriage licenses are valid only for a few months at most. So if you wait too long to tie the knot, you may have to obtain another license.

Opting for a prenuptial agreement

Some couples negotiate prenuptial agreements before they get married. In these agreements, couples establish their own rules for their marriage and possible divorce. Some couples view this preparation as better than leaving it up to a third party, such as a judge, to determine who gets what if the marriage ends. Usually, prenuptial agreements relate to money and other property.

Couples most often use prenuptial agreements when one spouse-to-be owns significantly more property than the other or has the ability to make significantly more income during the marriage. More and more business owners also are using prenuptials as a way to help protect their businesses from the repercussions of a possible divorce. Frequently, couples with prenuptial agreements have been married before, understand that marriage doesn't always mean living happily ever after, and want to avoid another expensive, protracted, and messy fight over property if divorce happens again.

Although the concept of a prenuptial agreement certainly has its practical merits, broaching the subject with your intended can be awkward. After all, who wants to talk about finances and legal agreements and the possibility of divorce when you're madly in love and everything is hearts and roses. Talk about putting a damper on your romance! Given that an estimated 50 percent of all American marriages end in divorce, and considering the emotional, not to mention financial, toll a divorce can take on everyone involved, spelling out the terms of your divorce before your marriage falls apart is really not a bad idea!

You can't negotiate child support and custody in a prenuptial agreement.

If you decide to prepare a prenuptial agreement, get an attorney's help so that you can be assured that the agreement is legally enforceable in your state. Each of you should have your own attorneys who can look out for your best interests and make certain that what you're agreeing to is fair to you. In fact, some states *require* separate attorneys. To save on costs, you and your future spouse may want to work out the general details before you meet with your attorneys.

States have different requirements for what makes a prenuptial agreement legally enforceable. Here are the more common ones:

- ✔ Both of you must participate in preparing the agreement, and you both must sign it.
- ✔ Both of you must fully disclose your assets and liabilities to the other, including anything you know that you will be inheriting or any significant

gifts you know you will be receiving in the future. Sharing this information ensures that each of you knows before signing the agreement what you're giving up and what you're getting.

✔ The agreement must be fair to both of you at the time it's negotiated.

✔ Both of you must be entering into the agreement because you want to, not because you're feeling coerced. Also, there can be no fraud involved.

A prenuptial agreement doesn't have to last forever. If things change in your lives and you and your spouse decide you want to amend the agreement or even void it, you can. But be sure to do it in writing and get the changes or the revocation witnessed and notarized.

Playing the name game

It used to be assumed that a woman took her husband's name when she married. Things are different now, and if you're a woman, it's perfectly acceptable to keep your own name, take your husband's, or combine the two. In fact, the law allows women — and men — to use any name they want.

If you choose to change your name, notify the Social Security Administration so that your Social Security number is transferred to your new name and you don't jeopardize your benefits. Also, get a new driver's license, tell your creditors about your name change so that you don't have problems with your credit record, and change your name on important documents such as bank accounts; brokerage accounts; estate planning documents such as your will, living trust agreement, living will, and durable power of attorney; and your passport. You may have to provide some agencies and offices with a certified copy of your marriage certificate in order to change your name. You should receive the certificate in the mail within a few weeks of your marriage.

Breaking Up Can Be Hard to Do

If it's become obvious that you're not going to live happily ever after, you have three ways to end your relationship:

✔ **Annulment:** An annulment makes it as though your marriage never happened. Usually (though not always), annulments occur relatively soon after a marriage.

✔ **Separation:** Living apart is usually an interim measure before a divorce, but some couples get a legal separation rather than a divorce.

✔ **Divorce:** Divorce legally ends your marriage and leaves both people free to remarry.

Pretend it didn't happen: Annulment

A legal *annulment* is a court action that voids a marriage and frees both partners to remarry. Annulments can involve agreements about spousal support as well as child custody and support.

In the not-so-distant past, when divorces were more difficult to obtain than they are now, annulments were much more commonplace. Now, they're most often sought by couples whose religion prevents them from divorcing.

A legal annulment is not the same as a religious annulment. If your church annuls your marriage, you're still legally married.

To get an annulment, you have to tell the court why you want one. Your reasons are your *grounds* for the annulment. Although the grounds for an annulment vary by state, they usually include fraud (your spouse lied to you prior to your marriage, and if you had known the truth, you would not have married that person), mental illness, forced consent or duress, failure to consummate the marriage, lack of consent to underage marriage, and bigamy.

Depending on the reason for annulment, if you have children from your relationship, they will be considered legitimate, and the court may award custody, order child support, and may order spousal support, too.

If you've been married for a "long time," you'll find it difficult to get an annulment. The definition of a "long time" can range from a couple of months to a couple of years, depending on your state.

Take some time apart: Separation

If your marriage is in trouble but you want to try to work things out, you may decide to give yourself and your partner some breathing room by separating. Maybe you think that being apart will help each of you assess your relationship and work on the problems that are contributing to your marital difficulties. Sometimes, distance does make the heart grow fonder.

Separating can also be a deliberate prelude to a divorce. You and your partner may be unable to get along with one another, and it may be clear that your marriage is over. Or your partner may simply leave without consulting you or despite your objections. Such action can instigate a divorce.

While you're separated, you're still married, and therefore, you still have all the legal rights and responsibilities that accompany marriage. Usually, separating is a private matter between you and your spouse, so ordinarily the court doesn't get involved. Some states, however, recognize *judicial separations* that do involve the court. This sort of thing is another option for couples whose religion prevents them from getting divorced. In a judicial separation, the court approves or decides the terms of a couple's separation, almost as if they were getting a divorce.

Some people separate with no intention of divorcing so that one spouse can remain covered by the other's health insurance policy.

If your marriage involves minor children, or if one spouse depends on the financial support of the other, and even if your separation is amicable, it's best to formalize your separation with a legal agreement that spells out how you're going to share responsibility for your children, details the separation's financial terms, and sets out other important duties that each of you may have to the other. That way, if either spouse fails to live up to the agreement and legal action becomes necessary, you have a written contract that provides tangible evidence of what was agreed to. If you and your spouse draft the agreement yourselves, each of you should hire your own attorney to review it for fairness and thoroughness and to spot any potential legal problems. Get the agreement witnessed and notarized to be extra sure that it stands up in court.

If you're the family's primary breadwinner and you and your spouse have children together, not having a written separation agreement can put you at risk for being accused of abandonment after your divorce proceedings begin. Such an accusation not only can affect the outcome of your divorce settlement but also can affect your custodial rights to your children. It even can result in a court awarding your spouse retroactive child support for the period of your separation, plus interest.

Call it quits: Divorce

Not all that long ago, society frowned on divorce and actively discouraged it by making getting divorced a difficult and expensive legal process. Couples were expected to stay together, for better or worse, and to divorce only if things became absolutely intolerable. Furthermore, state laws required that the spouse who filed for divorce had to provide grounds for the divorce by accusing the other of adultery, desertion, mental cruelty, abuse, or other such failings. If the other spouse contested the divorce, the spouse who filed had to prove the grounds, and sometimes, the other spouse would counter-file and make his or her own allegations. Divorce could get really messy — and expensive, too.

Society's attitudes toward divorce started shifting in the 1960s. People began to recognize that sometimes marriages just didn't work out and that the mud-slinging and emotional upheaval associated with fault divorces wasn't good for anyone except lawyers. So, a growing number of states began recognizing *no-fault divorces.* To get a no-fault divorce, all a spouse usually has to do is claim irreconcilable differences, irretrievable breakdown, or separation. Today, 30 states allow fault divorces, 40 states permit no-fault divorces, and 15 states allow only no-fault divorces.

In some states, if you file a fault divorce and your spouse doesn't want the divorce to proceed, your spouse can try to prove to the court that he or she did not do whatever it is that you allege in your divorce petition. However, most judges don't stop a divorce from moving forward simply because one spouse doesn't want the marriage to end.

Understanding the divorce process

When you file for divorce, you actually initiate a civil lawsuit against your spouse. To settle the lawsuit, you have to come to an agreement that addresses the basic issues in a divorce: how to divide up your marital property, whether either of you gets spousal support (for how long and how much), and if you have minor children from your marriage, how to deal with their custody and support. Before your divorce is final and your agreement legally binding on both of you, the court must approve the agreement.

Like most lawsuits, your divorce may never go to trial. But if you, your spouse, and your attorneys are unable to negotiate all aspects of your divorce agreement outside of court, a trial is scheduled, and the judge decides things for you.

Is an attorney necessary?

If your divorce is of the no-fault variety and you and your spouse are comfort-able working out its terms together, you probably don't need much legal help. But both of you should hire attorneys before you begin working out the details of your divorce so that each of you has a clear understanding of your individual rights and obligations, is aware of anything you should do or shouldn't do before divorcing, and understands any special issues you may need to con-sider. For example, if all your credit is in your spouse's name, you'll probably have trouble borrowing money or getting a credit card in your own name after you're divorced. So, if possible, you may want to delay your divorce until you've had time to build credit in your own name. Also, your attorneys may be able to suggest ways to divide up your marital property and debts that you may not otherwise think of. For example, you may decide to use mediation to help you work out the terms of your divorce.

Your attorneys should review the divorce agreement you create before it's final to make certain that you haven't inadvertently created potential prob-lems for either spouse and so that each of you can be assured that it's fair.

There are times when getting legal help with your divorce is absolutely essential, particularly if you and your spouse are too estranged to work together; if your marital property is substantial or especially complex (so that dividing it up may be problematic); or if taxes are an issue. If your divorce negotiations also involve decisions about spousal support and/or child custody and support, legal help is always a good idea.

If you have a hard time asserting yourself with your spouse, or if you feel especially guilty about the divorce, getting an attorney's help can ensure that you're not shortchanged in your settlement.

Who gets what?

Unless you've signed a prenuptial agreement and waived your property rights, your state's property laws entitle both spouses to a share of any marital property. Most states are *separate property* states, but nine are *community property* states: Arizona, California, Idaho, Louisiana, Nevada, New Mexico, Texas, Washington, and Wisconsin.

Separate property states

Separate property states use the concept of *equitable distribution* — that is, what is fair — to decide how a couple's property and debt are divided up when they divorce. "What's fair" is determined on a case-by-case basis according to specific criteria your state has already established. Fairness can mean that you and your spouse split the value of your property and debt 50/50, 75/25, 90/10, or whatever. Examples of the typical criteria that a separate property state uses to determine an equitable split include the following:

- How much each of you earns and could earn in the future
- Your current standard of living as a couple
- How much separate property each of you owns
- The value of your marital property
- The contribution each of you has made to your marriage (Homemaking is considered a job and therefore is taken into account.)
- The employee benefits either of you are entitled to
- The length of your marriage
- Your age and health
- Whether or not there are minor children involved and who will have custody of them
- The degree to which each of you contributed to the end of your marriage (This is a factor in only some states.)

Both community and separate property laws say that if you receive an inheritance or gift while you're married, it's yours alone and is not treated as marital property when you divorce. Also, both kinds of laws view property that you bring to your marriage as yours alone, unless you later commingle it with marital property.

Community property states

If you live in a community property state, the property that you acquire during your marriage and the income you earn belong to *both* of you. It generally doesn't matter whether only one spouse paid for something or whether you earned more than your spouse. You're each joint owners of your property — and your debts, too.

The philosophy behind community property law is that it takes two to make a marriage and that as a team, one way or another, you both helped create the wealth that you built during your marriage as well as any debts you may have racked up. Divorcing spouses in community property states are usually expected to divide up equally both their marital property and the debt from their marriage; however, judges in community property states do have latitude to order other arrangements.

Obviously, property settlement negotiations in separate property states can be much more complicated than in community property states.

Who gets the house?

It's not a hard and fast rule, but usually, if you have custody of the kids, you get the house unless you and your spouse agree to a different arrangement. Sometimes, a property agreement stipulates that the spouse with custody can stay in the house until the children all reach the age of 18, at which time the house must be sold and the sale proceeds split between both former spouses according to the terms of their agreement.

What about pensions and other retirement benefits?

In community property states, pensions and other retirement benefits earned during a marriage are viewed as belonging equally to both spouses. In separate property states, how you divide up these assets is something to be negotiated.

When a couple gets divorced, regardless of what kind of property law their state recognizes, if they have included one another in their wills, their divorce automatically voids that part of their wills.

Spousal support

When traditional marriages were more commonplace and a couple divorced, the husband was usually expected to provide his former wife with enough income throughout her life so that she could live in the same style she enjoyed when she was married. That obligation only ended if she remarried, or in some states, if she began living with another man.

Today, however, with more women working outside the home and collecting their own incomes, it's no longer assumed that a divorced woman receives alimony or spousal support from her husband; and in most states, men as well as women can now receive spousal support. In addition, the traditional "for the rest of your life" support is being replaced by temporary alimony that's provided long enough to help a spouse get an education or build a post-divorce career so that he or she can be financially independent.

If your spouse can't earn a living or a significant disparity exists between what you earn and what your spouse earns, and if that disparity is expected to continue, then the court may require that you make long-term support payments to your ex.

Like other aspects of your divorce negotiations, you and your spouse can work out your own agreement about whether or not either of you receives spousal support, and if so, how much and when. If you can't, or if the court doesn't feel that your agreement is fair, it makes this decision for you. Some states require that support payments be based on a percentage of how much the bigger earner makes, while others leave the size of payments to the discretion of the court.

If your unmarried live-in relationship ends, one partner may sue the other for *palimony* — a share of the property you acquired while you were together and/or financial support. If minor children are involved, the parent with custody may also sue for child support. Palimony is not recognized by all states, and even when it is, the right to palimony is usually difficult to prove.

What follows are some other important facts about spousal support:

- ✔ If you're concerned that your former spouse may not live up to the terms of your support agreement, you can ask him or her to post a bond guaranteeing the payments.

- ✔ If your former spouse doesn't pay up, you can ask the court to get the payments reinstated and to collect the payments that you didn't receive. Depending on your state, the court can collect payments by ordering your ex-spouse's employer to garnish his or her wages; placing liens on property that your former spouse may own; and tapping the funds in your ex's bank accounts. Remember, however, that bureaucracies work slowly, so after the court agrees to help you, it may be a long time before you see any money. Another option for getting your due in some states is to ask the court to find your ex-spouse in contempt of court; if this happens, your ex is sent to jail. The best advice when your former spouse falls behind on his or her spousal support payments is to consult the attorney who helped you with your divorce or talk with another family law attorney.

✔ You can ask the court for an increase in the amount of spousal support you're receiving if you have a legitimate reason for needing more money. The court probably will not consider your desire for a larger wardrobe or an expensive vacation to be adequate reasons! However, the court may agree to your request if:

  • Your spousal support agreement doesn't provide for automatic adjustments to keep pace with inflation, so you need an increase just to keep your financial head above water.

  • You've become too ill to work.

  • You've been injured and can't work temporarily.

✔ If you're paying support and want to reduce your payments, the court may give you the okay if you provide it with a good reason.

✔ If you're making spousal support payments, they are tax deductible. If you're receiving them, you must include them in your gross income when doing your taxes.

Who gets the kids?

If you and your spouse have minor children, your divorce negotiations also involve decisions about how to handle their care and support after you're divorced. Discussions about their care have to address two basic issues: physical custody and legal custody. If you have physical custody, the children spend most of their time with you. If you have legal custody, you have the right to make all final decisions about how your children are raised — their education, religion, health care, and so on. But depending on your post-divorce relationship, you're free to allow your former spouse to have input into your decisions. If you have physical custody of your kids, you most likely have legal custody, too.

If you have physical custody of your children, your spouse probably has visitation rights, which means that he or she is able to spend time with them. The specifics of those visitation rights, including the exact days of the week, holidays, and other special times, are spelled out in your custody agreement.

The attitude of the law toward child custody has changed over the years, just as every other aspect of divorce has changed. In the 19th century, children were viewed as their father's property, so they tended to go with Dad when their parents split. Starting in the 20th century, most states began to view both parents as having an equal right to the physical and legal custody of their children, and therefore, custody decisions were supposed to be based on what was in the "best interest of the children." In reality, however, the courts tended to favor mothers over fathers. That bias is changing somewhat as more mothers work outside the home, as parents share the care of their children more equally, and as more fathers begin to assert their rights to raise their children. *Joint custody,* or sharing the physical and/or the legal custody of children, has therefore become an increasingly popular option for divorcing parents, and nearly all states permit joint custody. In fact, in some states, a judge can *order* couples to share joint custody of their children.

Many joint custody agreements include a provision that requires ex-spouses to use mediation when they're unable to settle issues related to their children.

Before deciding on joint custody, be sure to consider the arrangement's potential pros and cons.

Joint custody pros:

- ✔ You and your former spouse both have the opportunity to remain actively involved in your children's day-to-day lives.

- ✔ Your children have an easier time maintaining an ongoing relationship with each parent, assuming you and your ex are willing to work with one another to support these relationships.

Joint custody cons:

- ✔ The arrangement is more expensive because both parents have to maintain separate homes for the kids.

- ✔ Shuttling back and forth between two homes may be stressful for your children.

- ✔ You and your spouse must interact, cooperate, and support one another's parenting styles, even if they're dissimilar.

However you decide to handle custody of your kids, the details of your agreement should be written out and should be part of your legal divorce agreement. That way, if you encounter problems later, the court can enforce the custody arrangement as it was established. To avoid confusion and to minimize the potential for conflict, the agreement should be as specific as possible regarding your individual rights and responsibilities as parents without being so rigid that the rules can't be bent occasionally if necessary.

If you and your spouse can't work out a custody agreement, the court does it for you after a custody hearing or trial. During the hearing, friends and family may be called to testify about your characters and about your individual relationships with your children. Also, experts such as social workers and psychiatrists may testify about your lifestyles, personalities, and so on. These hearings can be emotionally grueling, not to mention expensive.

The judge's custody decision is based on what he or she believes is in your children's best interest. That decision, however, is guided by state-established criteria, which usually include:

- ✔ The age and physical health of each parent
- ✔ The mental health of each parent
- ✔ The age and sex of the children
- ✔ Which parent has been the primary care provider for the children
- ✔ The quality of home and community each parent can offer the children
- ✔ The work and travel schedules of each parent
- ✔ Whether either parent has a history of drug or alcohol abuse
- ✔ The emotional bonds the children have established with each parent

If your children are old enough to have a preference, the judge may talk with them to find out their opinions.

Increasingly, the courts are recognizing the rights of gay parents in their custody decisions.

Although rare, if the court decides that neither you nor your spouse can do a good job of raising your children, it will award custody to someone else, a relative when possible.

After a custody agreement has been approved by the court and is final, you and your ex-spouse are legally bound to abide by all of its terms, which means that if you have custody of your child and your ex-husband has visitation rights, you can't deny him those rights because you're angry with him or you don't like his new girlfriend. If, however, you feel that the arrangement you agreed upon is not working out and is detrimental to your child, you can petition the court to modify your agreement.

If you have reason to believe that your ex may be harming your child or may be considering kidnapping, inform the court immediately. It may suspend or cancel your ex-spouse's visitation rights, or the court may allow visitation to continue but only in a supervised setting with a third party present.

The Parental Kidnapping Prevention Act makes kidnapping by a noncustodial parent a federal offense. If you believe that your ex-spouse has kidnapped your child, call your local police, your state attorney general's office, and the office of the U.S. Attorney General immediately.

According to the Uniform Child Custody Jurisdiction Act, all states are required to enforce a child custody agreement made in another state.

Child support

Child support payments are intended to help provide a minor child with the same standard of living after a divorce as he or she enjoyed prior to the divorce (when the child lived with both parents). Up until recently, the father was almost always responsible for child support payments. But now that two-paycheck families are commonplace, generally, the parent with physical custody of the kids receives financial support payments from the other parent.

The federal government requires all states to establish and use a standard formula for determining the minimum amount of child support one parent must pay the other. Each state is free to establish its own formula. State formulas tend to take into account the following criteria:

- The income that each parent earns, although in some states, only the income of the noncustodial parent is considered
- The number of minor children the couple has
- The needs of each minor child, including basic needs like food, clothing, shelter, routine medical care, lessons, and educational opportunities

The amount of child support you (or your former spouse) receive is flexible as long as the minimum determined by the formula is met. If a child has special needs such as medical problems not covered by insurance, the court may order support payments that are higher than what the formula indicates. If you and your spouse are able to work out your own agreement regarding child support, the court simply uses its formula to make sure that your agreement is fair.

If the amount you're receiving in child support is not adequate to meet your child's needs, you can ask the court for an increase. To keep pace with changes in cost of living, many agreements include an automatic annual cost-of-living increase. Another option is to peg automatic increases in child support to stages in a child's life. The theory here is that as a child grows older, the cost of raising him or her increases.

If you're making child support payments and changes in your life — a pay cut or prolonged illness, for example — make it difficult if not impossible to continue paying the amount of child support you agreed on, ask the court to let you make smaller payments. It may grant your request for a limited amount of time or indefinitely, deny your request, or possibly order you to use your savings, liquidate assets, or find a better-paying job so that you can continue the same level of payments.

Theoretically, child support payments must be spent on the care of the children, not on other things.

Here are some other things you should know about making child support payments:

- Child support payments aren't viewed as taxable income.

- You can't claim child support payments as tax deductions.

- You can't claim your minor children as tax deductions unless they live with you more than half of the year or unless your former spouse gives you the deductions by completing an IRS Form 8332.

- If you're obligated to make child support payments, federal law requires that you provide your minor children with medical insurance unless equal or better insurance coverage is available for a comparable or better price, or unless you and your former spouse agree on a different arrangement approved by the court.

- Unless your child support agreement says otherwise, your obligation to pay child support usually continues until your child becomes a legal adult — age 18 or 21 depending in your state — even if your ex-spouse marries a millionaire! However, in some states, the obligation can continue while your child is in college or trade school. Even so, by the time your child is in his or her early 20s, your obligation will be over unless you've agreed to a different arrangement.

- Dying isn't necessarily an acceptable reason for not supporting a minor child! You're expected to make adequate provisions for that possibility by including your child in your will, setting up a trust for your child, naming your child as a beneficiary of your life insurance policy, and so on. If you die without having provided for the support of your minor child, your child can sue your estate for support!

- If your ex-spouse is paying child support and files for personal bankruptcy, the obligation of child support is unaffected. Also, your ex-spouse can't use bankruptcy to wipe out any delinquent child support payments that he or she may owe to you. If your ex-spouse files for bankruptcy, contact your family law attorney as soon as possible to find out if you should do anything to ensure that the payments continue.

Deadbeat Dads . . . and Moms

According to a report by the U.S. Census Bureau, in 2002, 13.4 million parents held custody of 21.5 million children under the age of 21 whose other parent lived somewhere else. About 59 percent of the custodial parents had obtained court orders for child support, and of these parents, less than half had received the child support payments they were entitled to in 2001; around 29 percent received only some of their child support, and 26 percent had received nothing at all. In most instances, children suffer significantly when custodial parents don't receive their child support or receive only part of what they're due. In fact, lack of child support is a leading cause of poverty among children living in single-parent households.

Over the years, as the problem of deadbeat dads and moms has worsened, placing children in jeopardy, the federal and state governments have looked for new ways to enforce existing child support agreements and to establish support orders where no agreement exists. For example, the federal Family Support Act was passed to require all states to enact laws mandating that all new and modified child support orders include a provision for automatic wage deductions. That way, if a parent falls behind on his or her child support payments, the parent's employer can be required to begin deducting money from the parent's paycheck, which goes to the custodial parent.

Federal law also requires that all states use proven methods of collection to ensure that parents get the support they're due. These proven methods include the following:

- ✔ Placing liens on the delinquent parent's real or personal property — real estate, vehicles, boats, and so on. Although a lien doesn't necessarily mean that the other parent sees any money right away, it does mean that the delinquent parent is unable to transfer, borrow against, or sell the property until he or she has taken care of the past-due child support.

  Usually, you can't place a lien on the primary residence of a former spouse or on any property that he or she may need to earn a living.

- ✔ Taking any state or federal tax refunds that the non-paying spouse is entitled to.

- ✔ Fining or jailing a former spouse for contempt of court.

- ✔ Tapping into any unemployment compensation payments, veteran's benefits, or other state and federal benefits that the delinquent parent may be receiving.

- ✔ Garnishing the delinquent parent's wages.

- ✔ Withholding, suspending, or restricting the use of driver's licenses, professional and occupational licenses, and recreational and sporting licenses held by noncustodial parents who owe past-due support.

- ✔ Denying a passport to anyone who owes more than $5,000 in past-due support.

- ✔ Reporting unpaid child support of more than $1,000 to the national credit reporting agencies.

State child support agencies must petition to include medical support in a child support order whenever health care coverage is available to the non-custodial parent at a reasonable cost.

If you're having trouble collecting child support from an ex-spouse, or if you're not getting any child support from a child's parent because you don't have a legally binding support agreement, get in contact with the Child Support Enforcement (CSE) program immediately by calling your state or local human services department. The CSE program is designed to collect support payments from parents who are legally obligated to pay child support. It can help you even if you don't have a legal support agreement with the child's father or mother or if you and the father or mother were never married. The program is a joint effort of the federal government together with state and local governments.

Although the specifics of the CSE program vary from state to state, no matter where you live, the program offers four basic services:

- ✔ It helps you establish the paternity of your child.
- ✔ It locates the child's father or mother (whoever is delinquent on payments).
- ✔ It establishes a child support order where no such agreement exists.
- ✔ It helps enforce existing agreements.

CSE offices must also make child support debts over $1,000 available to credit bureaus when they request the information. In some states, credit bureaus request this information regularly.

The CSE personnel in your area also know how to use other federal laws that may be helpful to you, or they can refer you to someone else who can tell you about them. These laws include

- ✔ The 1992 Child Support Recovery Act, which makes it a federal crime for a parent to willfully avoid making child support payments to a child living in another state if the amount owed in back child support is more than $5,000 and if that amount has been past due for more than a year. Those found guilty of violating this law face imprisonment and fines.
- ✔ The Uniform Interstate Family Support Act (UIFSA), which makes an order of support in one state enforceable in all others. UIFSA spells out specific processes for initiating interstate enforcement actions. The enforcement process can be initiated in your own state or in the state where the father or mother of your child now lives.

✔ The Personal Responsibility and Work Opportunity Reconciliation Act (PRWORA), established in 1996, which mandates the creation of a national *new hire registry.* Employers are required to report new employees to state and federal new hire databases to make it easier for child support to be withheld from wages and to better track parents who owe child support and move to a new state.

✔ The Deadbeat Parents Act, signed into law in 1998, which allows a non-custodial parent who willfully avoids paying child support for a child living in another state to be charged with a misdemeanor if the amount of the past-due child support is at least $5,000 and has been owed for more than one year. If convicted, the parent can be incarcerated for up to six months and/or fined up to $5,000. Under the law, a parent can be charged with a felony if he or she travels out of state or to another country to avoid paying child support (assuming the child support has gone unpaid for more than one year and amounts to more than $5,000); or if the parent willfully fails to pay child support to a child who lives in another state, owes more than $10,000 in past-due support, and has owed that support for more than two years. Parents convicted of a felony can be incarcerated for up to two years and/or fined up to $25,000.

Unmarried Women and Child Support

If you're unmarried and have a child, most states expect the father to assume all of the legal responsibilities that come with paternity, whether you're living together or not. If the child's father denies paternity, you can sue him, and he has to prove that he's not the father either by submitting the results of blood tests or DNA tests or by proving that he's sterile or impotent and could never have fathered a child. After paternity is established, the CSE program can help you obtain and enforce a legal support order.

The Uniform Parentage Act has been adopted by more than a third of all states. It allows any interested party, not just the mother, to file a paternity suit on behalf of a child.

Chapter 5

Parenting and Child Care

- -

In This Chapter

▶ Understanding the rights and responsibilities of parenting

▶ Opting for foster care and legal guardians

▶ Pointing out the consequences of abuse and neglect

▶ Creating a family through adoption or surrogacy

▶ Handling in-home child care arrangements

- -

*G*one are the days when most children lived in two-parent households and moms stayed home. Today, kids are as likely to live with one parent as two, and moms as well as dads are working outside the home. Women are less dependent on their husbands for financial support, and quality child care is a serious issue for many, many parents.

Here's another important development: Although the majority of couples who want children use the "old-fashioned way" to begin their families (or they adopt children), a growing number of couples are turning to science to help them become parents.

Regardless of how you start your family, and regardless of whether or not you're a single parent or you share parenting responsibilities with a partner, you should be aware of your parental rights and responsibilities. This information is particularly important given that recent years have seen a trend at both the national and the state levels to expand parental rights, better enforce existing parental responsibility laws, and pass new ones.

To Be or Not to Be a Parent

For some couples, starting a family is the logical next step after marriage, but others may not want children at all. Whatever your decision, it's one you're free to make for yourself.

According to the U.S. Supreme Court, the decision to have or not have a child is a private, personal one. If you're a woman, no one, not even your husband, can force you to have a baby, and you have the right to use contraceptives to prevent getting pregnant. If you do become pregnant, no one can force you to have an abortion either.

Disagreements about whether or not to have children can be grounds for divorce in some states.

In 1973's landmark decision, *Roe vs. Wade,* the Supreme Court ruled that all women have a constitutional right to a safe, legal abortion. Specifically, the ruling stated that during the first trimester of a pregnancy, the state may not limit or regulate this right other than to insist that an abortion be performed by a licensed physician. Beginning in the second trimester, however, the court ruled that states may place limits on that right, but only to protect a woman's health. It also ruled that to protect a fetus, beginning in the third trimester — the point at which a fetus can survive outside a woman's body — the state can limit a woman's access to an abortion or even prevent her from having one, unless an abortion is necessary to preserve the woman's health or life.

In 1992, the Supreme Court reaffirmed its decision in *Roe vs. Wade* but ruled that states may place restrictions on abortions as long as they don't impose "an undue burden" on pregnant women. As a result, some states now require women who consent to an abortion to wait 24 hours before having one, and some states require minors who want an abortion to either notify a parent or guardian of their intention or get written permission from a parent or guardian to have the medical procedure.

Being a Parent Is Serious Stuff

When you think about having a baby, you may be more apt to romanticize the idea of a child than you are to consider the serious implications of what you're about to do — that you're not only increasing the size of your family but also assuming new legal responsibilities and obligations. In fact, starting a family is one of the most significant steps any of us will ever take.

Although you can divorce your spouse and rid yourself of many of the legal obligations that come with marriage, you can't divorce your kids! They're for keeps, or at least until they become legal adults at age 18 or 21, depending on your state.

Legal obligations

As a parent, you have a constitutional right to make basic decisions about how your minor children are raised, including where they're educated, how they're disciplined, where they live, the values you impart to them, and so on. But you also have a legal obligation to provide for their basic needs — health, education, and well-being — while they're minors or until they turn 18 or 21, depending on your state. In some cases, this obligation can last even after your child becomes an adult (if your child is seriously disabled and unable to support him or herself, or if your child would be on welfare without your support, for example). And there are times when your parental obligations end early, such as if your child is legally married before age 18 or becomes an *emancipated* minor. An emancipated minor is a child whose parents have voluntarily surrendered their legal rights and responsibilities in regard to the care, custody, and support of the child. The child is free to make his or her own decisions and provide for his or her own financial support.

Education

Your child must attend school for a minimum number of years. In most states, your child must begin school at age 5 or 6 and remain in school until age 14 or 16.

If you want to home school your child, be sure it's legal in your state, and know what your state requires of home-schoolers.

Some states, including Kansas, Michigan, and Texas, have adopted parents' rights legislation in response to what some parents, policymakers, and politicians view as an undermining of their right to determine what kinds of information their children will receive in school and at what age their children will receive it. For example, some parents object to certain types of school-based health and sexuality education.

Medical care

Generally, part of your responsibility as a parent is to make sure that your child receives necessary medical care. This responsibility doesn't mean that you're obligated to provide specific care just because a doctor recommends it. For example, if your doctor suggests that regular allergy shots will make your daughter sneeze less or that your son's teeth can be straightened with braces, it's up to you to decide whether or not you want to provide her or him with the recommended care.

In most instances, you have the right to consent to any medical care your child receives. Your consent is not necessary, however, if:

  ✔ Your child needs emergency care, and you're not immediately available.

  ✔ Your child is pregnant and needs prenatal care or wants treatment for a sexually transmitted disease or alcoholism.

  ✔ Your child needs lifesaving medical treatment, and you refuse to give your consent. A court can intervene and mandate the treatment.

Your state can require that your child receive certain immunizations. Usually, if you don't provide them, your child isn't allowed to attend school, which puts you in violation of your state's education requirements for minor children.

Some states will exempt a child from having to receive certain immunizations if such immunizations are dangerous to the child's health or if your religion prohibits them.

If physical, emotional, or financial problems prevent you from meeting your parental obligations, you have the right to ask the state to care for your child. Usually, your child is placed in foster care. But before making such a request, consult with an attorney because if you're not careful, your parental rights may be terminated, and after you lose them, they can be tough to get back.

Discipline and liability

As a parent, you have the right to use *appropriate* discipline with your minor child. But if your discipline, or your failure to discipline, threatens the life or the physical well-being of your child, then your state can take your child away from you and even prosecute you.

If you're unable to control your child, you have the right to ask the court for help. It won't step in if you're simply having trouble getting your son to keep his room clean — the problem must be much more serious than that. If your child is endangering him or herself or others, however, and if your child has a history of problems, then the court may declare your child *in need of services* and begin actively supervising him or her.

Parents can be held liable for the consequences of a minor child's actions — vandalizing property or intentionally harming someone, for example — especially if the state can prove that the parents were aware of what their child was doing and did little or nothing to stop the child.

A Michigan couple learned this lesson the hard way when a jury convicted them of violating a city ordinance that requires parents to *exercise reasonable parental control* over children under 18 years of age. The court fined each parent and ordered them to pay more than $1,000 in court costs because their son repeatedly smoked marijuana and stole several thousand dollars from his family's church, among other things.

In most states, though, a parent's legal liability is usually significantly less than the actual dollar value of any damages that the child may cause.

Defining the Roles of Legal Guardians and Foster Parents

If you're unable to meet your parental responsibilities and don't want to put your child in foster care, another option is to appoint a *legal guardian,* a close friend or relative perhaps, to care for your child. The guardian assumes all of your legal rights as a parent and must be approved by a court.

To help ensure that the guardian cares for your child according to your wishes, and to make sure that you'll have no trouble reassuming your role as parent when you're ready, hire an attorney to help you draw up a contract defining the terms of the guardianship, including its duration, conditions, and any specific instructions you have for the guardian.

Foster parents care for children when their parents are unable or unwilling to care for them or when the children are victims of abuse or neglect. Children may live with foster parents until they can return to their biological parents or until adoptive parents can be found.

Foster parents have most of the duties and rights of a child's birth parents. They receive a stipend from the state to help pay for the cost of caring for a foster child.

Protecting Against Abuse and Neglect

All states have parental child abuse and neglect laws. *Neglect* is generally considered to be failure to provide a child with adequate shelter, clothing, food, "reasonably necessary" medical attention, and supervision. For example, if you leave your minor child home alone while you go to work or to a party, don't keep your child clean, or deny your child food for a period of time, then you may be charged with neglect. Whether or not it's neglect depends somewhat on the age of your child. For example, you're more apt to be charged with neglect if you leave your 3-year-old child home alone than if you leave your 16-year-old alone.

Abuse most commonly refers to situations where you, or another adult responsible for your child, intentionally harm the child physically or emotionally. Simply allowing a child to suffer also qualifies as abuse. Abuse can also include sexual abuse and extreme verbal abuse, especially in public. Although we're all aware of situations in which adults so physically mistreated a child that there was no doubt in our minds that the child had been abused, in other instances, things may not be so clear-cut. In fact, what may seem like abuse to one person may be viewed as "appropriate discipline" by someone else.

If you kick a child out of your home, you may be charged with abuse and neglect, depending on your state's laws.

If you suspect that a child is being abused or neglected, you have a legal responsibility (no matter what state you live in) to report your suspicions to your police department or to your local, county, or state child protection agency or welfare agency. All states as well as the District of Columbia have laws that require certain professionals such as doctors, nurses, teachers, social workers, clergy and so on — people most apt to come into contact with a child who is being mistreated — to report suspected cases of child neglect or abuse. These states have also established specific reporting laws, and most of them require professionals to reports suspected abuse right away.

All states have laws to protect individuals from being sued for making good faith reports of suspected child abuse or neglect.

If a court finds that a child is being abused or neglected, the child is usually placed in temporary foster care with the goal of reuniting child and parents after the problems contributing to the neglect or abuse are addressed. When, however, the abuse or neglect is particularly bad, or if it's an ongoing problem, the state may terminate the parents' rights, and the child is put up for adoption.

The Ins and Outs of Adoption

Many couples who are unable to have biological children decide to adopt instead. When they do, they assume all of the legal rights and responsibilities that come with being a parent.

Although adoptive parents are most often married, as society's definition of a family changes, state laws regarding who can adopt change, too. Single people can adopt in many states, and in a growing number of states, unmarried couples, both heterosexual and homosexual, are also becoming adoptive parents.

Some states have special requirements for adults who want to adopt. For example, they may require that the adopting parents be a minimum number of years older than the child they want to adopt — ten years older in California, for example. Also, some states require that adopting parents be residents of the state for a certain period of time in order to adopt there.

A single man or a gay or lesbian couple may have a harder time adopting a child than a single woman or a heterosexual couple, everything else being equal. This imbalance is because states require judges to consider what is in a child's best interest when deciding with whom to place a child, and some states allow sexual orientation to be an explicit consideration. Even when it isn't an explicit consideration, sexual orientation may play a role in some judges' decisions. Also, some states have passed laws to prohibit adoptions by a single gay or lesbian individual or by gay or lesbian couples. These states include Florida and Mississippi. Utah bans adoptions by all unmarried couples, whether heterosexual or homosexual. Even in states where no such laws are in place, the potential complications make it advisable to get legal help with a gay or lesbian adoption.

Each state also has its own set of criteria for what makes an adoption legal. Individuals who participate in illegal adoptions face prosecution. Legal adoptions usually have the following characteristics:

- ✔ The adoption must follow state laws.
- ✔ Usually, if the child's biological parents are married, they must consent to the adoption. If they're unmarried, the mother must provide her consent; whether or not the father is required to give his consent varies from state to state.
- ✔ If a court determines that the adoptive child's biological parents are *unfit* to raise the child, then their parental rights must be terminated.

> ✔ The adoptive parents can't pay excessive fees to an intermediary or to the adoptive child's biological parents.
>
> ✔ A court must approve the adoption.
>
> ✔ The family court approving the adoption must believe that it's *in the best interest of the child.*

Most states have a waiting period for a mother who puts her child up for adoption; this way, she can be sure that she wants to take that step.

Adoption.com (`www.adoption.com`) is a one-stop resource for prospective adoptive parents as well as birth parents and individuals who were adopted. Among other things, it includes information about the basics of adoption and the various types of adoption; links to hundreds of adoption agencies, adoption facilitators, and attorneys; information and links to adoption support groups; information on the rights of adoptees; photolistings of children waiting to be adopted; and e-mail lists, newsgroups, bulletin boards, and chat groups. The site also provides resources for birth parents and adopted individuals who want to get in touch with their birth parents.

The types of adoptions

There are three basic types of legal adoption: agency adoptions, related adoptions, and private adoptions.

Agency adoptions

Agency adoptions are arranged by public and private agencies and are legal in all states. Usually, the agencies are licensed or regulated by the state. The children placed by public agencies usually have become wards of the state because they were taken away from their parents, orphaned, or abandoned. In contrast, the children placed by private adoption agencies are usually given up voluntarily because the parents can't afford to raise them, believe they're too young to start a family, and so on. If you work with an agency to adopt a child, you have to go through a formal process designed to help the agency ensure that you will be a good parent.

Agency adoptions typically provide adoptive parents with more legal safeguards than private adoptions. However, they're also more apt to place restrictions on whom they will help adopt. For example, an agency may not work with individuals over a certain age.

Some states regulate the fees that an agency can charge an adopting couple. But no matter what the state, adoptive parents who are adopting a child who isn't born yet are expected to pay the costs of the birth mother's pregnancy and any adoption-related expenses she may incur.

Private adoptions

Private adoptions are legal in most states. Usually, an adoption facilitator, a doctor, lawyer, or someone else in contact with the biological parents of a child arranges for the adoption, but sometimes, the birth parents and the adoptive parents deal with one another directly.

If you decide to adopt a child through a private adoption, be sure that the person you work with is reputable and that you have an attorney review all of the paperwork.

With a private adoption, you can adopt a child who lives in your state, in another state, or even in another country. But because out-of-state and international adoptions tend to be more complicated, they also cost more than the typical in-state, private adoption.

If you're considering a foreign adoption, find an agency that specializes in them. It will know how to locate a baby and how to deal with the inevitable bureaucratic red tape (like obtaining an immigration visa for your new child) in both countries.

Related adoptions

Related adoptions take place when relatives adopt a child. The parents of the child may have died or may be unable to care for their child due to illness, drug use, or other problems. Adoptive relatives, like any adoptive parents, must go through a process laid out by the state to make the adoption legal.

Fathers and adoptions

Most states require that if a woman decides to put her child up for adoption and knows who the child's father is, then she must let the man know about her plans. His consent may or may not be necessary to go through with the adoption. However, if the child's mother and father aren't married, and if he has helped support the child and has maintained regular, ongoing contact with the child, then he probably has the right to withhold his approval. In addition, the court will probably grant his request if he asks for the right to raise the child by himself.

Your options if you're adopted

If you're adopted, at some point in your life, you may become curious about your birth parents and may even want to meet them. The ease with which you'll be able to do so depends in part on whether your adoption was *traditional* (or *closed*) or *open.*

In a *closed adoption,* the birth and adopting parents may share information with one another, and the adopting parents may even send the birth parents photos of the child they adopted, letters about the child, and so on, but neither set of parents has any identifying information about the other — no names, residence addresses, and so on. In an *open adoption,* however, although the birth parents give up all their parental rights and responsibilities in regard to their child, the two sets of parents typically know more about one another. For example, they may share phone numbers and even visit one another. The birth parents may send photos and letters to the child and may stay in touch with the child as long as they are alive.

Many agencies let the parents decide together how much and what kind of contact the birth parents will have with the adoptive parents and with the child. Also, in some states, adopted children who are at least 18 years old may learn the identity of their birth parents if everyone agrees to reveal the information.

Traditionally, adoptions have always been highly confidential so that the privacy of everyone involved is protected. So, if your adoption was a traditional one, learning about your birth parents may be more difficult but not necessarily impossible. You have to work through a court, and you may need the help of an attorney who knows how to cut through the bureaucratic red tape.

If you're adopting a child through an open adoption, you and the birth parents may decide that you can be at the birth of the child if he or she is not already born.

Using a Surrogate

Scientific advances have given many men and women who in the past were unable to start a family the chance to become parents. Although these advances are offering new hope to would-be parents, the laws regarding how these advances should be used and the rights of those who use them are still being defined.

If you're unable to conceive a child or cannot carry one to term, you may decide to use the services of a female surrogate. Depending on your particular complication, the surrogate may be artificially inseminated by your husband's or partner's sperm and will then give birth to the baby for you, or an egg you donate may be fertilized by your husband or partner *in vitro* and be implanted in the surrogate who will later give birth to the child. If the problem lies with your husband or partner, then you may want to use a male surrogate or a sperm bank to help you start a family.

If you're having problems conceiving and want to get information and advice from other couples that have faced the same or similar problems, visit www. fertilityplus.org.

If surrogate parenting is legal in your state, find out if any particular laws govern the relationship between you and the surrogate. For example, you may be prohibited from paying a surrogate because the exchange of money is viewed as equivalent to baby-selling.

Be careful about using a broker to help you with the surrogate process. If the broker's only service is locating possible surrogates, in the eyes of the law, the broker may be selling babies. In such a situation, you and the broker can be prosecuted.

Always hire an attorney who is familiar with the applicable laws of your state to prepare an airtight contract for you. Given the emotional nature of your relationship with one another and all the things that could go wrong, you need a legal agreement whether you know the surrogate or not. The agreement should address issues such as your responsibilities and the surrogate's while she is pregnant; the financial terms of your agreement (whether you're paying for all the surrogate's pregnancy-related medical expenses, for example); confidentiality, parental, and custodial rights; and how you will resolve any disagreement that may arise. Don't rely on any paperwork that a broker, doctor, sperm bank, or surrogate may provide.

An airtight contract is especially important if you work with a female surrogate. State in the contract that you want the surrogate to waive all her rights to the child after it's born; otherwise, she may have a change of heart after the baby is born, and you may find yourself in court battling for the baby. If the surrogate provided the egg, she's the baby's biological mother, and your husband or partner is the father; therefore, before you can adopt the baby and become its legal parent, the surrogate must waive her parental rights. If you end up in a court battle with a surrogate, she may get visitation rights, custody, and even child support, depending on the nature of her role in bringing the baby into the world, whether or not there was a surrogate contract, and exactly what the contract said.

Generally, the potential for legal problems doesn't exist to the same degree when you work with a sperm donor or a sperm bank. If you work directly with a sperm donor, it's unlikely that he will assert his parental rights to any child he may father because doing so means that he also assumes all of the legal obligations that go with being a parent. If you work through a sperm bank, sperm bank donors usually don't have any parental legal rights or obligations. Many states give sperm donors no parental rights. In fact, if your husband or partner consents to your being artificially inseminated with donor sperm, most states view your husband or partner as the child's legal father.

Child Care

Finding quality child care is a big problem for many parents today. So, you may find it somewhat reassuring to know that to help ensure a basic level of safety and care at day care centers, most states and many local governments require that the centers be licensed and meet certain minimum standards for child-to-caregiver ratios, nutrition, sanitation, and safety. To find out about the rules for child care providers in your area, look in the government listings section of your phone book under "Child Care Providers" or "Family or Social Services."

In many states, day care centers operated by a religious entity don't have to be licensed.

Hiring home-based child care

You may decide to forego day care centers and hire a caretaker to watch your child in your home. It's a good idea to draw up a written contract between you and your home-based child care provider that stipulates the employee's responsibilities, hours of work, and compensation.

Hiring someone to care for your child in your home brings with it several other obligations to the federal government, besides your federal tax obligations. You must:

- ✔ Give the caretaker a W-2 form to fill out and return to the IRS.
- ✔ Pay the caretaker minimum wage.
- ✔ Report certain information to the agency in your state that is charged with maintaining a Directory of New Hires under the Personal

Responsibility and Work Opportunity Act of 1996. The information includes the caretaker's name, address, and Social Security number, and any other information specifically required by your state's agency. You must report this information within a specific period of time — up to 20 days after the date that you hire the caretaker, depending on your state. The reporting is intended to help with the enforcement of child support court orders.

Don't forget your tax obligations

If you're lucky enough to be able to afford in-home child care, don't learn the hard way that you need to comply with many federal reporting and taxing requirements. In addition, your state may have its own requirements.

Federal law requires that if you pay your child's at-home caregiver more than $1,400 in a calendar year, then you must pay *nanny taxes.* These federal employment taxes include Social Security, Medicare, and federal unemployment taxes. You must also pay these taxes if you hire any kind of household help, including housekeepers, gardeners, cooks, and so on.

Au pairs

Hiring an *au pair* to live at your home and help care for your children is an option that many couples use to resolve the issue of quality child care. Au pairs are usually young European women (although there are male au pairs, too) between the ages of 18 and 25. They come to the United States for a maximum of 12 months on exchange visitor visas to live with a family, provide child care, and take at least six semester hours of academic credit at an accredited post-secondary educational institution. All this comes in exchange for a private room, meals, a weekly stipend tied to the minimum wage, 1½ days off each week plus a full weekend off each month, two weeks' paid vacation, and $500 toward the cost of the au pair's education in the United States.

Because an au pair is not considered a foreign worker but rather a participant in a cultural exchange, you don't have to pay his or her Social Security or other taxes.

The United States Information Agency (USIA), which is located within the State Department, works with a number of nonprofit organizations in this country who help match families with au pairs. Visit the agency's Web site at www.exchanges.state.gov/education/ jexchanges/private/aupair_wage.htm for a list of these organizations including their contact information. The site also provides detailed information regarding your responsibilities when you hire an au pair.

In addition to the nanny taxes, you will probably have to pay state unemployment taxes and maybe state disability taxes, too. To find out whether these are requirements in your state, contact your insurance agent or your state's department of labor or employment, which can also tell you about any other tax-related obligations you may have.

For a complete explanation of your federal tax obligations when you hire a caregiver for your child, including instructions on how and when to pay the taxes, go to the IRS Web site at www.irs.org and download Publication 926, *Household Employer's Tax Guide*.

Don't ignore your tax obligations to the IRS. If you do and the IRS finds out, you may find yourself owing that agency a lot of money. You're liable for all the taxes you don't pay plus interest — at a high rate — and you also have to pay substantial penalties on the back taxes. Contact the IRS at 800-829-1040 to find out the terms and conditions of your reporting and tax obligations.

Chapter 6

The Law and Your Job

*U*nless you've won the lottery or your proverbial rich uncle has left you a small fortune, you probably spend most of your waking hours working at a job. Even Snow White's seven dwarfs went to work!

Whether you're gainfully employed or looking to be employed, you should be aware that the federal government has passed many laws to protect your rights in the workplace. These laws cover everything from being hired and fired, to your rights on the job, to the minimum you're paid, to safety at work. Your state has also passed laws that affect you and the workplace. Many of these laws reinforce or expand the rights provided by the federal laws.

The U.S. Department of Labor maintains a Web site at www.dol.gov. Among other things, it offers comprehensive, detailed information about the federal laws and regulations that affect you as an employee.

Applying for a Job

To explain how employment laws may affect you, I start where all employees start — with the job application process.

The interview or job application

Generally, in a job interview, you cannot be asked questions that have nothing to do with your job qualifications, including questions about your age, gender, ethnic origin, race, color, religion, political affiliations, whether or not you have any children or intend to have them, your medical history, or whether you have any disabilities. State and local laws may also prohibit discrimination on the basis of your marital status or sexual orientation.

Most anti-discrimination employment laws apply to employers with 15 or more employees. However, local and state laws often apply to employers with fewer workers.

Employers can ask you personal questions if they relate to a job's *bona fide occupational qualifications* and if the same questions are asked of all applicants for the same job.

References

State laws limit the kinds of information that a past employer can provide to a prospective employer. Generally, a past employer can provide only information about the following: the position you held, the salary you received, the dates that you worked for the former employer, the reason you left the job, and the circumstances surrounding your departure (you were doing a great job but wanted more challenges; you couldn't get along with anyone; and so on). In other words, a past employer can provide essentially just enough to verify what's on your résumé or job application and comment on your past job performance, as long as those comments are verifiable.

Background checks

A prospective employer can conduct a background check on you if the information sought is strictly job related. Also, according to the federal Fair Credit Reporting Act, a prospective employer can review a copy of your credit history as part of the decision-making process. For example, a prospective employer may review your credit history if the job you're applying for requires you to handle large sums of money. However, the employer must get your written permission upfront to review your credit record information, and if you're turned down for the job you apply for in whole or in part because of that information, then the employer must give you the name and contact information of the credit reporting agency that provided your credit record.

Affirmative action

An *affirmative action plan* (AAP) is a plan that outlines how a business recruits, hires, and promotes minorities and women in order to improve workplace disparities that are the result of discrimination or to make amends for past discrimination. Most private employers are free to decide for themselves whether or not to have an AAP. Government agencies are required to have them, and employers with government contracts — local, state, or federal — may be required to have them, too. If, however, an employer that is not required to have an AAP is sued for discrimination and found guilty, the employer may be required to implement such a plan.

An employer can review your credit history if he's deciding whether to hire, promote, demote, or fire you. However, the employer must get your written permission first.

Testing

Depending on the job you're applying for and the state you live in, certain types of pre-employment tests are legal, including job-related intelligence or skills tests and drug tests, so long as all applicants are required to take the same tests. This section describes the rules regarding other kinds of tests.

The Americans with Disabilities Act (ADA) says that you cannot be required to take a medical or psychological test as part of the application process. But you can be required to take one after you've been offered a job, assuming that all other individuals being hired for that same job category are required to take the exam, too. If the tests show that you have a disability that may interfere with your ability to do the job you've been offered and that hiring you will create an "undue hardship" on the business, the employer has the right to rescind the offer. The employer must hire you, however, if "reasonable accommodations" can be made that will allow you to perform the job satisfactorily. Also, after you have been hired, your employer can't require you to take a medical exam or answer questions about your disability unless such questions are job related and reflect your ability to properly conduct the employer's business.

Here is the legal lowdown on some tests and requirements you may encounter:

- ✔ **Drug testing:** Drug screening tests are permitted under federal law; however, some states have laws that restrict drug testing or have established guidelines for such testing.

- ✔ **AIDS testing:** You can be required to be tested for AIDS, but only after you've been offered a job. If you test positive, the employer cannot take back the offer unless he can prove that there's a job-based reason why someone who is HIV-positive should not be hired.

- ✔ **Fingerprinting and photographs:** Some states allow employers to require fingerprinting and photographs when they're hiring for certain kinds of positions, including police officers and child care workers, but usually only after the employer has made a job offer.

- ✔ **Lie detector tests:** The Federal Employee Polygraph Protection Act (EPPA) says that private sector employers can't require you to take a lie detector test, also called a *polygraph exam,* unless you're applying for certain kinds of positions, including jobs in the security industry (armored cars, security alarms, and security guard firms that protect facilities, materials, or operations affecting health or safety, national security, currency, or the like) and jobs with pharmaceutical and other firms authorized to manufacture, distribute, or dispense controlled substances that will give you direct access to the controlled substances. Lie detector tests may also be given to current employees of those firms with access to persons or property that are the subject of an ongoing investigation. Employees suspected of being involved in a workplace incident that causes economic damage to their employers or who had access to the property that is the subject of an investigation can also be required to submit to a polygraph test. The EPPA doesn't apply to public sector employers. Also, most states have their own laws governing the use of polygraph tests.

  When a lie detector test is administered, the EPPA sets strict standards for who can conduct the test, how the test can be conducted, and how the test results can be used.

Some states require employers to obtain written permission from a job applicant before certain medical tests are conducted.

Dealing with Job Offers That Come with Conditions

If you're a white-collar professional and are offered a new job, as a condition of employment, your prospective employer may want you to sign an agreement called a *covenant not to compete.* This agreement restricts your ability to work for one of the employer's competitors or to begin a business that competes directly with your employer if you voluntarily leave your new job or are fired from it. Most agreements of this type apply to a limited geographic area and are good for only a limited period of time.

Obviously, a covenant not to compete benefits your new employer and not you because it limits your options should you and the employer part company. So, avoid signing one if you can. If you can't avoid it and you really want the job, it's a good idea to hire an attorney to review the agreement before you sign it. The attorney can suggest changes you should try to negotiate, or he or she can negotiate them for you.

If you do sign a covenant not to compete and later violate it, your former employer has the right to sue you and possibly your new employer as well. But if the court determines that the terms of the agreement were overly stringent or restrictive, it may let you off of the hook or order you to comply with new, less onerous restrictions.

You may also be asked to sign a confidentiality agreement as a condition of your employment. Such an agreement may require you to not divulge certain proprietary information such as special formulas, business plans, product details, or copyrights. Be sure you understand exactly what you're agreeing not to do before signing.

Legal Issues on the Job

After you're hired, it's important that you understand your rights in the workplace. And where better to start than with your first paycheck!

Getting paid: Show me the money!

The Fair Labor Standards Act (FLSA) establishes the federal minimum wage for most employees. Currently, the federal minimum hourly wage is $5.15. However, lower minimums apply if you're under age 20, a full-time student, a worker with disabilities, an employee who receive tips, or a youth worker (a student who is at least 16 years old and who is enrolled in a vocational education program).

The FLSA also determines which employees are eligible for overtime pay. Those employees must be paid time and a half if they work more than 40 hours in a workweek. In August 2004, those rules were overhauled for the first time in more than half a century. The changes apply to any business that generates gross revenues of more than $500,000.

What the FLSA doesn't require

You may be surprised to hear that the FLSA doesn't require your employer to provide you with any of the job benefits and job-related information on the following list. Whether or not you receive them may be something for you and your employer to negotiate, or your eligibility for such things may be determined by the nature of the job you're hired to perform. Also, your state may have a law that requires some or all of the benefits on this list.

✔ Overtime pay for work on Saturdays, Sundays, holidays, or on your regular days of rest

✔ Vacation pay, pay for holidays, severance pay, or sick pay

✔ Meal or rest periods

✔ Holidays off

✔ Vacations

✔ Pay raises or fringe benefits

✔ Discharge notices when you're let go, a reason for your being discharged, or immediate payment of your final wages

Presently, 18 states have minimum wage laws that are more generous than the FLSA. Employers in those states must apply the more generous standards to their employees.

The following sections outline the new federal standards that employers must use to determine which of their employees are eligible for overtime pay. Eligible employees are classified as *nonexempt,* and those who are ineligible are classified as *exempt.*

Employees eligible for overtime pay

According to the FLSA, most employees who make less than $455 a week ($23,660 a year) are eligible for overtime, regardless of whether the employee is a blue-collar or white-collar worker and regardless of whether or not he or she is a supervisor. Police, firefighters, and other first responders are included among the workers who are nonexempt.

Employees ineligible for overtime pay

Many employers may find the rules complicated and confusing, so if you're uncertain about whether or not you should be receiving overtime pay, get in touch with your state's Wage and Hour Division office, your state's department of labor office, or contact an employment law attorney. The following categories of workers are ineligible for overtime pay according to FLSA's updated rules.

- ✔ All employees who earn more than $100,000 a year

- ✔ Teachers, doctors, and lawyers

- ✔ Except for salespeople, employees in most executive, professional, or administrative positions who earn between $23,660 and $100,000 a year

- ✔ Individuals in management positions who manage at least two employees and are entitled to hire or fire individuals, or who can recommend that someone be hired or fired

- ✔ Employees in administrative positions with decision-making authority who are in change of some sort of operation for their employers

- ✔ Employees whose primary job responsibilities are computer-related and involve the implementation, analysis, development, or application of computer systems or designs

- ✔ Salespeople who regularly work outside of their employer's places of business

- ✔ Employees in jobs that require imagination, invention, originality, artistic, or creative endeavors

If you work for a public sector employer, in most cases, when you're eligible for overtime, your employer can offer you *comp time* — time away from your job that's equivalent to the additional money you would receive in your check otherwise. Usually, you have the right to choose whether you want to receive overtime pay or comp time.

What to do if you're not being paid correctly

If you're a nonexempt employee and you don't believe that you're being paid fairly according to the requirements of the FLSA, you can file a complaint with the Wage and Hour Division (WHD) of the U.S. Department of Labor, either by mail or at any WHD District office. Be sure to file your complaint within 18 months of the date that the violation occurs. In your complaint you must provide the following information:

- ✔ Your name, address, and a daytime phone number

- ✔ Your job title and a description of the kind of work you do

- ✔ The rate and frequency of your pay. (For example, you're paid a salary of $2,000 twice a month, or you're paid weekly at the rate of $10 per hour.)

- ✔ The number of hours you actually work each week

✔ A description of the violation/s you are alleging and the date/s of the violation/s

✔ The name, address, and phone number of your employer, as well as the nature of the employer's business — restaurant, software developer, retailer, and so on

After your complaint is received, WHD staff reviews it to determine whether you were a nonexempt worker at the time of the violation, whether you were performing work that was covered by the FLSA, and whether a violation may have been committed. If the staff determines that a potential FLSA violation was committed, it will investigate.

If the WHD's investigation determines that there's a "reasonable belief" that the law has been broken, and if the violation is something that the WHD can rectify, then it will investigate your employer. Depending on the outcome of the investigation, you may receive back wages, and your employer may face civil or criminal action. Employers who violate minimum wage and/or overtime pay requirements may be required to pay up to $1,100 per violation.

If you don't receive back wages as a result of the investigation or if the WHD decides not to conduct an investigation, you're entitled to file a lawsuit in federal court to recover the wages you believe you should have received. (You can sue your employer in state or federal court for twice the amount of the back wages and overtime you are owed.) Don't try filing the lawsuit on your own. Hire an employment law attorney who has specific experience handling cases similar to yours.

If you have any questions about the complaint process or about the FLSA in general, visit the WHD Web site at www.dol.gov/esa/whd or call the WHD toll-free help line at 1-866-487-9243. The help line is available from 8 a.m. to 5 p.m. in your time zone.

Although the WHD has regional offices in all states as well as in the District of Columbia, you can also contact its main office about your complaint. The address for that office is: Department of Labor, WHD, Frances Perkins Building, 200 Constitution Avenue, Washington, DC, 20210.

When do I get my paycheck, and why did you take out so much?

All states have laws regulating how and when you must be paid. Most require that employees be paid at least twice per month.

When you get your paycheck, you may be surprised to discover that it's not for the amount you had expected. That's probably because you forgot about paycheck deductions. For example, the federal government requires your employer to withhold federal income and Social Security taxes from your paycheck. Your state may make similar requirements of your employer.

Depending on your state, your employer may be allowed to deduct certain expenses from your paycheck (such as pay advances and the cost of job-related tools, equipment, and uniforms), as long as the deductions don't cut into your minimum wage or overtime pay. The same rule applies to instances when an employee working at a retail outlet is held responsible for cash shortages. And if you give your okay, your employer can deduct things like charitable donations, union dues, insurance premiums, and contributions to retirement accounts, even if these deductions do bring your pay below the minimum wage limit.

Most states prohibit employers from docking an employee's pay for discipli-nary reasons; however, some states allow employers to deduct money from an employee's paycheck to compensate for monetary losses that the busi-ness may have suffered due to the employee's dishonesty or negligence. These deductions must be spread out over a series of paychecks so that the amount the employee receives during a given pay period does not fall below the minimum wage.

Job benefits

Being able to pay your bills because you're getting a regular paycheck is cer-tainly the most important benefit of being employed. Depending on the com-pany you work for, however, your job may provide other benefits as well, including a paid vacation, insurance, and a retirement plan. Although most additional job benefits are optional for employers, employers who offer these benefits are usually expected to make the same benefit or benefit package available to all employees within a particular category. Therefore, an employer may offer different benefit packages to employees in different categories. For example, an employer may offer one set of benefits to all exempt employees and a different benefit package to all executives paid over $150,000 per year.

Some states require employers to offer their employees health insurance.

No federal law requires employers to provide their pregnant workers with paid maternity leave. But because pregnancy and childbirth are technically considered disabilities, you can use paid disability leave during your pregnancy or childbirth if your employer offers paid disability leave. Some states require employers to provide up to 16 weeks of unpaid maternity leave.

A must-have job benefit: Family and medical leave

Under the Family and Medical Leave Act (FMLA), the federal government requires all employers with at least 50 workers and most public agencies to allow qualified employees — employees who have worked for at least 12 months and at least 1,250 hours for a particular employer — to take off up to 12 weeks per 12-month period without pay for such things as

- The birth of a child
- The adoption of a child
- Assuming responsibility for a foster child
- The care of a spouse, child, or parent with a serious health condition
- Recuperation from a serious health problem such as an illness or injury that prevents an employee from working

You're entitled to take any paid vacation or personal time you may have accrued during your FMLA time off. In addition, under certain circumstances, your employer can require that you use any vacation or sick leave you may have accrued during your FMLA leave, assuming that your employer's policy regarding vacation and sick time off covers the reason or reasons why you want to take the FMLA leave.

Preparing for FMLA leave

The FMLA requires you to provide your employer with 30 days' notice of your need to take paid time off when you can anticipate the need. Also, when the FMLA time off is for a serious medical problem, your employer can require that you provide the following as a condition of your leave:

- Medical certification confirming that you have a serious medical condition. However, your employer is not entitled to review your medical records.
- Second or third medical opinions (at your employer's expense) and periodic medical recertifications.
- Periodic reports during your FMLA leave regarding your medical status and your intent to return to work.

Taking FMLA leave

If you take advantage of the FMLA, your employer must maintain your health insurance. You may be asked to reimburse your employer for the cost of the insurance if, at the end of your leave, you decide not to return to work. If you do return, you must be allowed to come back to your old job or to an equivalent one with the same pay and benefits. (See the next section, "Returning from FMLA leave," for more info on what to expect when you return to work.)

While you're on leave, your seniority and other benefits don't accrue, and you can't collect unemployment insurance. Also, your employer can count your accrued vacation, sick leave, and personal days toward your requested leave of absence.

Returning from FMLA leave

If you take time off under the FMLA, with a few exceptions, you're entitled to be reinstated in your same position when you return to work at the end of your leave. The exceptions include:

- ✔ You state in no uncertain terms that you do not intend to return to work after your leave has expired.

- ✔ Because of a corporate reorganization or some other change, your job is eliminated while you are on leave.

- ✔ You're highly paid — your salary is within your employer's top ten percent pay bracket — and reinstating you in your former position would cause serious economic harm to your employer.

- ✔ You're unable to return to work when your FMLA leave is up due to a physical or emotional problem or for some other reason. At that point, you're no longer covered by the FMLA.

- ✔ You fail to provide your employer with medical certification that you're well enough to return to work. Under certain conditions, your employer can require that you provide it with a medical certificate stating that you are well enough to return to your job.

In limited circumstances, if you're a key employee and your return to work will cause "substantial and grievous economic injury" to your employer's operations, your employer can refuse to reinstate you after you take FMLA leave and your health coverage is maintained. A *key employee* is defined as an individual among the highest-paid 10 percent of employees within 75 miles of your work location.

Your employer can't refuse to return you to your former position or eliminate that position in retaliation for your FMLA leave.

Some states have laws similar to the FMLA. Many of these laws are more generous than the FMLA. For example, a few states and Puerto Rico require that employers provide temporary disability insurance to their workers during leaves of absence.

If you have questions about the Family and Medical Leave Act, contact the National Partnership for Women and Families, which publishes a brochure on the topic. You can read the brochure online at www.nationalpartnership. org, or you can write to the organization at 1875 Connecticut Avenue, NW, Suite 710, Washington, DC, 20009.

Dealing with Employment-Related Discrimination

At some point in your working career, you may believe that you have been the victim of employment-related discrimination. In most cases, your first response should be an informal one — bring the problem to the attention of the person you believe discriminated against you or to that person's supervisor. What happened may have been an innocent mistake on his or her part, or you may have misconstrued the situation. Give everyone the benefit of the doubt and an opportunity to clear the air and/or rectify the situation. If the problem remains, you can continue to try to resolve it informally by "working your way up the ladder."

If you suspect discrimination, it's important that you get advice as soon as possible from your state's anti-discrimination agency or an employment law attorney for the following reasons.

- ✔ Time limits are in place for filing complaints and lawsuits related to employment discrimination.

- ✔ Some states require that you file a complaint with them before filing one with the Equal Employment Opportunity Commission (EEOC), while others require exactly the opposite.

- ✔ You need to find out what information you need to prove your claim.

If you're unable to locate your state's anti-discrimination agency or an employment law attorney, you can also contact the EEOC. The EEOC can help you understand if you have the grounds to file a formal complaint against your employer, inform you of your rights, and explain your options. (See the sidebar "The Equal Employment Opportunity Commission," later in this chapter.)

The Equal Employment Opportunity Commission

The Federal Equal Employment Opportunity Commission (EEOC) enforces federal anti-discrimination laws relating to discrimination on the basis of disability, pay and other compensation, national origin or ethnicity, pregnancy, race, religion, and sex.

Contact the EEOC's main office in Washington, D.C., or the regional office closest to you if you have a question about any of the laws that help protect you from being discriminated against when you apply for a job or after you're hired, or if you want to file a formal complaint against an employer because you believe you were discriminated against.

EEOC
1801 L St., NW
Washington, DC 20507
202-663-4900, 202-663-4944 (TTY)

Dial 1-800-669-4000 or 1-800-669-6820 (TTY) to be connected with your EEOC local office. To request EEOC publications, dial 1-800-669-3362.

If the EEOC does find reasonable cause, it will contact the employer and attempt to work out a settlement. If the EEOC is unable to resolve the issue out of court, it may file a lawsuit on your behalf; however, the EEOC files very few lawsuits. Assuming the EEOC wins on your behalf, and depending on the basis of the lawsuit, the employer may be ordered to hire you, reinstate you, promote you with a raise that's paid retroactively, reimburse you for the missed salary, and/or pay your legal fees. The employer can also be fined or penalized in some other way.

If you lose your case, depending on your state, the court can order you to pay the legal fees your employer accrued while defending itself against your lawsuit. This penalty is rarely handed down, and the lawsuit must be clearly frivolous, that is, have no basis in law or fact, to reach this conclusion.

If you want to file a lawsuit against your employer, you must file a claim first. Claims can be filed with the EEOC by mail or by calling the EEOC office nearest you. Call 1-800-669-400 to be connected with that office. You can also visit the office to file your claim in person.

If you file a complaint against your employer with the EEOC, you cannot be fired, demoted, or discriminated against for doing so.

If you file a formal complaint, the EEOC notifies your employer about the complaint, and if the commission decides that your allegation merits further investigation, it may collect additional information related to your charge. After the commission completes its research, the EEOC discusses the evidence with you or with the employer as appropriate. It may also select the case for mediation, assuming you and the employer are willing to try to resolve your disagreement using this process. Mediation offers you a faster means of resolving your problem than using the regular EEOC investigation process. If you agree to mediation and it's unsuccessful, the EEOC can continue its investigation.

If the EEOC's investigation shows that your rights were discriminated against, it notifies you and the employer of its finding and works with the employer to try to develop a remedy for the discrimination. If a remedy can't be agreed upon, the EEOC decides whether to file a lawsuit against your employer in federal court. On the other hand, if the EEOC and your employer identify a remedy for your problem, you can't file a lawsuit. However, you can file a lawsuit if the employer doesn't live up to its agreement with the EEOC.

If the EEOC finds no *reasonable cause* that discrimination did occur, it issues you a *right to sue* letter, and you're free to hire an attorney and file a lawsuit in federal court if you wish. You must do so within 90 days of receiving the letter. (The attorney you hire may be willing to take your case on contingency if your case is a strong one.)

To help find an employment attorney who can help you pursue your claim, contact the National Employment Lawyers Association at 415-296-7629 or go the organization's Web site at www.nela.org.

If you file a complaint with the EEOC and it doesn't act on your complaint within 180 days, then you can request that it issue you a right to sue letter.

Sexual Harassment

Beginning in the 1960s, women began to move into the workplace in growing numbers, and we began to hear about the problem of employment-related sexual harassment, although sexual harassment in the workplace was nothing new. Under pressure from women's groups and progressive elected officials and others, federal and state governments as well as employers were eventually forced to acknowledge the problem, and laws were passed to address sexual harassment. Now, with the law on their side, women (and men, too) are less reluctant to remain silent when they're harassed.

Sexual harassment is against the law. Title VII of the Civil Rights Act of 1964 views it as a form of employment discrimination, and the Civil Rights Act of 1991 provides victims of sexual harassment with the legal grounds to sue for damages. Also, many states have their own laws outlawing sexual harassment, and the laws of other states define sexual harassment as a form of sexual discrimination.

If you believe that you're being sexually harassed, you should follow the advice outlined in the previous section on employment-related discrimination. If your state has laws regarding sexual harassment, you should contact the appropriate agency as well as the EEOC.

Sexual harassment isn't always obvious. Although the stereotypical case involves a lascivious boss chasing his secretary around the desk, sexual harassment doesn't have to include physical contact or overt verbal advances. According to the EEOC, sexual harassment includes the following:

✔ Leading you to believe that you'll lose your job, be passed up for a promotion, or receive less desirable work assignments if you don't respond positively to a sexual advance — whether physical or verbal. This kind of harassment is considered *quid pro quo* sexual harassment (that's Latin for something given or done in exchange for something else — an even trade). Only someone who is in a supervisory or managerial position over you — someone with a certain degree of power over you — is capable of committing this form of harassment.

✔ Creating an intimidating, hostile, or offensive work environment that makes it difficult for you to perform your job. Sexually lewd comments, sexually explicit materials, or unwanted physical touching are all examples of things that can create this kind of environment.

Generally, something must happen more than once — a pattern must be established — before it can be considered sexual harassment. And because reasonable people can disagree about what is sexually offensive, the law also considers the intent of the person accused of sexual harassment. So, if you believe that you're being harassed, keep a record of each incident and include what happened, who did it, and where and when the incident occurred. If there were any witnesses to the incident, be sure to note them as well.

Employers are legally obligated to address instances of sexual harassment that come to their attention. Generally, employers are considered legally liable for instances of *quid pro quo* sexual harassment. Also, because they're expected to create and maintain a non-hostile environment for their workers, employers may also be legally liable for any harassment that takes place in a hostile or offensive work environment, even if the employers aren't aware of the particular instances of harassment.

You can be a victim of sexual harassment even if the harassment is not directed at you. For example, you may be the victim of sexual harassment if, at your expense, a co-worker is promoted or given better work assignments in exchange for sexual favors.

If the sexual advances of your manager or supervisor are unwelcome but you comply with them, the law may still view the advances as sexual harassment.

Safety on the Job

Federal law says that you have the right to "safe and healthful working conditions." These conditions are established and protected by the federal Occupational Safety and Health Act, which is enforced by the Occupational Safety and Health Administration (OSHA). Nearly every private sector employer is required to maintain a reasonably safe workplace for its employees and to meet OSHA's health and safety requirements.

Reporting unsafe conditions

If you believe an unsafe or unhealthy situation exists at your place of work — employees aren't being adequately protected from certain toxic or carcinogenic chemicals or equipment isn't being regularly inspected and maintained, for example — you can bring the matter to the attention of your employer, or you can become a whistle-blower by filing a complaint with the Occupational Safety and Health Administration (OSHA). (A whistle-blower is someone who brings his or her employer's illegal or unsafe activities to the attention of a government agency or office with enforcement powers. As a whistle-blower, you have the right to have your name withheld from your employer.)

Complaints can be filed in several ways. You can

- File online at www.osha.gov/as/opa/worker/complain.html.
- Download a complaint form at www.osha.gov/as/opa/worker/complain.html, and then fax or mail it to the main OSHA office or your regional office.
- Telephone OSHA's main office or your regional office.

If you contact OSHA, officers evaluate your information to determine whether your complaint merits an on-site or an off-site inspection. If an inspection is not necessary, OSHA conducts its investigation via phone and fax. With this type of investigation, officers contact your employer to discuss the hazards you have alleged, and then they follow up with a fax or a letter. Within five days, your employer must identify in writing whether or not it finds any hazards; if hazards exist, your employer must inform OSHA of what it has done or plans to do to correct them. You receive a copy of the employer's response to OSHA, and if you're not satisfied with it, you can request an on-site inspection.

Your state may have its own workplace health and safety agency and laws. Those laws may provide you with more protections than OSHA does and may impose stiffer punishments on employers who violate those rights. Therefore, if you believe that your rights have been violated, contact your state attorney general's office to find out if your state has any laws that apply to your problem and if it does, what your rights are under that law and what redress you may be entitled to. You may also want to consult with an employment law attorney about whether you're better off seeking redress using your state law or OSHA.

As long as you're not acting out of maliciousness, your employer can't fire you or harass you in any way for blowing the whistle on violations.

Dealing with accidents

Despite an employer's efforts to provide a healthy and safe workplace for its employees, on-the-job accidents and health problems do happen. And if you're the victim, you probably have the right to receive workers compensation payments.

In general, workers compensation provides you with replacement income, reimburses you for any medical expenses you rack up as a result of your problem, and pays for any physical or vocational rehabilitation you may need. Depending on the severity and permanence of your problem, your compensation may also include temporary or permanent disability. Dependents of individuals who are killed or become seriously ill because of on-the-job hazards are also entitled to benefits under the workers compensation program.

Most state laws require that you inform your employer of an on-the-job injury within 30 days of the injury or within 30 days of learning of the injury — for example, you learn that the dust you breathe in while doing your job has damaged your lungs.

Some states exempt very small employers from having to provide workers compensation. Others exempt certain types of workers from such coverage, including independent contractors, domestic workers, and farm workers. If you fall into one of these exempt categories and are injured on the job or become sick with a work-related illness, you may have to sue the employer to get any financial help.

What Your Employer Has the Right to Know about You

With the advent of technology that makes it easier and easier for government, private marketers, and even employers to peek and pry into our lives, our individual privacy is increasingly jeopardized. But laws do exist that can help us preserve some of our privacy in the workplace. For example, many states limit the rights of employers to use video and audio surveillance techniques to monitor employees' activities at work. State laws also exist that limit the ability of employers to read their employees' e-mail as well as employees' personal mail that may be delivered to the workplace. Generally, at a minimum, these laws require employers to tell their employees that they will be doing these things.

Although federal law prohibits employers from monitoring their employees' personal calls, employers are allowed to monitor employees' conversations with clients and customers. In some states, however, employers must let their employees know that their conversations are being recorded or monitored. Employers are also permitted to obtain a record of the calls their employees make at work and the length of their calls.

Some states have their own laws restricting employers' ability to listen to their employees' phone calls.

Computer software also allows employers to monitors what their employees have stored on their computers and even to see in real time what is on their employees' computer screens, as well as monitor employees' use of e-mail and the sites they visit on the Internet while they're at work. There is even software that can tell employers in data entry or other intensive word processing industries how many keystrokes per hour their employees are performing; still other software can tell employers how much time their employees spend away from their computers. Talk about Big Brother watching!

Don't assume that a deleted e-mail message is gone forever. It's not. Also, don't assume that just because your employer has a system that designates certain e-mail as confidential or private that any messages with this designation are safe from monitoring.

In an effort to check up on you, your employer may

- ✔ Listen to your voice mail.
- ✔ Search you or your property at work if the search is work related. (This option may not be permissible in some states.) But to avoid accusations of invasion of privacy, assault, intentional infliction of emotional harm, and the like, employers should let their employees know that they may be searched before they conduct a search, conduct their searches in an nonintrusive manner, and take care not to injure an employee during a search. In other words, searches should be conducted with discretion and good judgment.

✔ Ask that you take a lie detector or polygraph test, but only if the employer has evidence that you were involved in a work-related situation that harmed your employer economically or in some other way. The federal Employment Polygraph Protection Act restricts the use of this kind of test. Many states also regulate or prohibit employers' use of polygraph tests.

✔ Require that a doctor examine you if there's any question about whether you're fit to perform your job. However, your employer is not entitled to receive the results of the exam or any tests that were run — only a report from the doctor may be passed along.

The Americans with Disabilities Act requires your employer to keep your medical-related information in a file that is separate from your personnel file and to restrict who can have access to that information.

✔ Conduct random drug testing, depending on the type of job you have and the industry you work in. For example, federal law says that airline pilots and transit workers can be required to submit to random drug tests without notice and can be fired if they refuse. The same holds true for nuclear reactor workers, peace officers, and other employees who work in a safety-sensitive or security-sensitive industry. Also, you can be required to take a drug test if your employer has good reason to believe that you're under the influence of drugs at any time while you're on the job. In all other situations, your employer must notify you before a drug test and must have a written policy for how the testing will be conducted and how the results will be used. Many states limit when employees can be drug tested and the particular kinds of testing that can be done.

The Federal Drug-Free Work Place Act says that all public and private businesses, as well as governmental agencies and nonprofit organizations that receive federal grants of any amount or federal contracts worth at least $25,000, must establish a drug-free education program for their employees and communicate with them about the program.

Accessing your personnel file

Among other provisions, the Federal Privacy Act gives federal government workers the right to review the contents of their personnel files, to copy whatever they want, and to challenge the information they may find in their files. Other federal laws give private sector employees in particular work situations access to certain information in their personnel files. Also, your state may have a law giving you the right to review the information in your personnel file, make copies of that information, and challenge its accuracy.

Calling It Quits

You can leave your job in several ways. Some are pleasant, like moving on to a bigger and better job, starting your own business, or retiring. Others are a lot less pleasant, like being fired or being laid off due to corporate downsizing, outsourcing, or job restructuring. You may also be laid off if your job becomes obsolete.

If you're like most employees, you're considered an *at-will* employee, which means that you can be fired at any time for just about any job-related reason without any notice or severance pay. So much for job security, huh!

But you still may have some rights as an at-will employee; exceptions to at-will employment and firing do exist. For example, depending on your state, your employer may have to provide *just cause* or *good reason* for firing you. Also, you can't be fired at-will if you have a contract with your employer that makes other provisions for your firing or if your employer has an employment policy that prohibits such firings.

If you're a government worker, civil service laws protect you from at-will firings. Also, most labor unions have contracts with employers that prohibit at-will firings of their members.

If you feel that your firing is the result of discrimination, you can attempt to get redress by contacting the EEOC (follow the advice presented earlier in this chapter). You can also consult with an employment law attorney.

If you feel that your firing was unfair but not necessarily discriminatory, you should contact an employment attorney to discuss whether you have any basis for filing a lawsuit. Be sure to discuss the matter with your employer first, though.

Severance pay

When you lose your job, you don't automatically receive severance pay. It's up to your boss to decide if you get severance and how much you get — unless your employer made a verbal promise to you, your employment contract provides for it, your employer's employment policy promises severance pay, or for many years, employees in your same position have received severance pay. If you're fired for misconduct, you probably won't get anything.

Your state may have a law that specifies when you must receive your final paycheck and whether the check must include payment for any vacation time you did not use. So, if you don't receive your last paycheck on a timely basis, or if it arrives but it's for the wrong amount, then contact your former employer. If that gets you nowhere, call your state employment agency for advice about what to do. It may suggest that you contact an employment law attorney.

Unemployment insurance

Unless you're fired for gross misconduct, you're probably eligible to receive unemployment insurance if you've been working at your current job long enough. How long is long enough varies from state to state. After applying for unemployment insurance, you can probably collect your benefits for at least 26 weeks. To apply for unemployment benefits, contact your state's unemployment insurance office.

If you leave your job voluntarily, you may be eligible to collect unemployment if you can prove that your employer made your work situation so intolerable that you had to leave.

Health insurance

Because of the Consolidated Omnibus Budget Reconciliation Act, better known as COBRA, you can remain on your employer's health insurance plan for up to 18 months after you leave your job, whether you're fired or you quit, assuming that your employer has at least 20 employees. Your family members can stay on the policy as well. However, you must continue to pay the full cost of your insurance premium. It's better than nothing!

You can be denied COBRA benefits if you're dismissed for gross misconduct.

Chapter 7

Driving and the Law

• •

In This Chapter

▶ Getting your license

▶ Obeying the rules of the road

▶ Knowing your rights when a cop pulls you over

▶ Dealing with accidents

▶ Fulfilling your responsibilities as a driver

• •

*D*riving is simple. Just turn the ignition key and step on the gas, right?
Wrong. Before you can get behind the wheel, you have some legal hoops
to jump through. Namely, you must get a driver's license and have insurance.
And to maintain your right to get behind the wheel, you must demonstrate
your willingness and ability to obey the rules of the road.

Getting Your Driver's License

In most states, 16 is the magic age for getting a regular driver's license,
although in most states, you can get a learner's permit at age 15. Also, some
states allow young people to get their licenses at an earlier age if they meet
certain conditions, such as passing a driver's education class or getting the
consent of their parents.

Although the exact process for getting a driver's license differs slightly from
state to state, it typically includes passing the following tests:

✔ A written test about the basic rules of the road. (Pretty much a no-brainer
if you're a passenger who pays attention when someone else is driving.)

✔ A behind-the-wheel test of your ability to drive. (Passing this test can be
a little trickier, especially if you're intimidated by having a stranger in
the seat next to you watching your every move!)

✔ A vision test. (You can't study for this one, so you either pass or you
don't.)

Your driver's license may come with restrictions, or restrictions may sometimes be added on later. The restrictions can be as insignificant as requiring that you wear your glasses or contact lenses whenever you drive, or if you have a chronic and potentially dangerous medical condition, the restrictions may limit when you can drive. If you ignore your restrictions and get pulled over by a police officer, your license can be suspended.

Your driver's license doesn't last forever, so you have to renew it periodically. If you're lucky, you can do it by mail and avoid the hassle of making a personal appearance at your state department of motor vehicles. If you're a senior citizen over a certain age, your state may require that you pass an eye exam and a driver's test every time you renew your license.

If you move to a new state, you may have to apply for a new driver's license within a certain number of days after your move, or you may be able to wait until your old license expires. Check with the department of motor vehicles in your new home state for details.

The Rules of the Road

Keeping your right to drive requires you to demonstrate that you're a responsible driver. If you don't, your license may be *suspended* (you lose it temporarily) or *revoked* (you're grounded for good). Grounds for suspension or revocation can include the following:

- ✔ Causing "too many" traffic accidents (every state has its own rules for what qualifies as "too many")
- ✔ Getting a lot of tickets for moving violations
- ✔ Driving without insurance
- ✔ Being convicted of driving while under the influence of alcohol or drugs

States share information on the records of their drivers. So, if you move, your new state may refuse to license you if your previous state has suspended or revoked your license.

If your license has been suspended or revoked, don't even think about driving. If you do and a police officer pulls you over, you'll be arrested and charged with either a misdemeanor or a felony depending on why you lost your license.

Uh Oh! Stopped by the Cops

Your three-hour drive to the beach is almost over. It's been an easy one — beautiful scenery and little traffic. You've been making great time. Life couldn't be better! Then all of a sudden, out of nowhere, a cop car with its lights flashing is right behind you. Talk about putting a damper on your trip!

If this happens to you, pull off the road as quickly and safely as possible and remain in the car unless the police officer tells you to get out. The officer will ask to see your driver's license and possibly your vehicle registration and proof of insurance. The officer should tell you why you've been stopped — it's your legal right to know. If the officer doesn't provide this information, ask.

If you're not sure that the person who stops you is really a police officer, ask to see his or her photo identification. Don't settle for a badge. If the "officer" refuses to show you an I.D. or, after seeing it, you're still not convinced, ask that the officer's supervisor be called or offer to follow the officer to the police station.

You can be stopped by a police officer if he or she has a *reasonable belief* or *reasonable suspicion* that you or someone in your vehicle is committing or has committed a crime. The crime can be any number of things, including driving too fast, driving with an expired license plate, reckless driving, driving while intoxicated, driving with a headlight out, leaving the scene of a crime, robbery, murder — you get the picture.

Searching your car

After you've been stopped, the police officer can't search your car unless you give your permission or unless the officer has *probable cause*. Probable cause is a kind of gray area; its definition varies widely among states, and those definitions are constantly changing. Generally, an officer has probable cause when he or she believes that your car contains incriminating evidence — evidence that you and/or your passenger are committing or have committed a crime. With probable cause, your vehicle can be searched without a search warrant.

Reasonable suspicion is easier to prove than probable cause.

A police officer's reason for stopping you affects whether or not he has probable cause to conduct a search. For example, being stopped because your headlight is out may provide less probable cause for a search than being pulled over because you've been driving erratically or at a high rate of speed.

The Fourth Amendment of the U.S. Constitution protects you and your belongings from unreasonable searches and seizures. Law enforcement officials must usually obtain a search warrant in order to search your home. But the Supreme Court has ruled that the Fourth Amendment provides you less protection when you're in your car.

If an officer looks through your vehicle window — a *plain view* search — and spies something that he or she considers to be possible evidence of a crime, like an open container of beer sitting on your seat or a half-smoked marijuana cigarette lying in the ashtray, the officer can take it as evidence. After spying potential evidence, the officer has the right to conduct a full-scale, warrantless search of your car.

If an officer begins searching your vehicle without apparent probable cause, ask to see his or her search warrant, but don't try to stop the search. If you're not shown a warrant and the officer continues the search and takes something from your vehicle, you can challenge the seizure in court.

Searching your person

The police have the right to frisk you or "pat you down" without a warrant if they have a reasonable suspicion that you may possess drugs or weapons and can articulate their reasoning to the courts. Although they can't search your clothes or your pockets, if they feel something suspicious, they can seize it; otherwise, the police need probable cause to search your clothing and your pockets. This restriction also applies to warrant-less searches of your car.

Getting Tickets

Even the most careful and conscientious drivers are likely to get a ticket for a traffic violation of some sort at some point in their driving careers. If you're lucky, your tickets will be for non-moving violations — parking tickets and tickets for mechanical defects, for example. You have to pay fines on these kinds of violations, but they don't damage your driving record. But tickets for moving violations such as speeding, reckless driving, and driving while intoxicated do go on your record and may possibly increase your insurance costs. If you get two moving violations within a certain period of time, expect to have your license suspended or revoked for a period of time.

Parking tickets may not be a big deal, but don't ignore them. If you accumulate enough unpaid tickets, a warrant for your arrest may be issued, or your car may be immobilized by the infamous Denver Boot. The Boot is essentially a mechanism that locks a wheel on your car so that you can't drive it. The only way to get it removed is to pay your tickets, so get your checkbook ready.

When you get a ticket, you have two options: fight it or pay it by the due date. If you decide to fight, you have to be arraigned in court on a certain date. At the arraignment, your rights are read to you, and you're asked to plead guilty or not guilty. Because you're fighting the charge, you say "not guilty." (Some states let you do this by mail.) If you've been charged with a serious moving violation, it's a good idea to hire an attorney to represent you. If you don't get an attorney, your case is a matter of your word against that of the police officer who ticketed you, which means that you're probably at a serious disadvantage.

If you're ticketed for a moving violation and you decide not to fight it, you're pleading guilty by paying the fine. That means that the cost of your insurance premium may go up, and the violation goes on your driving record.

Accidents Happen

If you're involved in an accident, regardless of whom you think is at fault, stop your vehicle and inspect the damage. Not stopping is a criminal offense. If you're convicted of a "hit and run," your driver's license may be suspended, or you may be fined and sentenced to jail.

If no one is injured and damage to the vehicles involved is very slight to nonexistent, you and the other driver can handle the situation yourselves without calling the police. Exchange your names, addresses, phone numbers, the names of your insurance companies, your policy numbers, your driver's license numbers, license plate numbers, and the makes, models, and years of your cars. If, however, someone is injured or killed, or if property damage is substantial, you must call the police, and an officer will file an accident report.

Most insurance companies don't pay claims without a police report. Don't sign any insurance forms related to an accident-related injury without first consulting an attorney.

Although all states require accident reports in the case of death or injury, each state has its own criteria for when an accident report is required.

When the police arrive, you must answer any questions the officers may ask. If witnesses to the accident are present, get their names and phone numbers but don't talk with them about what you think happened. If you end up in court as a result of the accident and a witness testifies, what you say at the scene can be used against you.

If you have the presence of mind to do so, make some notes about your accident while everything is still relatively fresh in your mind. For example, you may want to draw a diagram of the accident and describe the weather, street conditions, and any other pertinent factors. This information can be helpful if you're sued over the accident or end up suing the other driver.

If you hit a parked car, you're expected to make a reasonable effort to locate the owner; at the very least, you're obligated to leave your name, address, and phone number on the car you hit and notify the police.

Drinking and Driving

As they say, drinking and driving don't mix. To deter drivers from using alcohol, state laws have become harsher in recent years. Presently, depending on the state you're convicted of drinking and driving in, your license may be suspended or revoked, and you may be jailed, fined, put on probation, or forced to enroll in a rehab program. If you've been convicted before for drunk driving, your penalty will be especially serious.

Every state has its own standard for determining when a driver is under the influence of alcohol and should not be behind the wheel, and the laws governing drinking and driving also apply to driving while under the influence of illegal drugs.

If you're stopped by a police officer and the officer suspects that you've been drinking, he or she will probably ask you to take a number of roadside impairment or sobriety tests, which can include walking in a straight line, reciting the alphabet backwards, or standing on one leg. You may also be asked to take a preliminary breath test, which gives the officer a measure of the level of alcohol in your blood. The results of these tests may provide the officer with sufficient probable cause to arrest you.

If you're arrested and taken to the police station, you may be asked to take a Breathalyzer test, which provides a more precise measure of your intoxication level.

Legally, you can refuse to take a roadside sobriety test. But the officer can arrest you anyway if he or she suspects that you're intoxicated because your speech is slurred, your eyes are bloodshot, you're weaving when you stand still, and so on. At the police station, you can also refuse to take a Breathalyzer, urine, or blood test; however, your refusal to take any of these tests can be used against you in court, and you may be subject to stiffer than normal penalties if you're convicted. Also, depending on your state, a blood sample can be forcibly withdrawn if you've been involved in a traffic accident in which someone was killed or seriously injured.

If you're involved in a car accident that results in death or serious injury, the officer may want a sample of your blood. Testing your level of intoxication by sampling your blood provides stronger evidence in court than the results of a Breathalyzer test.

When you get a driver's license, your state assumes that you've given *implied consent* to be tested for alcohol use. Usually, the concept of implied consent also applies to testing for the use of drugs while you're driving.

The Responsibilities of Owning a Vehicle

If you own a vehicle, you must follow certain rules if you want to keep your vehicle on the road and keep yourself out of legal hot water.

Register your car

When you buy a car, you must register it right away. Also, you probably have to renew the registration every year. In most states, registration is contingent on proof of liability insurance (skip down to the section "Maintain valid insurance" for details on this).

Get it inspected

To help ensure that your car meets the minimum safety standards established by your state, you must have your car inspected regularly (usually annually) either at a state-authorized repair shop or dealer, or at a government inspection station. Your car also may have to meet certain environmental standards. If your car doesn't pass muster, you're given a specified period of time in which to bring it up to standards and to get it reinspected; otherwise, you can't continue driving it. If you don't get your car's problems fixed and you keep it on the road, you're subject to fines.

Maintain valid insurance

All states have financial responsibility laws. Most of these laws require that drivers have liability insurance, but others allow drivers to provide proof that they have other means of paying for a state-specified amount of damages in the event of an accident.

Liability insurance helps protect you legally and financially if an accident is your fault and someone is injured or killed and/or you cause serious property damage. Your insurer pays the legitimate claims of the injured party and defends you in court if you're sued. Usually, your insurer also protects you if someone driving your car with your permission is involved in an accident.

For extra protection, you can purchase additional insurance, such as uninsured motorist coverage (pays your expenses when you're hit by an uninsured driver); collision coverage (pays for the physical damage to your vehicle); and comprehensive coverage (pays for non-accident-related damage to your vehicle, such as if a tree falls on your car, your car is pounded by hail, your car is stolen, and so on).

Some states have no-fault laws for liability insurance. In these states, policyholders are reimbursed by their own insurance companies when they're injured in an accident regardless of who caused the accident. This kind of insurance, however, restricts the ability of anyone injured in an accident to sue the person at fault.

Although most no-fault insurance policies apply only to personal injury claims, a few also apply to property damage.

Chapter 8

Privacy: Do You Really Have Any?

- -

In This Chapter

▶ Recognizing the good and bad sides of federal privacy legislation

▶ Guarding your identity

▶ Understanding how federal anti-terrorism laws may affect you

- -

As Americans, we cherish our privacy. We value the right to lead our lives with a minimum of government interference and to keep the details of our private lives to ourselves. Privacy is central to our concept of freedom. But often, without our knowledge or permission, information about some of the most personal aspects of our lives — financial data, demographic characteristics, buying habits, medical history — is collected by the government, private companies, and high-tech snoops. Much of this information is uncorroborated, which means that it may be incorrect. Yet it may be used to make decisions that can affect our lives in important ways. For example, we may be denied the job we want or the insurance we need, or we may even be arrested because of erroneous information in a database somewhere. Furthermore, if an identity thief steals our personal and financial information — a crime that was not a major threat when the first edition of this book was written — our financial lives can be ruined, and it can take many months, if not years, to recover from the impact of the crime.

Ironically, as much as we value our privacy and as much as it is threatened every day, few federal laws actually help protect it. Those that do tend to be narrowly focused, full of loopholes and exceptions that have been added by powerful special interests, and without real teeth. Some privacy laws are also woefully outdated because they were written before personal computers became ubiquitous, before technology facilitated the creation of the sophisticated databases that exist today, before it became routine for businesses and other organizations to exchange files of information online, and before so much information about us was available for the taking on the Internet. Furthermore, in its War on Terrorism, the federal government now has powers to invade your privacy without your knowledge or permission. For example, if you're suspected of having a connection with terrorism, the FBI and the CIA can monitor your conversations and search your home without your knowledge or permission, and they can even force your local librarian to tell them what books you've been reading!

In this chapter, I tell you how the federal government and the private sector gain access to your information and what they may do with it, and I fill you in on the laws that have been passed to help protect you. This chapter explains identity theft — a growing threat to your privacy — and reviews the various steps you should take if you're a victim of that crime. I arm you with numerous practical tips for protecting your personal and financial information and also detail how HIPAA (the Health Insurance Portability and Accountability Act) may jeopardize the security of your health-related information and how the war on terrorism may undermine your privacy.

Who Knows What About Me?

What follows are just some of the ways that your private information is collected, shared, and even sold despite the existence of federal privacy laws:

- ✔ Companies comprising the billion-dollar information industry make big bucks collecting consumer data from the Census Bureau, credit applications, product warranty cards, magazine subscription cards, and public records to create detailed consumer profiles. They sell this data to marketers. Although federal laws place some limits on what companies can do with your personal information, businesses in the information industry are effectively free to do what they want.

- ✔ Some companies specialize in selling information to employers. For example, to help them make hiring decisions, an employer may query a database company to find out if a job applicant has ever filed claims for on-the-job injuries. If the applicant has, he or she may be labeled a potential troublemaker and not get hired, even though the individual may have had a good reason for filing the claim. As another example, an employer may ask a private database company to tell it whether an applicant has ever been arrested. Most likely, if the applicant has been, he or she will be denied a job — even though the database may not show that the applicant was acquitted!

- ✔ Federal agencies regularly collect, store, manipulate, and share massive amounts of data about us — our medical histories, educational backgrounds, financial status, employment histories, criminal histories, and so on. Sometimes they enhance their information with information from private databases. Since September 11, 2001, anti-terrorism laws have given the federal government greater freedom to invade our privacy. For more information on such legislation, turn to the section "Post-9/11 Inroads into Your Privacy: The Patriot Act," later in this chapter.

- ✔ Some federal agencies create detailed *profiles* of certain groups of people — tax evaders, welfare cheaters, and terrorists, for example. Then they compare the consumers in their databases to these profiles in order to identify the people they're looking for. *Profiling* has been widely criticized by privacy advocates because the technique is not foolproof and therefore has disrupted the lives of many innocent people.

  Profiling is subject to very few restrictions, and you have little recourse if you're the victim of a profiling error.

- ✔ Identity thieves steal Social Security and/or driver's license numbers, bank and credit card account numbers, and other financial information as a way to steal your money, charge up your credit cards without your knowledge, increase the credit limits on your accounts, benefit from your health plan, and so on. All this is done without your knowledge.

- ✔ Medical providers, insurance companies, and others in the medical industry store highly sensitive information about your mental and physical health in computer files, not locked cabinets, and they share that information with one another via e-mail. These storage and communication methods make information highly vulnerable, and as a result, countless individuals may have access to your personal health information.

Depending on your state, you may have certain privacy rights in the workplace. Also, the federal government bars employers from tapping your phone conversations or listening to your private conversations at work without telling you ahead of time.

In light of these modern-day challenges to our privacy, it may surprise you to know that the word "privacy" isn't even mentioned in the Constitution! Perhaps the explanation is a simple one — in the 18th century, our privacy could only be threatened in few ways, and the Founding Fathers believed that Amendment Four of the Constitution, which protects Americans from "unreasonable searches and seizures," pretty much took care of any potential problems.

So far, elected officials have been unwilling to pass laws that will truly help us protect our privacy. Therefore, the burden is on each of us to do what we can to protect it ourselves. Although there's no foolproof way to do that, you can start by being aware of the privacy-related laws that do exist and of the steps you can take both to limit who has access to your personal information and to minimize the damage an identity thief can do to your finances.

The Federal Privacy Act

The federal government is this country's biggest collector of information about us. Just stop to think about the kinds of personal data you share when you fill out your income tax return every year; apply for Social Security, Medicare, or other government benefit programs; fill out an application for a student loan; or participate in a Census Bureau survey!

The federal Privacy Act was passed in 1974 to limit the ability of federal agencies to collect, use, and disseminate our personal information. The law says that, when practical, agencies must collect only "necessary" information and that when you provide information about yourself, the agency must tell you how the information will be used. The Privacy Act also says that before an agency can share your information with another agency, it must get your written permission. The law gives you some other rights as well, including the right to

- ✔ Obtain a copy of the data file that a federal agency maintains on you

- ✔ Dispute the accuracy and completeness of the information in that file

- ✔ Have file information corrected, updated, or deleted

How to find out what's in your information file

To find out whether or not a federal agency maintains a file on you and, if so, what's in that file, write a letter to the agency's Privacy Act officer or to the head of the agency. Clearly stipulate in your letter that you're making your request pursuant to the federal Privacy Act and describe as best you can exactly what records you're asking for. Your request can be as general as "all records you're maintaining on me" or as specific as "a copy of my complete file." Also, write "Privacy Act Request" on the outside of your envelope to expedite your request.

Be sure your letter includes your full name, address, and Social Security number, and attach to it a copy of your driver's license. If your request is too vague, the agency will notify you, and agency personnel should be able to help you restate your request with greater specificity.

Some agencies have very specific procedures for making record requests. For example, your signature on your request letter or on the request form that the agency may require you fill out may have to be notarized. So, before you make your request, it's a good idea to write to the agency and ask for a copy of its request requirements.

The Privacy Act is so vaguely worded and includes so many loopholes and exceptions that it's really of little value to consumers. Depending on what you ask an agency for, loopholes in the Privacy Act may allow it to deny you the information you seek.

Although the law doesn't specify how quickly an agency must respond to your request to know what's in your data file, most agencies have a ten-day response policy. If a month goes by and you still haven't heard anything, you may want to write the agency another letter and enclose with it a copy of your first letter.

How to amend your file

When the agency sends you the information you've requested, it should also include instructions for how to challenge the information if you believe it's out-of-date, incorrect, or incomplete. Typically, you're instructed to do the following:

1. Write to the agency official who released the information to you.

2. Clearly spell out the problem you've identified and how you want it corrected or what you want added.

3. Include copies of documentation that justifies your request for an amendment to your data file.

If an agency allows you to request a change in your file by phone or in person, put your request in writing, too. A written request can be helpful if your request ends in an appeal.

After you make your request for an amendment, the agency should respond within ten days of receiving it. The agency may respond by telling you about any additional information it needs. It may agree to your request or deny it. If your request is denied, you must be told why and be provided with instructions for appealing the agency's decision.

If your request is denied, you have the right to prepare a short statement regarding what you disagree with in your file and to have that statement made a permanent part of the agency's record on you.

The Privacy Act doesn't spell out a specific procedure that agencies must follow when an agency's decision is appealed. The law, however, does require that each agency establish its own appeals process. (You use the same process if the agency denies your request for information and if the agency denies your amendment request.)

If the agency denies your appeal, you can sue the agency in federal district court. You must file your lawsuit within two years of an agency's final denial. If you win your lawsuit, you may be able to recover court costs and attorney's fees.

Privacy Act shortcomings

The federal Privacy Act falls far short of protecting consumer privacy. Here are some reasons why:

- ✔ The law is worded vaguely and therefore is open to interpretation.

- ✔ The law includes many exemptions to the ban on agencies sharing information about you without your written consent. A particularly problematic exemption is one that allows a federal agency to share consumer data with another agency when it's done for "routine use." Just about anything can be justified as routine!

- ✔ The Office of Management and Budget (OMB) has responsibility for monitoring and enforcing this law. Its powers to do so are extremely limited, however, and as a consequence, agencies tend to ignore and abuse the provisions of the Privacy Act.

The Right to Financial Privacy Act

The federal Right to Financial Privacy Act (RFPA) was passed in 1978 to help balance the need of federal law-enforcement agencies (the FBI, Department of Justice investigators, Treasury Department investigators, and Social Security Administration officials, for example) to review a consumer's bank records as part of a criminal investigation and a consumer's desire that his or her financial information be kept private. The law doesn't apply to state law-enforcement agencies, only federal ones.

According to the RFPA, federal law-enforcement officials can gain access to your bank records either by obtaining your written permission (if you provide your permission, it's good for up to three months) or by getting an administrative or judicial subpoena, court order, or search warrant.

If officials try to gain access to your bank records via a written request, subpoena, court order, or summons, they must serve or mail you a copy of their documentation at your last known address on or before the day that the bank is served with the request and then wait ten or fourteen days, depending on how you've been notified, before they can look at the information. The officials must also give you a written explanation of why the information is being sought and of your legal right to challenge the information request. (If law-enforcement officials use a search warrant to get access to your bank records, the law allows them to notify you after the fact — as much as 90 days after the bank has been served. Also, under broadly defined conditions, the agency can get extensions of this notification deadline in 90-day increments.)

The RFPA gives you the right to challenge in court a federal law-enforcement agency's efforts to access your bank records. To win your challenge, you have to demonstrate that the agency doesn't need the information or that it has violated the provisions of the RFPA. You need an attorney's help to take this action.

The RFPA doesn't apply to state or local law-enforcement officials. So in the absence of a state law prohibiting access entirely or one that limits access, state and local law-enforcement officials can go to your bank, present appropriate identification, explain the purpose of their visit, and review your records — all without your knowledge or permission!

The federal Financial Services Modernization Act

The federal Financial Services Modernization Act (FSMA) law, also known as the Gramm-Leach Act, allows financial services companies such as banks, insurance companies, brokerage houses, mortgage companies, auto financing companies, and so on to affiliate in order to function as "financial supermarkets." Usually, *affiliated companies* are owned or controlled by the same company — they're part of the same corporate family. The FSMA allows these affiliated companies to share with one another information about your finances, spending patterns, investments, account numbers, health-related information, and so on. You have no control over this exchange. However, the FSMA also gives *you* some rights in regard to the companies' sharing your information with unaffiliated businesses.

Your rights under the FSMA

The FSMA says that the financial services companies you do business with must provide you with three different types of notices:

A privacy notice

This notice must identify what information the companies collect about their customers. That information can include information that their customers put on their applications; information that the companies may have obtained about their customers from other sources, such as from credit reporting agencies; and information about their customers' transactions. The privacy notice must also indicate with whom the financial services companies share their information and how they protect that information.

If you're a *customer* of a financial services company — meaning someone who has an ongoing relationship with the company, as defined by the FSMA — then you're automatically entitled to receive this privacy notice every year for as long as the relationship continues. However, if you're a *consumer* of a financial services company — meaning you do business with the company on a one time basis or periodically, according to the FSMA — then you're only entitled to receive a privacy notice when the company shares your information with companies that it's not affiliated with it, although there are some exceptions.

The FSMA privacy notice must also let you know that the federal Fair Credit Reporting Act (FCRA) gives you the right to opt out of having a financial services company share with its affiliates information related to your creditworthiness — your credit report or a credit application, for example. Under the FCRA, you don't have the right to opt out when it comes to other kinds of information.

The more your personal and financial information is shared and sold by businesses, the more likely it is that your privacy will be violated and the information will fall into the wrong hands.

Your state may have a law that provides you with more protections than the FSMA does.

The FSMA prohibits affiliated financial companies from selling your account numbers to third parties. However, affiliated companies are free to provide third parties with your account information if the third parties are going to market the financial companies' products and services.

An opt-out notice

This notice must let you know that you have the right to opt out of having financial services companies share your information with third parties that they're not affiliated with and must tell you how to exercise this right. The opt-out notice may come to you in the mail or via e-mail if you regularly do business with a financial services company online. As a customer of such a company, you're entitled to receive this notice automatically each year; otherwise, you will only receive it occasionally.

Pay close attention to the instructions in the notice regarding exactly how to opt out. If you don't follow the instructions to the letter, your account numbers will be withheld, but your personal information still will be shared with others.

If you're a *customer* of a financial services company and you don't opt out when you first receive the opt-out notice, you can contact the company later to opt out. However, the company may share your personal information until you take action.

Under the FSMA, although you can opt out of having financial services companies share your information with non-affiliated companies, you have no control over what affiliated companies share with one another.

The FSMA doesn't require that financial services companies use a standard type of opt-out notice. Therefore, it's up to you to review all of the inserts you receive with your account statements and credit card bills and any other information you may receive in the mail from financial services companies you have done business with or have an ongoing relationship with. You also need to read carefully the subject headings on the e-mails you receive from these companies so that you can determine whether any of that information includes opt-out instructions. Making opting out even more complicated, the law doesn't require that the notices be sent out at a certain time of year. However, it does require that opt-out notices be "clear and conspicuous."

An explanation of security policies

The third type of notice that financial services companies must provide for their customers is an explanation of security policies. This information must explain how affiliated financial services companies protect the personal information they maintain on you.

If your FSMA rights are violated

Under the FSMA, you don't have the right to sue a financial services company that violates your rights. In most instances, the most you can do is write a letter of complaint to the business and complain to one of the federal agencies charged with enforcing the FSMA. If you file a complaint, the federal agency will review the complaint and conduct an investigation if it believes there's sufficient basis for one. If the agency finds that a financial services company has violated the FSMA, it may decide to take administrative or legal action against the company.

If your FSMA-related problem is with a bank or savings and loan, Chapter 10 provides information about how to register a complaint with the appropriate federal agency.

If your complaint is with a stock brokerage, contact

> Securities and Exchange Commission
> Investor Education and Assistance
> 450 Fifth St., NW
> Washington, DC 20549
> 202-942-7040
> www.sec.gov/complaint/selectconduct.shtml

If you've got a beef with a commodities futures exchange or with a registered company engaged in futures and commodity option trading, contact

Commodity Futures Trading Commission
Three Lafayette Centre
1155 21st St., NW
Washington, DC 20581
202-418-5000
www.cftc.gov

To complain about an insurance company, contact your state's insurance commission. If you can't find contact information for that office in the government listings of your local phone book, call the National Association of Insurance Commissioners at 816-842-3600 or visit that organization's Web site at www.naic.org.

If your FSMA complaint is related to a non-bank mortgage lender, loan broker, certain types of financial or investment advisors, a tax preparer, providers of real estate settlement services, or a debt collector, get in touch with the Federal Trade Commission at www.ftc.gov or at 1-877-382-4357. You can also write to the FTC at Bureau of Consumer Protection, 600 Pennsylvania Avenue, NW, Washington, DC 20580.

Your state may have a law allowing you to bring a lawsuit if your FSMA rights have been violated. Consult with a consumer law attorney about your options.

The Federal Identity Theft and Assumption Deterrence Act

The federal Identity Theft and Assumption Deterrence Act (ITADA) makes identity theft a federal crime. Identity theft occurs when someone steals your personal and/or financial information — your bank account number, credit card account numbers, Social Security number, driver's license number, ATM or PIN number, and so on — and uses it to, among other things,

- Run up your credit cards.
- Get a loan in your name.
- Drain your bank accounts.
- Obtain new credit in your name.
- Benefit from your insurance.
- Obtain a cell phone.

- ✔ Initiate utility service.
- ✔ File a fraudulent tax return.

Identity theft is one of the fastest growing crimes in this country. An estimated 7 million consumers were victims of the crime in 2003, and according to a national survey, one-half of all identity thefts are committed by friends, relatives, or co-workers of the victims.

Identity thieves can steal your information in any number of ways. For example, they may eavesdrop on your phone conversations, pick up the receipt you carelessly leave by an ATM machine, steal your wallet, copy an account number from the credit card you use to make a purchase or from the store copy of the charge receipt, rifle through your garbage or your mail, trick you into providing your personal or financial information over the phone or online, hack into your computer, or get your information over the Internet. Your identity may also be stolen at work. For example, one of your co-workers with access to your personnel file may steal information contained there.

Unfortunately, catching an identity thief can be extremely difficult. If the criminal can't be found, then the ITADA is of little value. Listed below are a couple reasons why this is true.

- ✔ The theft of your identity can happen without your knowledge, unlike many other types of crimes. By the time you realize that an identity thief has victimized you, it may be virtually impossible to determine the thief's identity. For example, you may not realize that you're a crime victim until you review your monthly credit card statement and notice charges you didn't make or authorize, until you discover new accounts in your credit report that you didn't open, until a retailer refuses to accept your check even though you have always maintained a healthy balance in your bank account, or until a debt collector calls demanding payment on a debt you know nothing about. Yikes!

- ✔ The law doesn't help you undo all of the damage that an identity thief can do to your financial life. He or she can destroy your credit history, cause your credit score to take a dive, and ruin your good name.

Some consumers have been arrested for crimes they didn't commit because of something that identity thieves did in their names!

An ounce of prevention

The best way to avoid having to deal with the repercussions of identity theft is to do whatever you can to keep your personal and financial information private.

To keep things as private as possible when it comes to your credit cards, follow this advice:

- Don't carry multiple credit cards and IDs in your wallet or purse. That way, if your purse or wallet is stolen, you have less for an identity thief to take.

- When you pay with a credit card, don't write your phone number, home address, or other personal information on the credit card sales slip, and don't provide the merchant with your driver's license number. Most national bankcard companies prohibit merchants from refusing to sell to you if you refuse to provide this information.

  Some state laws prohibit merchants from writing your phone number, address, and other information on your sales slip when you pay with a national bankcard like MasterCard or Visa. These laws also apply to retail store charge cards and gas cards.

- Review each credit card billing statement as soon as it arrives, looking for charges you didn't make. If you believe that the charges may be the result of identity theft, follow the instructions in the section "What to do if you're a victim of identity theft" in this chapter.

- Be aware of when your billing statements are supposed to arrive so that if one of them doesn't show up on time, you can call the appropriate creditor. An identity thief may have changed the billing address for the account.

- Whenever possible, use cash instead of credit to pay for your purchases. When you pay with cash, you don't leave behind a receipt with your account information on it — information that could get into the wrong hands. Also, when you pay with cash, you minimize the likelihood that any of your personal information will end up in a business's database where it could be vulnerable to an identity thief.

To protect your Social Security number:

- Leave your Social Security card at home or in a safety deposit box unless you absolutely need it.

- Avoid sharing your Social Security number with others unless it's absolutely necessary to do so. The number can be used by an identity thief to open bank accounts, obtain credit cards, access your insurance policy, and so on. Although your employer and the financial institutions you do business with have some legitimate need for your Social Security number, other businesses may simply want it for their records. Therefore, when you're asked for your Social Security number, politely ask why it's needed and what will happen if you choose not to provide it.

- Don't have your driver's license number or Social Security number printed on your checks.

  If your state uses Social Security numbers as driver's license numbers, ask if you can use an alternate number on your license. Most states will comply with the request.

In addition to protecting your credit cards and Social Security number, take the following other precautions to keep your personal stuff away from prying eyes.

- Every six months, order a copy of your Equifax, Experian, and TransUnion credit reports and review them for any indications that someone has been using your accounts or has obtained new credit in your name. If you find signs of fraud, get in touch with the credit reporting agency to report the fraud right away.

- Purchase a paper shredder and shred all papers that contain your name and address, account information, PIN or ATM numbers, Social Security numbers, and so on. These papers include charge receipts, bank statements, checks, ATM receipts, credit applications, tax-related forms and correspondence, statements from your doctors, and insurance-related information containing your personal information and/or your policy or group number. Don't toss them into your trash or a recycling bin.

- Don't share your personal and financial information over the phone unless you initiated the call or unless you know with whom you are speaking and feel certain that the caller has a legitimate need for the information. If you receive a call from someone who wants information from you and who claims to represent an organization that sounds familiar and/or legitimate, ask the caller to send you a written request for the information. If the caller is an identity thief and/or if the organization is illegitimate, you probably won't ever receive the information.

  Some identity thieves may try to steal your information by claiming that they're with an organization that is well known and has a good reputation. However, the organization they claim they're with isn't the one you're familiar with and has a slightly different name. The identity thieves hope that you won't notice the difference and will let your guard down and give them the information they want from you. In fact, this type of mis-representation has become such a problem that some national organizations feature alerts on their Web sites warning visitors about fraudulent groups using names very similar to theirs.

- Never share your personal and financial information over the Internet unless you know for certain that the site you're visiting is secure. Secure sites show an unbroken lock or key somewhere on the page. Also, never respond to an unsolicited e-mail requesting that you provide your personal or financial information for "verification" or "account update" purposes.

✔ Minimize the amount of paperwork and documents containing your personal or financial information that you keep at work. If you keep this kind of information at your workplace, store it in a locked drawer or locker.

✔ Ask your employer about the kinds of procedures it has in place to protect the personal and financial information it maintains on you. Also find out how your employer disposes of that information.

The highest incidence of identity theft occurs in the workplace!

✔ When you're offered the opportunity, opt out of having your information shared with others. That information could include the information in your credit history, your buying habits and credit transactions, your address and phone number, your Social Security number, your Internet usage if you pay your bills online, your e-mail address, and so on. The more your information is shared and sold, the more likely that it will wind up in the hands of an identity thief. The sidebar "Opt for all opt-out opportunities," later in this chapter, explains some of the ways that you can opt out.

And if taking all those precautions still isn't enough to make you feel safe, here are a few more privacy protection suggestions.

✔ If you're planning to be out of town for several days, arrange to have the postal service hold your mail or ask someone you trust to pick it up for you each day. Otherwise, an identity thief may steal mail left sitting in your mailbox.

✔ Don't participate in phone and mail surveys unless you really want to. And if you do, understand that the information you provide may be bought and sold many times and could become part of numerous private and possibly government databases.

✔ When you use your ATM or PIN number, guard it carefully so that people near you can't see the number. Also, never share these numbers with anyone and don't write them on your ATM or debit cards or store them with those cards.

✔ Let your state and federal elected officials know that you want them to close the loopholes in existing privacy-related legislation. Demand that they pass new legislation that provides you with more protection from both governmental and private sector invasions of your privacy.

What to do if you're a victim of identity theft

Take action immediately if you believe that an identity thief may have victimized you. The sooner you act, the less potential damage will be done to your financial life. The Fair and Accurate Credit Transactions Act, which was passed in 2003 to amend the Fair Credit Reporting Act, gives victims of identity theft specific rights and proscribes certain actions they can take to minimize damage to their finances. However, even with the help of this new law, undoing the damage caused by an identity thief and getting your financial life back under control may be a long, emotional, and frustrating struggle. That's because the *burden of proof* (proving that you're a crime victim) rests with you; the legal authorities and creditors aren't always as helpful as they should be, and because identity thieves can be hard to catch, they can continue to victimize you.

Opt for all opt-out opportunities

You have several ways to opt out of having your personal and financial information shared between companies without your knowledge or permission. That information may include your account balances and credit transactions, your buying habits, Social Security number, Internet usage, and contact information. Some of the following opt-out opportunities were created by federal law; others by trade groups as a sign of good faith to consumers.

✔ **Add your name to the Direct Marketing Association's (DMA) opt-out lists.** The organization maintains opt-out lists for direct mail, telemarketing, and e-mail solicitations. The DMA's Customer Assistance page, `www.dmaconsumers.org/consumeras sistance.html`, provides links to and information about opting out of these types of solicitations. Although being on these lists doesn't totally eliminate unwanted solicitations, it will significantly reduce the number of unwanted solicitations you receive.

For e-mail solicitations, the DMA requires you to opt out again every two years. To continue opting out of receiving phone and direct mail solicitations, you have to contact the DMA again every five years.

✔ **Add your home phone number as well as your cell phone number to the Federal Trade Commission's Do Not Call registry.** You can do so by visiting `www.donotcall.gov` and following the on-screen instructions.

You can register up to three numbers at a time online. You can also add your numbers to the registry by calling 1-888-382-1222. However, you must call that number using whatever phone number you want registered, which means that if you want to register multiple numbers, you must make multiple calls. Your phone numbers remain in the registry for five years.

✔ **Contact your state attorney general's office of consumer protection to find out if your state has established its own opt-out program.**

✔ **Let the three national credit reporting agencies know that you don't want to receive any prescreened offers for credit, insurance, and other financial products.** Simply call 1-888-567-8688, and that one call will take care of all three companies. Using the information in consumers' credit files, credit reporting agencies create prescreened lists of consumers with certain characteristics — income level, age, credit score, and so on, and then they sell those lists to other companies. In turn, those other companies market their products and services to the names on the prescreened lists. If you've ever received a letter letting you know that you have been pre-approved for a credit card, a line of credit, or insurance, for example, your name was on a prescreened list.

When you realize that your identity has been stolen, you'll probably have to contact many offices, talk with lots of people, and fill out any number of forms. Some of the people you contact may promise to do certain things on your behalf. Therefore, it's a good idea to maintain detailed records of who you spoke with and when, what may have been promised, relevant deadlines and phone numbers, and so on. This information will be helpful if you decide to sue a creditor, credit reporting agency, or some other organization because it violated your privacy rights and contributed to the theft of your identity, or because you asked it to do something to help you undo the damage done by an identity thief and it didn't follow through on its promises. (You may have other reasons to sue.) When you or the person you speak with by phone promise to do or not do something, follow up your conversation with a letter restating what was agreed to. Send your letter via certified mail with return receipt requested. Also, if you have to take unpaid time off from work to deal with the loss of your identity, or if you incur out-of-pocket expenses related to the theft, keep detailed records of your expenses.

If you're ready to tear your hair out in frustration over trying to resolve your identity theft problem, you may want to get in touch with a California-based nonprofit organization called the Identity Theft Resource Center at 858-693-7935. The center is dedicated to helping people prevent and recover from identity theft. You can check out the center's Web site, `www.idtheft center.org`, for information about how to prevent identity theft and recover from it.

The following sections explain the most important steps you need to take if you're the victim of identity theft.

Contact credit reporting agencies

Contact the fraud alert hotline for one of the three national credit reporting agencies. The company you contact will add a fraud alert and a victim's statement to your credit file and will also notify the other two credit reporting agencies so they can do the same. To reach the fraud hotlines of the three major credit reporting agencies, call:

- Equifax: 1-800-525-6285
- Experian: 1-888-397-3742
- TransUnion: 1-800-680-7289

After a fraud alert is added to your credit files, each of the credit reporting agencies must send you a free copy of your credit report so that you can review it for additional signs of credit fraud — inquiries you didn't initiate, accounts you didn't open, charges you didn't make on your known accounts, and so on.

Some fraud alerts are better than others

When you ask a national credit reporting agency to add a fraud alert to your credit file, ordinarily, the alert will be a *standard alert,* which lasts 90 days. However, you can also ask that an *extended* alert be added to your credit files. This second type of alert lasts for seven years. However, to add an extended alert, you must provide the credit reporting agency with a copy of an *identity theft report.* According to FACTA, the identity theft report can be a copy of the report you filed with a local, state, or national law enforcement agency, or it can be a copy of a completed ID Theft Affidavit. You can obtain the affidavit form at the FTC's Web site, `www.ftc.gov`. However, the affidavit doesn't qualify as an *identity theft report* unless it has been filed with a federal, state, or local law enforcement agency and the agency accepted it.

An extended alert is attached to your credit file and credit score so that whenever a creditor checks them out, it's aware of the fact that you're an identity theft victim. Also, when your file has an extended alert, creditors must call you or contact you via some other method you've approved whenever they receive a request to increase your credit limit on an existing account, open a new account in your name, or carry out some other credit-related transaction in your name; creditors have to make this contact in order to confirm that the individual initiating the change or transaction is really you. On the other hand, with a standard alert, all creditors are obligated to do is use "reasonable policies and procedures" to make certain that you, not someone else, initiated the change or transaction.

An extended fraud alert entitles you to two free credit reports in the first year of the alert, and it also restricts prescreened offers for five years. An extended alert is really the best way to protect your credit in the future.

If you don't receive a free credit report from each of the credit reporting agencies after you file a fraud alert, contact whichever agencies didn't send you a report and ask for one. If you find any signs of fraud in any of your credit reports, contact the appropriate credit reporting agency right away by phone and in writing to get the incorrect information removed.

After your credit record information is corrected, order copies of your credit file every couple months to ensure that the problem information doesn't reappear and to make certain that you don't notice additional signs of fraud. When you're sure that all problems associated with the theft of your identity have been cleared up, review your credit record every six months.

Call the police

Report the identity theft to your local police or to the police in the community where the theft took place. Let the department know that you want to file a police report and make certain that the report lists each fraudulent account. Keep a copy of the report for your own records.

You may have problems getting the police to agree to let you file a police report because many police departments are reluctant to help consumers who are victims of identity theft. They may drag their feet or refuse to help you because of the nature of the crime, because the crime may have been committed outside the department's jurisdiction, and/or because the department is short-handed and wants to focus its resources on other kinds of crimes. In fact, the national nonprofit Identity Theft Resource Center (www.idthcftcenter.org) reports that only one-half of all the identity theft victims it works with have been able to secure a police report. To date, only California has a law requiring police departments to take police reports from all local ID theft victims. The sidebar titled "Getting the cooperation you need from the police" provides advice for obtaining a police report and for what to do if you can't get one.

Under the Fair and Accurate Credit Transactions Act (FACTA), an identity theft victim has the right to ask a creditor and anyone else that the identity thief may have done business with using your information for copies of the thief's application and transactions. You may need this documentation to help uncover the person who is ruining your good name. However, businesses have the right to request that you provide them with a copy of your police report before they give you the information and documents you request.

Get fraudulent information blocked

Ask each of the credit reporting agencies to block the reporting of any fraudulent information you may have found in your credit reports. If you do, the blocked information can't be shared with creditors and others who review your credit file. To get a block, write to each of the national credit reporting agencies and specify the particular information you want blocked. Also state in your letter that you don't want any credit-related transactions you initiate blocked. These transactions could include applying for additional credit, charging a purchase on one of your credit cards, getting a bank loan, and so on. Attach to your letter proof of your identity and a copy of the police report related to the theft of your identity. Chapter 10 provides addresses for each of the three national credit reporting agencies. After they receive your letter, the agencies must add the block to your credit file within four business days.

For the best protection, get fraudulent information blocked and ask that both types of alerts be added to your credit file.

Close compromised accounts

Close all accounts that have been tampered with or that were opened fraudulently, including credit card accounts, bank accounts, home equity lines of credit, utility accounts, and so on. Ask that the accounts be reported as "closed at the consumer's request." Otherwise someone who reviews your credit history may conclude that your creditors closed the accounts because you didn't keep up with your payments. Contact the creditors immediately by phone and then follow up in writing soon after. Send your letter via certified mail with a return receipt requested.

If you close an existing account and open a new replacement account, don't use the same PIN or password if there are fraudulent charges or other transactions associated with the closed account. The same person who fraudulently used the accounts that you closed may commit more fraud using the new accounts, so using the same PIN or password just creates more problems for yourself.

For new, unauthorized accounts (accounts that an identity thief opened in your name) and for accounts you opened, ask the company if it accepts the FTC's ID Theft Affidavit (available at www.ftc.gov/bcp/conline/pubs/credit/affidavit.pdf). This form was designed to help you close unauthorized accounts and get rid of debts that are wrongfully attributed to you. If the company doesn't accept the FTC's form, ask the company to send you the fraud dispute form it uses.

If your ATM card has been lost, stolen, or otherwise compromised, cancel the card as soon as you can and get a new card with a new PIN.

No federal law limits the amount of losses you can claim when your checks or bank account number are stolen or if you lose your checks. However, your state may have such a law. Contact your state banking commission/department or the consumer protection office of your state attorney general to find out the specifics.

If your checks have been stolen, or if you believe that someone has stolen your bank account number, contact your bank immediately to close the account. Ask that the bank notify the check verification services it works with. For extra protection, you also should contact the following major check verification services yourself.

- ✔ Certegy, Inc.: 1-800-437-5120
- ✔ Check Rite: 1-800-766-2748
- ✔ Chex Systems: 1-800-552-1900
- ✔ International Check Services: 1-800-631-9656
- ✔ National Processing Company: 1-800-526-5380
- ✔ SCAN: 1-800-262-7771
- ✔ TeleCheck: 1-800-366-2425

Getting the cooperation you need from the police

When you're the victim of identity theft, it's important that you report the incident to the police department in the community where the theft occurred and get them to file a complete report on the crime. Many creditors won't help you resolve your identity theft problem if you don't have a police report. Also, credit reporting agencies won't block fraudulent accounts and information related to those accounts without a police report.

Unfortunately, some police departments can be slow to respond and less than helpful to ID theft victims. In part, it's because the authorities know that their chances of finding an identity thief are not great and because the police department may be understaffed due to budget cuts. Therefore, police department personnel are more apt to spend their time dealing with violent crimes or crimes that are easier to solve than most cases of identity theft.

If the police department you contact seems to be dragging its feet when it comes to providing you with a police report, the following advice can help you see action.

✔ **Provide the police department with as much documentation about the crime as you can.** Not only will the information help you convince the department that you truly

are a crime victim, but it will also make it easier for the police to file a complete report. Examples of documentation to provide include copies of your credit reports containing the fraudulent information, letters from debt collectors trying to collect fraudulent debts incurred in your name, and a copy of your completed and notarized FTC ID Theft Affidavit.

✔ **Educate the police about the high rate of identity theft by referring whomever you speak with to the FTC's Consumer Sentinal database.** The police can use the database to find out about other identity theft complaints in your community and elsewhere. If there are a lot of complaints in your area, or if there's a pattern to the complaints, the police may take your problem more seriously.

✔ **Don't take no for an answer.** If the police department drags its heels about preparing a police report for you or tells you that it can't, explain again why you need one. If you still get nowhere, contact your county police department, and if it balks as well, ask your state police department for a report. If you strike out with everyone, get in touch with a consumer law attorney.

Contact the FTC

File an identity theft complaint with the FTC by going to www.consumer.gov/idtheft or by calling the commission's identity theft hotline at 1-877-438-4338. You can also write to the FTC about your identity theft at Identity Theft Clearinghouse, Federal Trade Commission, 600 Pennsylvania Avenue, NW, Washington, DC 20580. Although the FTC will not take action against an identity thief on your behalf alone, the information you provide may be helpful to law enforcement officials who are trying to locate and arrest identity thieves. Also, when you file a complaint, the FTC puts you in touch with other identity theft resources that may be helpful to you.

Feeling confused about how to get back your good name? Call the FTC's identity theft hotline at 1-877-438-4338. A counselor will advise you about the best ways to deal with your identity theft problem.

Trying to recover from the theft of your identity isn't easy. You need all the help you can get! Therefore, check out the FTC's publication, *ID Theft: When Bad Things Happen to Your Name.* Not only is this publication loaded with helpful information that goes beyond the scope of this chapter, but it also includes forms you can use to keep track of the actions you take over time to address your identity theft problem. You can read or download a copy of the publication at www.ftc.gov/bcp/conline/pubs/credit/idtheft.htm, or you can order a copy by calling the FTC at 1-877-382-4357.

Protecting your identity when you go online

There are no 100-percent definite ways yet to protect your personal and financial information from identity thieves and cybersnoops when you go online, but by applying the following practical and easy-to-use tips, you can at least make it more unlikely that your information gets into the wrong hands.

- ✔ **Use a secure browser to help protect the privacy of your online transactions.** A secure browser scrambles or encrypts your information when you send it over the Internet. Look for a lock icon on the browser's status bar when you send private information, and keep your browser software updated.

- ✔ **Always check out a Web site's privacy or security policy when you visit it for the first time.** If the site doesn't have such a policy, don't spend any time there. The policy should explain what information may be collected at the site, how that information may be used, and whether or not your information may be shared with third parties.

- ✔ **Minimize the amount of personal and financial information you store on your computer.** Tech savvy identity thieves don't have trouble stealing that information either when you're away from your computer, when you're conducting financial transactions, or when you're filling out surveys or other forms online. Before you get rid of a computer, delete all personal and financial information using a "wipe" utility, which overwrites everything you have on your hard drive. Simply deleting the information may not get rid of it.

- ✔ **Be careful what information you send via e-mail, especially when it comes to credit card and bank account numbers, PIN numbers, your Social Security number, and other critical information.** Although it may seem like the information you send via the Internet goes directly from your computer to the recipient's computer, in fact, the information actually makes several stops on the way to its final destination and a skilled identity thief can intercept it at any point. Furthermore, a record of what you send stays on your computer and on the computer system of the company that transmitted the information. Also, current laws allow a government agency such as the IRS or the FBI to gain access to that information if necessary.

✔ **Never open documents or download files sent by people or organizations you don't know.**

✔ **When choosing a password to get online, avoid the obvious ones.** Passwords such as your birthday, your first or last name, part of your driver's license number, and so on are easy enough for cybersnoops to figure out. A safer choice is a password that includes a combination of upper- and lowercase letters, a random series of numbers or symbols, or a combination of these things. Also, changing your password regularly is a good way to protect your accounts and information.

✔ **Avoid automatic login options that save you having to reenter your password and username each time you enter a Web site.** Also, whenever you leave a site, always log off. If you don't and your computer is stolen, it will be easier for the thief to access your information.

✔ **Install virus protection software on your computer and update it regularly and whenever you learn of a new virus.**

✔ **Install firewall protections on your computer, especially if you have a high-speed Internet connection such as DSL or cable.** That sort of connection leaves your computer connected to the Internet 24 hours a day, whether you're actively online or not. A firewall makes it more difficult for computer hackers to access the personal and financial information you have stored on your computer.

The Federal Health Insurance Portability and Accountability Act

The multifaceted Health Insurance Portability and Accountability Act (HIPAA) gives you the right to privacy under certain conditions when it comes to:

✔ Your medical record information

✔ Conversations between you and your doctor

✔ Conversations your doctor has with nurses and other medical personnel about your care and treatment

✔ Information about you that your health insurer has in its paper or computer files

Health care providers, health insurance companies, HMOs, and most employer group health plans must abide by HIPAA's requirements as long as they store and transmit patient information electronically. HIPAA also applies to Medicare and Medicaid.

HIPAA doesn't apply to the Medical Information Bureau. For an explanation of the Medical Information Bureau, jump to the sidebar of the same name that appears later in this chapter.

HIPAA places certain obligations on covered businesses and other organizations when it comes to the information they collect and maintain on you. For example, the law says that they must

✔ Provide you with a written notice explaining how your medical record information may be used or shared (for example, if it will be used for marketing purposes). Ordinarily, you receive this information when you visit a medical provider for the first time, or it comes through the mail from your insurer. Regardless, you can request the information at any time.

✔ Give you an opportunity to decide whether or not you want to give your permission for your medical record information to be used or shared for certain purposes. Generally, your medical information can't be shared with your employer, used or shared for things like sales calls or advertising, or used or shared for certain other purposes without your written permission. The form you sign to provide your permission must explain who will see your information and what it will be used for.

A health care provider or other organization covered by HIPAA isn't required to get your permission to share your medical information with others if that information is required for your treatment, for the payment of the care you receive, or for "health care operations." This exception is a big loophole in HIPAA.

HIPAA requires health care providers to

✔ Provide you with a report regarding how and when they shared your information and the reason it was shared.

✔ Allow you to view your medical records and give you a copy of those records upon your request. In most instances, after you make your request, you must be provided a copy of your records within 30 days.

However, a medical provider can extend this period an additional 30 days if it explains why the extra time is needed. Also, the provider has the right to charge you for the cost of copying and mailing your records to you.

If you find an error in your medical records, you're entitled to have it corrected, assuming your doctor, hospital, or another medical provider agrees that there is indeed an error. If the provider doesn't concede that an error exists, you can have a note added to your records indicating your disagreement.

What to do if your HIPAA rights are violated

If your HIPAA rights are violated, you have no rights under that law to sue for the violation of your privacy. The only thing you can do is file a complaint with your medical provider or health insurer and a complaint with the federal Office of Civil Rights (OCR). After you file your OCR complaint, the Department of Health and Human Services or the federal Justice Department may decide to sue on your behalf. The privacy notices your health care providers and health insurer are obligated to provide you with must explain how to file a complaint.

You can file a complaint with the OCR in writing, by fax, or via e-mail. However, the OCR prefers that you use its Health Information Privacy Complaint form, which is available at www.hhs.gov/ocr/hipaa.

If you don't use the OCR's complaint form and present your complaint in a letter, be sure to provide the following information:

✔ Your name, full address, home and work telephone numbers, and e-mail address

✔ The name, full address, and phone number of the person, agency, or organization you believe violated your health information privacy rights

✔ A brief description of the violation — explain how, why, and when you believe that your health information privacy rights were violated

✔ Anything else that you feel is relevant to your complaint

Be sure to sign your name and date your letter. And don't forget to keep a copy of the letter for your own records.

If you mail your complaint form or letter to the OCR, send it to the OCR's regional office responsible for the region of the country where the violation of your rights took place. You can obtain the address of that office or get answers to other questions about the complaint process by calling 1-800-368-1019.

Your state may have a law that entitles you to sue for a violation of HIPAA. The state law may also give you more privacy rights than does HIPAA.

When doctor-patient confidentiality can be violated

Regardless of what HIPAA says, there are times when your doctor can use — or may even be legally obligated to share with others — what you tell him or her or what he or she learns from your medical exams and tests. For example:

- ✔ If you sue your doctor, you may have to share your medical records with your attorney, and your doctor may be able to use your medical record information against you.

- ✔ If you have a contagious disease, to help protect others, your doctor must report your illness to the appropriate health authorities.

- ✔ If you're treated for a gunshot or a stab wound, usually your injury must be reported to the police because it's assumed that your wound is crime-related.

- ✔ Generally, if information you've shared with your doctor leads him or her to suspect that you're going to commit a crime or hurt someone, your doctor must notify the appropriate legal authorities.

- ✔ If you have a sexually transmitted disease such as syphilis or gonorrhea, your doctor must report your condition to the health authority in order to protect the health of others.

Also, if a doctor treats a child who he or she suspects is the victim of child abuse, the doctor is legally required to report the suspicion to the proper authorities to help protect the child.

Post-9/11 Inroads into Your Privacy: The Patriot Act

Since the tragedies of September 11, 2001, the privacy of every American citizen is in greater jeopardy than ever. The reason for this vulnerability is that, in a rush to prevent future acts of terrorism at home, Congress has adopted a number of new laws that many consumers, privacy watchdog groups, and others believe tip the delicate balance between combating domestic terrorism and preserving our civil rights in favor of the government's right to know.

The federal Patriot Act was hurriedly passed into law in the fall of 2001 without undergoing adequate scrutiny by lawmakers. Not until it was passed did some legislators begin to understand the scope and potential impact of the law they had voted for and how it would further undermine many of the already weak federal privacy laws intended to protect consumers. In fact, to date, more than 300 American communities have passed resolutions against the Patriot Act stating that they will not comply with some or all of the law's requirements.

After the Patriot Act went into effect, Congress later passed another new law to combat terrorism, nicknamed Patriot II. Both laws have been criticized by both sides of the political spectrum for their encroachments on the civil liberties and privacy of Americans. Combined, these two laws do the following:

✔ Establish the crime of domestic terrorism and make political organizations that promote particular social or political causes — anti-war organizations, gay rights organizations, and privacy rights organizations, for example — vulnerable to government surveillance, wiretaps, and even criminal action. For example, if you're a protestor, you could be jailed indefinitely if law enforcement authorities decide that your protest is an act of domestic terrorism.

✔ Allow the FBI to investigate you for a criminal matter even if the agency doesn't have probable cause that you committed the crime and assuming that the agency asserts that the investigation is for "intelligence purposes."

✔ Increase the rights of law enforcement personnel to search your private property in secret. Specifically, under certain circumstances, authorities can obtain a search warrant, enter your residence or your business without notifying you first of their intentions, and photograph your property. Depending on the circumstances, they may even be able to take some of your property without your permission.

✔ Make it easier for law enforcement personnel to force third parties to turn over your medical, mental health, financial, library, and school records. It also makes it easier for law enforcement to eavesdrop on your phone conversations and spy on you via the Internet, possibly capturing your passwords and monitoring where you go on the Internet, who you send e-mails to and who e-mails you. To gain access to such information, all the government has to do is allege that it needs the information for an ongoing terrorism investigation. The government doesn't even have to provide proof of its allegation.

If the federal government orders a third party to turn over records about you, the third party is barred from disclosing that fact to anyone. This rule means that you won't know if your records have been searched.

✔ Jeopardize consumers' financial privacy by encouraging members of the Federal Deposit Insurance Corporation (FDIC) to report to the FBI, DEA, and IRS if the deposit or spending patterns of their account holders change in significant ways. FDIC members are also encouraged to create and maintain profiles of their account holders.

✔ Weaken the secrecy of a grand jury by allowing any federal official or bureaucrat to share grand jury testimony or wiretap information.

✔ Redefine the term "financial institution" from referring to a bank to referring to any business whose "cash transactions have a high degree of usefulness in criminal, tax, or regulatory matters," including car dealerships, gambling casinos, stock brokerages, insurance agencies, credit card companies, jewelers, airlines, and the U.S. Postal Service.

Other federal privacy laws you should know about

A few other privacy-related federal laws you should know about include:

✔ **The Computer Matching and Privacy Protection Act,** which regulates the freedom of federal agencies to compare consumer information in one database to information in another in an effort to reduce waste, fraud, and abuse. The law says that if the computer matching reveals something negative about you, before an agency can take action, it must notify you and give you a chance to respond. This law doesn't affect computer matching done for tax and law-enforcement purposes.

✔ **The Video Privacy Protection Act,** which prevents retailers who rent videos from disclosing or selling their customers' video-rental records without obtaining customers' prior approval or unless a court order requires them to do so.

✔ **The Electronic Communications Privacy Act,** which was passed in 1986 to broaden the scope of the Wiretap Act and other federal wiretap laws and to protect the privacy of electronic communications, including video, text, audio, and data transmissions.

✔ **The Driver's Privacy Protection Act,** which restricts public disclosure of the personal information contained in your state department of motor vehicle's records.

✔ **The Telecommunications Act,** which requires telephone companies to get consumers' approval before using information about their calling patterns to market services to them.

In Chapter 10, I discuss the strengths and weaknesses of another important federal privacy law, the Fair Credit Reporting Act.

Part III
The Law and Your Money

The 5th Wave   By Rich Tennant

"...and don't tell me I'm not being frugal enough. I hired a man last week to do nothing but clip coupons!"

In this part . . .

You'll find four chapters in this part that relate to your financial life as well as your business life if you happen to be an aspiring entrepreneur or if you already own a small business. The first chapter covers the key legal issues small-business owners should be aware of, and the next two chapters address credit and personal finance issues. I also provide a chapter on the things to know and watch out for when buying and selling a home.

Chapter 9

So You Want to Be an Entrepreneur!

*A*side from falling in love, perhaps no other experience in life can be as intoxicating and as exciting as starting your own business. You dream of the possibilities! You count the money you'll make! You can almost taste your success! Donald Trump, watch out!

Despite your optimism, it's important for you to know that although thousands of businesses are started every year, more than 50 percent of them fail within four years, and 63 percent go bust in six years. Although some of the reasons behind this high rate of failure aren't within the scope of this book, one important explanation is that new business owners don't spend enough time planning to be in business and learning about the laws that affect them. Such oversights can be costly, if not financially fatal, for the typical small business owner.

If you're looking for a business opportunity to sink your teeth into, be alert for scams. Whether they're marketed online, sold by aggressive telemarketers, or promoted through classified advertising or on television infomercials, the income potential of these "business opportunities" is often wildly exaggerated, and you'll typically get little or nothing for your up-front cash payment.

In this chapter, I don't tell you how to finance or manage your business in order to maximize your chances for success. But I do explain some of the key legal issues that the typical small business owner should be aware of. To get a more complete picture of your legal obligations and rights, turn to Chapter 6, which discusses employee rights in the workplace and also covers the things that employers are required to do and are barred from doing in regard to existing employees as well as potential employees.

Illustrated with colorful and lively graphics, the Business Owners' Idea Café, www.businessownersideacafe.com, which describes itself as taking a "Fun Approach to Serious Business," is full of practical information for aspiring entrepreneurs as well as current business owners. The site allows you to schmooze with other business owners, access business-related resources, and get advice from business experts.

Getting Off to the Right Start

One of the first and most fundamental decisions you have to make when you're planning to begin a business is the legal structure that your business should have: sole proprietorship, partnership, corporation, or some variation. Don't downplay the importance of this decision. It affects any or all of the following:

- ✔ The cost of starting and running your business

- ✔ How much direct control you have over your business

- ✔ The degree to which you're personally liable for any debts your business takes on

- ✔ Whether or not you're personally liable for any lawsuits filed against your business

- ✔ The ease with which you're able to get loans or investment capital to help finance your business

- ✔ The taxes you have to pay

The legal structure of your business even affects the kind of bankruptcy you can file! Although I realize that bankruptcy isn't something most aspiring entrepreneurs want to be thinking about when they're focused on getting a business started, given the high rate of business failure, you would be naïve not to acknowledge the possibility.

Before making a final decision on the best legal structure for your business, it's a good idea to schedule an appointment with a business attorney or a CPA. At this meeting, not only can you get detailed information about the pros and cons of each structure in light of your particular business, but you can also find out about other issues and concerns that you should be aware of. To prepare you for that meeting, what follows is a quick rundown of your business structure options.

Sole proprietorships

Sole proprietorships are easy and inexpensive to start, making them far and away the most popular way to organize a business. To begin a sole proprietorship, all you really need to do is start acting like a business. You don't have to fill out any official paperwork or pay any fees, but you have a few extra IRS forms to file each April. Come tax time, all you need to do is complete a Schedule C showing your business revenues and expenses and your net income or loss.

Depending on the kind of business you have, your local government may require you to obtain special licenses, even if your business is a sole proprietorship.

If you take a business name that is different from your own — Accurate Accounting or Caring Child Care, for example — you may have to file that name with your county or with your secretary of state. This assumed name is your *DBA,* which stands for "doing business as." Filing a DBA helps ensure that you don't use someone else's business name and that another business doesn't take yours. It also lets people who do business with your company know exactly who they're dealing with.

When you run a business as a sole proprietorship, you're its chief cook and bottle washer and everything in between. You have 100 percent control. In fact, in the eyes of the law, you *are* your business; there's no distinction. Your business debts are your personal debts. And if your business is sued, it's really you who's sued. In other words, if you structure your business as a sole proprietorship, you're *personally* liable for all your business debts and legal problems because your personal and business assets are one and the same. This fact is the single most significant drawback to a sole proprietorship.

Obtaining adequate financing for your business is another problem that stems from your business identity overlapping your personal identity. Because your business doesn't have a credit history separate from your personal credit history, if you already have a lot of credit or if your credit history is damaged, you will have a tough time borrowing money to help pay for your business's operations and fund its growth.

It's legal but not wise to run your sole proprietorship out of your personal checkbook. If the IRS audits you, you may have a difficult time proving which expenses were business-related and which were personal.

Partnerships

If you're in a business with one or more persons, you can structure it in two basic ways: a partnership or a corporation. If you choose to establish a partnership, you're opting for a legal structure much like a sole proprietorship. For example, you and your partners are each personally liable for all your business's financial and legal liabilities. Also, as with a sole proprietorship, your share of your business's income or loss needs to be reported on your personal tax return.

A partnership must file an annual report with the IRS indicating how much it earned or lost in a tax year as well as each partner's share of that profit or loss.

Advantages and disadvantages of partnerships

Having partners can be advantageous because they can bring to a business expertise, contacts, and money that a single owner may not have. Partners also share liability for a business's debts and legal problems. Being in a partnership can be problematic, however, because the actions of one partner legally obligate all partners as business owners, and each partner can also be held personally liable. If your partnership incurs a debt that it's unable to pay, or if it's sued and cannot pay the judgment, whether the debt or lawsuit is the consequence of one partner's action doesn't matter in the eyes of the law. Each partner is personally liable.

Here's an example of partner liability and how it can affect you: Suppose your partner uses the company credit card to wine and dine potential clients while he's at a week-long, out-of-town conference. To impress them, he eats at only the best restaurants and buys expensive bottles of wine.

When you open the company's credit card bill a month after your partner has returned, you're both astounded at your partner's profligate spending and concerned about how your business will ever come up with the money necessary to pay off the bill in the time required because you've only been in business for six months and money is very tight. You're also worried because you know that if your business can't pay the bill in full, the credit card company has a legal right to collect directly from either you or your partner — from whomever has the money.

A partnership is very much like a marriage: The actions of one partner can have a profound effect on the other. So, when choosing a partner, be sure to select someone who shares your business philosophy, is willing to communicate honestly and openly with you, and whose judgment and honesty you trust implicitly.

The benefits of formalizing your partnership with a written agreement

Your partner may be a business associate, a friend, or even a spouse. Regardless, to help ensure that your relationship is a happy one, it's advisable, but not legally required, for you to negotiate a written partnership agreement. Although you still have a partnership whether you formalize your relationship with a written agreement or not, preparing a formal partnership agreement can provide you a number of important benefits:

- Negotiating the terms of your agreement forces you to define your working relationship and address issues you may otherwise overlook.

- If partnership problems do develop (and what close relationship doesn't have them?), a written agreement can help you resolve them before your relationship deteriorates in bitterness and acrimony, or even in court.

- If you decide to end your partnership, a written agreement can help you do it in a matter that is fair to both parties.

If you don't have a written agreement, the general terms of your relationship are defined by the Uniform Partnership Act, which has been adopted in some form by all states except Louisiana. Its guidelines, however, may not meet the particular needs of your partnership.

Partnerships can be established to accomplish a very specific business project — a real estate deal, for example. After the project is completed, the partnership is dissolved.

One type of formal partnership is the *limited partnership.* Limited partners contribute investment capital to a partnership but don't have the right to become involved in the management of the business. Their liability is limited to the amount of their investment.

Whatever type of partnership you decide on, after you and your partners have talked through the general terms of your business relationship, it's best to hire an attorney to prepare your formal, written agreement. The attorney knows what to include and how to avoid typical partnership pitfalls. Spending money on an attorney at this stage of your business relationship is money well spent because it's a lot cheaper to get legal help to prevent problems from developing than it is to hire an attorney to resolve them.

At a minimum, your agreement should address the following:

- The rights and responsibilities of each partner
- What each partner is contributing to the business and the value of the contributions
- How decisions will be made

✔ How business income and debts, as well as profits and losses, will be shared

✔ How business property will be owned

✔ How the books and other records will be kept

✔ How disputes should be resolved

✔ Provisions for dissolving the partnership, expanding it, buying out a partner, and bringing in a new partner

Unless you make other provisions in your partnership agreement, your partnership will automatically be dissolved if a partner leaves or dies or if a new partner is added.

Corporations

Unlike either a sole proprietorship or a partnership, a *corporation* has a legal identity apart from its owners. This business structure therefore minimizes or avoids many of the legal and financial risks and headaches associated with sole proprietorships and partnerships. Owners of a corporation have limited liability for the actions of the business, and corporations typically have an easier time obtaining the funds they need to operate and expand.

Setup and paperwork

The advantages of incorporating come at a cost: It takes time and money to set up and maintain a corporation. At a minimum, starting a corporation requires you to prepare and file articles of incorporation with your secretary of state's office, pay a filing fee, and write a set of corporate bylaws. After your business has been established, you must maintain proper corporate records (including minutes of shareholder meetings), file annual reports with your secretary of state, and file the necessary state and federal taxes for your business. You must keep your personal finances totally separate from your business's finances. No running your business through your personal checking account or "loaning" yourself money from the till.

If a shareholder (owner of a corporation) dies or leaves (sells his or her share of the business), or if another shareholder is brought in (new or existing shares are sold), the corporation continues to exist, unlike what happens in similar situations when a business is a partnership.

A corporation is owned by its shareholders. In most states, a corporation can have just one shareholder (you), or it can have more shareholders. In fact, selling shares can be a good way to raise funds for your business and represents a business financing technique unique to corporations.

The corporate vocabulary

If you incorporate, you'll be exposed to a whole new business vocabulary. Here are some of the most important terms you need to become familiar with:

The players:

- ✔ Board of directors: Set corporate policy and make long-term decisions for the corporation.

- ✔ Officers: Manage the day-to-day operations of the business and implement policies set by the board.

- ✔ Shareholders: Own the corporate stock; as owners, they elect the directors, amend bylaws, amend articles of incorporation, remove directors, and vote on other basic corporate issues.

The paperwork:

- ✔ Articles of incorporation: Filing this paperwork formally establishes a corporation.

This document usually reflects the corporation's name and purpose, the names and addresses of the persons filing the articles (the incorporators and the name of the *registered agent,* the person to receive official notices related to the corporation), and the number of authorized shares. In some states, you can obtain a standard, fill-in-the-blanks articles of incorporation form from your secretary of state; in others, you have to write your own based on your state's requirements.

- ✔ Corporate bylaws: Written by the board of directors, this document spells out basic rules for the corporation. It can be amended as necessary.

- ✔ Stock certificates or shares of stock: The written indication of ownership in a corporation.

Liability and drawbacks

As I've already indicated, one reason for structuring your business as a corporation is that your personal liability for your business's actions is limited. For example, if your business defaults on a loan or is sued, you don't lose any more than your investment in the company. In reality, however, especially if your corporation has few shareholders, if it's new and has no financial track record, or if its track record isn't strong, you probably will have to personally guarantee any debt that your business takes on, which means that you're liable just as if your business was a sole proprietorship or partnership.

If you fail to run your corporation as a legal entity that is totally separate from you (for example, you commingle your business and personal assets in one bank account), you may be held personally liable for your business.

Double taxation is the key drawback to incorporating. A corporation pays federal taxes on its earnings (and possibly state income tax, too). After paying its taxes, the corporation may decide to distribute some of its earnings as dividends to its shareholders. If it does, the shareholders also pay taxes on that income. So, if you organize your business as a corporation, you may pay taxes twice: first a corporate tax and then an individual tax.

If your business is relatively small (no more than 35 shareholders) and meets a number of other federal criteria, you may want to structure it as a Subchapter S corporation, which is a hybrid of the traditional type of corporation. The key advantage of this alternative corporate structure is that it allows you to avoid double taxation.

A Subchapter S corporation doesn't pay federal corporate income taxes. Instead, rather than pay taxes on the dividends they receive from the corporation, the corporation's shareholders pay federal taxes on their share of the corporate profits — at their personal rate.

The *limited liability company* is another hybrid business structure that's a cross between a corporation and a partnership. For legal purposes, the limited liability company is a corporation; but for tax purposes, it's a partnership. This legal structure is also free of the disadvantages of both Subchapter S corporations and limited partnerships. But it has its own drawbacks, which are too complicated for me to get into here without thoroughly confusing you. So, talk to your CPA or lawyer about the possibility of forming a limited liability company, if you're interested.

At the federal Small Business Administration's Web site, `www.sba.gov`, you can find out about the myriad federal rules and regulations you may need to comply with when creating your own business, download government forms, find out about business opportunities that may be right for your business, and get information about government-backed loans and other federal assistance that your business may be eligible for. The site also provides advice and information about starting, financing, and managing a business, as well as links to the SBA offices nearest you.

Franchises

Some aspiring entrepreneurs choose to get into business by purchasing the rights to a proven concept rather than starting from scratch with their own ideas. Buying a franchise with an established and respected reputation can put you somewhat ahead in the game of money-making, and given that franchise opportunities abound for just about every kind of business you can think of, you have a good chance of finding one that interests you.

Legally, when you buy a franchise, the *franchisor* is selling you a license to begin and run the type of business it is franchising. Typically, your purchase includes the right to the franchise's trademark, trade names, products, and so on. You also purchase certain benefits and rights, which can include training, start-up assistance, discounts on supplies and merchandise, advertising support, ongoing management assistance, and sometimes even a building and land.

In essence, when you buy a franchise, you're buying a valuable business partner with a financial stake in helping you become a success. Because you're usually expected to pay the franchisor a percentage of your profits, the more successful you are, the more money the franchisor makes.

In exchange for receiving certain rights and benefits, you're expected to meet specific requirements set by the franchisor. They generally include the following: maintaining a certain level of business quality, spending a certain percentage of sales on business marketing, buying certain products or supplies from the franchisor, and using certain signage.

There are good franchises and not so good franchises, so before you buy one, check it out carefully and make certain that it's actually a good deal for you. Review the information a franchisor sends you as well as the franchise agreement and any other contracts you'll be expected to sign. Pay special attention to the franchisor's disclosure statement, or Uniform Franchise Offering Circular (UFOC). The Federal Trade Commission requires a franchisor to provide a potential buyer with a copy of its disclosure statement at their first meeting — at least ten days before a franchise agreement is signed or before any money changes hands.

Always review a franchise contract with an attorney before you sign it. The contract should clearly spell out all purchase details, including the rights and responsibilities of both you and the franchisor. Depending on the amount of money involved, you may even want the attorney to negotiate the contract for you.

A disclosure statement provides a wealth of information, so read it carefully. Among other things, it tells you the history of the franchisor, the track record of its franchises, and the names of the franchisor's corporate officers and their business backgrounds, including any criminal convictions, bankruptcies, and civil judgments.

The disclosure statement also spells out all relevant costs you will be expected to pay, the kinds of assistance the franchisor will provide you, under what conditions you can sell or lose the franchise, and so on. This statement must also include a copy of the company's latest audited income statement and balance sheet, so that you can use the information to help you evaluate the franchisor's financial stability.

Your state may place special requirements and restrictions on a franchisor. Call your state attorney general's office to find out about them.

Visit the federal Small Business Administration's Web site (www.sba.gov) to get the complete scoop on its small business services and loan programs. You can also download e-books, other free SBA publications, and business forms. This site also has links to other Web sites that are useful to business owners. If you're a female business owner, visit the SBA's Online Women's Business Center at www.onlinewbc.gov; here you can find information on programs and resources specifically aimed at female entrepreneurs.

Working out of Your Home

Personal computers, the Internet, and e-mail, as well as an acceptance of home-based businesses as legitimate, professional enterprises, have made it easier for many entrepreneurs to run successful businesses out of their homes.

These lucky people get to work in their bathrobes, tan while they take phone calls, multi-task to the sound of wind chimes, and weed their gardens during lunch. Yeah, right! But they do get to avoid commuting to and from an office, and they're spared the pressure and politics of the corporate world.

Steer clear of home business opportunity scams. Like other business scams, they make promises like "Make BIG BUCKS with OTHER PEOPLE'S MONEY using your answering machine." If you fall for that line, I've got a bridge I'd like to sell you.

Planning ahead

If you decide to begin operating a business out of your home, you should do all of the up-front planning and research recommended for any other entrepreneur starting a business. But to avoid getting into legal hot water, you need to check out some additional things:

- ✔ Does your community or housing development prohibit home-based businesses or certain types of home-based businesses?

- ✔ Does your business have to comply with local zoning ordinances, regulations, licensing requirements, or codes? If your business is in violation of one of these codes and it comes to the attention of your local government, you can be fined or even have your business shut down.

Some condominiums and planned communities have special rules regarding home-based businesses. They can be more restrictive than your state or local government's rules and regulations.

If you're lucky, you live in a community that's "home-based business friendly." Recognizing that most home-based businesses are non-polluting financial assets that generate little if any neighborhood traffic or noise, such communities place few if any restrictions on home-based businesses. Other, less enlightened communities may only allow you to operate a home-based business under certain conditions, or their zoning ordinances may effectively prevent you from running certain kinds of businesses out of your home. For example, these ordinances may limit traffic in a neighborhood, restrict or prohibit business signage in a residential neighborhood, impose on-street parking requirements for a business, and more.

If your community has laws that affect your ability to operate a home-based business, consider asking your local government to grant you a *variance* from those laws. A variance exempts your business from having to obey such laws.

Dealing with taxes and insurance

Taxes and insurance are two other issues that you may need to make special provisions for if your business is home-based. Although your basic business insurance needs are no different than if you operated out of a more traditional office space, don't assume that your homeowner's insurance policy covers your business property if it's stolen, damaged, or destroyed in your home office. And don't assume that your policy can help you if someone visiting your business or making a delivery is injured while on your premises. Just ask your insurance agent or broker if you need another policy.

Although you're liable for the same kind of taxes owed by any other business with a legal structure like yours, when you use a part of your home exclusively and regularly as a business, you can claim it as a tax deduction along with associated expenses, such as a portion of your home's utilities. To get the most up-to-date IRS information regarding taxes and home offices, call the IRS at 1-800-829-1040 and ask for Publication 587, *Business Use of Your Home*.

You can download IRS tax forms and information by going to www.irs.gov.

Making Nice with the IRS

As the saying goes, nothing in life is certain but death and taxes. You can't escape the grim reaper *or* the IRS!

Ignorance is *not* bliss when it comes to taxes, especially if you're a business owner. It's your responsibility to understand what kinds of taxes your business must pay, and then you must make sure to get them paid on time and in full. Not doing so can be a mistake with expensive and even fatal consequences for a business, because the IRS has the power to impose hefty penalties on businesses that don't pay their taxes and high rates of interest on the unpaid tax debt. In addition, the agency has many powerful collection tools at its disposal, including the right to seize your property, levy against your bank accounts, and even shut you down.

Order IRS Publication 583, *Starting a Business and Keeping Records,* to get an overview of your tax obligations according to the IRS.

There are three basic types of federal business taxes: income taxes, self-employment taxes, and employment taxes. Your state may impose its own taxes, too. The exact kind of taxes you have to pay depends on the structure of your business and, among other things, on whether or not you have any employees.

- ✔ **Income taxes:** No matter what legal form your business takes, you have to pay taxes on your business income. The specific income tax obligations of each type of business are reviewed earlier in this chapter.

  If you're a sole proprietor or in a partnership, it's a good idea to make quarterly estimated tax payments instead of having to come up with a lot of money every April 15th. Quarterly estimated payments are essentially down payments on the income taxes that you may owe and are based on your income from the previous year.

- ✔ **Self-employment taxes:** Sole proprietors and partners pay their Social Security taxes once per year by making an annual lump sum payment when they file their tax returns.

- ✔ **Employment or payroll taxes:** If you have employees, you must deduct federal income taxes, Social Security taxes, and Medicare taxes from your employees' paychecks, and you also have to match the Social Security portion.

  The IRS requires employers to withhold payroll taxes from their employees' wages and then deposit the total amount in an account at a depository bank. In turn, the bank sends your tax payments to the IRS on a periodic basis.

Payroll taxes represent a potential problem area for many businesses. Some neglect to deduct the taxes from their employees' wages or don't deduct enough; others make the deduction but deposit the tax money in the businesses' bank accounts rather than with a depository bank, using the money to fund their operations and growth. Usually these businesses view their use of the money as nothing more than a loan and fully intend to deposit the money with the depository bank by the time the taxes are due to be paid. In reality, however, as many a small and not-so-small business has learned the hard way, coming up with the money may be easier said than done. Many businesses therefore find it impossible to catch up after they fall behind on their payroll taxes, and when the IRS notices that they haven't been paying, the agency does whatever it can to collect, including holding all "responsible persons" 100 percent personally responsible for the debt and all related penalties and interest. "Responsible persons" can include the business's owners, officers, and bookkeeper — anyone who signs the checks.

To help you meet your payroll tax obligations, consider hiring a payroll service to help you. This kind of company handles all tax calculations, completes the paperwork, prepares employees' paychecks, keeps track of your payroll records and prepares quarterly state and federal tax forms as well as year-end forms.

Getting behind on payroll taxes is one of the major reasons why small businesses fail. If you develop payroll tax problems, consult a tax attorney immediately. If the IRS is threatening to seize your property or shut you down, call a bankruptcy attorney instead.

Knowing Your Employees

Employers can get themselves in hot water with the IRS by treating employees as independent contractors for tax purposes. An independent contractor is a self-employed person who provides a service to your business, usually on an hourly or project basis, but who is not controlled, supervised, or directed by you. If you use the services of an independent contractor, you don't have to worry about collecting and paying that person's payroll taxes, but you do have to complete and file an IRS 1099 form on any independent contractor to whom you pay at least $600 in any tax year.

Hiring foreign workers

If you want to hire temporary or permanent workers from other countries for your business, no matter what their nationalities, you must work your way through a complicated process. This process involves the U.S. Department of Labor's Division of Foreign Labor Certification, the department's Employment and Training Administration, the U.S. Bureau of Citizenship and Immigration Services (CIS) (formerly known as the Immigration and Naturalization Service), and the local office of your state's workforce agency.

From start to finish, this process can take a couple years, although in states such as California, Texas, and New York, where a lot of immigrant hiring occurs, it can take even longer. For a more detailed explanation of the process as well as downloadable forms, go to www.workforcesecurity.doleta.gov/foreign/hiring/asp. You may also want to consult with a labor attorney who has specific experience in getting foreign workers into the country legally.

Although the IRS has established 20 separate criteria to help employers distinguish between independent contractors and employees, the distinctions between one type of worker and another can still be puzzling.

Get copies of *Topic 762 — Independent Contractor vs. Employee,* produced by the IRS, and Publication 15-A, *Employer's Supplemental Tax Guide* to see how the IRS distinguishes between employees and independent contractors. You can read these publications online or order hard copies at the IRS Web site: www.irs.gov.

If the IRS decides that someone you've been treating as an independent contractor is really an employee, you're expected to pay the payroll taxes you should have been withholding, plus interest and penalties. If you have misclassified many workers, and if the IRS decides to go back in history and discovers that you've been misclassifying employees as independent contractors for a long time, your tax debt can be substantial. Furthermore, because certain federal laws only apply to businesses that employ a certain number of employees — for example, the Family Medical Leave Act (must have at least 50 employees) and the Americans with Disabilities Act (must have at least 15 employees) — you may also find that after the IRS has begun reclassifying your workers, your business has to begin complying with laws that can cost you even more money.

If your misclassifications are significant, you may not be able to recover from your mistakes. Bankruptcy may be your best option if you're unable to come up with the money to cover back taxes, interest, and penalties.

Patents, Trademarks, and Copyrights

Depending on the nature of your business, patents, trademarks (or intellectual property rights), and copyrights may be important to you. Why? Read on.

By the way, for a more in-depth look at the topics covered in this section, pick up a copy of *Patents, Copyrights & Trademarks For Dummies* by Henri Charmasson (Wiley).

Patents

Patents provide inventors (and society in general) a number of important benefits. For example, they encourage people to invent. Without patents, we may never have had the telephone, the computer, the airplane, and other innovations that have helped transform society.

Patents also make it easier for inventors to attract the money they need to transform their invention into something that they can market and sell or license.

Patents can only be granted for new and useful inventions and discoveries related to the following:

- ✔ Processes
- ✔ Machines
- ✔ Manufactured articles
- ✔ Compositions of matter, which refers to chemical compositions and compounds as well as some mixtures of ingredients — medicines, for example
- ✔ Improvements in any of the above

If you invent something new — how about a better mousetrap? — and if you want to "exclude others from making, using, or selling" your invention, then you must complete a patent application and file it with the U.S. Patent and Trademark Office in Washington, D.C.

In the application, you have to describe your invention in considerable detail, including how to make and use it. You may also have to provide a prototype. After you file your application and pay the fee, a lengthy review process, which can take at least a year to complete, begins. If you're granted a patent, you have to pay other fees as well, but your patent is valid throughout the United States and in all of its territories and possessions.

You can prepare the application yourself, but you're probably better off hiring a registered patent attorney or patent agent to help you. Although they don't come cheap, their knowledge of federal patent law and of the inner workings of the Patent and Trademark Office itself can be a timesaver and can give you a better shot at getting your invention patented.

If you choose to hire an attorney or agent to assist you, according to law, only attorneys and agents recognized by the U.S. Patent and Trademark Office can represent inventors before the office. The Patent and Trademark Office maintains a registry of approved attorneys and agents, which can be purchased for a small fee through the Superintendent of Documents, Government Printing Office (GPO), Washington, DC 20402.

If you're approached by a company claiming to be an invention marketing business, check it out carefully. To get their hands on your money, these businesses exaggerate the potential of your invention, do a haphazard patent search, get you a worthless patent, and do little if any marketing.

When you get a patent, what you're actually getting is time — 20 years after your application is filed — to develop your idea into something you can make money from. And you get the right to exclude others from doing the same. Meanwhile, your application information is available to the general public so that others can use the information to try and develop their own new inventions, which they, in turn, can try to patent. And so it goes. . . .

If someone violates your patent, the federal government will not help you enforce the patent or bring legal action against the violator. You have to file a lawsuit in federal district court to collect damages and/or to prevent further infringements on your patent.

Ideas can't be patented, but an idea can help create something that can be patented.

Trademarks

A *trademark* is something that you can use to identify your business's product and distinguish it from others. A trademark can be a name, symbol, shape, device, or even a word. Service marks are similar to trademarks but apply to a business service. Well-known trademarks include Apple, Häagen-Dazs, and Kodak. McDonald's is a highly visible service mark.

Before you attempt to establish a trademark, make sure that no one else is using the trademark you want.

Although you don't have to go through an application process to get a trademark (you get one simply by being the first to use it, and you keep it as long as you continue using it), it's a good idea to register your trademark with the U.S. Patent and Trademark Office. Being federally registered gives you the right to sue in federal court and recover treble damages for unlawful use of your trademark. Registration involves completing an application, providing samples of your trademark, and paying a fee.

You can also get a state trademark, but a federal trademark provides more protection and is good in all states. A state trademark is good only in the state that grants it.

You can apply for a patent or trademark online at the Web site of the U.S Patent and Trademark Office, www.uspto.gov. The site also allows you to monitor the status of your application after it's filed.

Copyrights

The Federal Copyright Act of 1976 allows copyrighting of original created works, including books, software, CD-ROMs, films, artwork, music, and so on, in order to prevent others from copying them without your permission and/or without paying you a fee.

Copyrighting something means that the entire time your copyright is in effect, you have the exclusive right to copy, perform, or display the copyrighted work. A copyright lasts for the life of the author plus 70 years, assuming "the work" was published after 1977. If your business commissioned the work, or if it was produced for your business by one of your employees, then the copyright lasts between 95 and 100 years.

In most cases, if one of your employees creates an original work as part of his or her job, the copyright belongs to you, the employer, not to the employee. So, if your business creates packaging for CD-ROMs, you have the copyright on the designs that your employees create while they're on the job. You're also free, however, to work out another arrangement with an employee by drawing up a written agreement to that effect, signed by both of you.

Copyright law allows for *fair use* of copyrighted material and establishes criteria for determining fair use.

An idea can't be copyrighted, but the expression of an idea in a work can be. Works whose value is totally utilitarian and not expressive in any way also can't be copyrighted. So, if you build a functional table in your workshop at home out of scrap wood with unique utilitarian features, you can't copyright the table; but you may want to patent it. A uniquely designed table whose uniqueness is not in its artistic qualities but in its utility may qualify for a patent. On the other hand, if you create a table out of an old tree, carving the table base into the shape of a tree trunk and carving branches to hold up the table's glass top, that table can have a copyright by virtue of its creative design.

Getting a copyright is significantly easier than getting a patent. In fact, there's no application process. As soon as you create a work that can be copyrighted, it's copyrighted! It's as easy as that.

If the need arises, you won't be able to sue someone for infringing your copyright unless you've first registered the copyright with the Library of Congress in Washington, D.C. Call 202-707-3000 for a copyright application or print one off from the U.S. Copyright Office Web site at www.copyright.gov. The Web site also offers much more detailed information about copyrights.

When Good Businesses Go Bad: Bankruptcy

I hate to close this chapter with a discussion of such an unhappy subject. But in fact, bankruptcy is a fitting final topic because thousands of small businesses end up in bankruptcy every year.

Businesses have a legal right to file bankruptcy as a way of protecting themselves from the collection actions of their creditors. Some businesses exercise this right because their financial problems are so severe that they can't remain in business. Others use bankruptcy as a way to stay in business.

The federal Bankruptcy Code recognizes many types of bankruptcy. The four most common types are Chapters 11, 12, and 13, which are all reorganization bankruptcies, and Chapter 7, which is a liquidation bankruptcy.

Bankruptcy is your best choice of action when . . .

- ✔ Your business owes back taxes, and the IRS is breathing down your neck, threatening to get its money by seizing your business or personal property, by taking money from your bank accounts, or by shutting your business down and liquidating its assets.
- ✔ Your business owes more to creditors than it can pay, and your creditors are unwilling to negotiate new debt payment plans that you can afford.
- ✔ Your secured creditors are threatening to take their collateral.
- ✔ Your business's landlord is threatening to evict you.

Getting your business back on its feet: Reorganization bankruptcies

Reorganization bankruptcies (Chapters 11, 12, and 13 bankruptcies) allow businesses to remain in business by working with the court and their creditors to develop a debt payment plan that enables them to repay much of their debt in a manner that they can afford over a three- to five-year period. (If your business files Chapter 11, you may get more time to pay off the debt.) While a business is in a reorganization bankruptcy, the court protects it from the collection actions of its creditors. If you file a reorganization bankruptcy, you're allowed to run your business without the court's interference while your bankruptcy is ongoing.

Each type of reorganization bankruptcy carries its own restrictions regarding what types of businesses are eligible. Chapter 13 reorganization is only available to sole proprietorships that have no more than $290,525 in unsecured debt and $871,559 in secured debt. Chapter 12 reorganization is available to family farmers. Partnerships and corporations must use Chapter 11 to reorganize.

Because Chapter 11 reorganization is significantly more time-consuming and costly than Chapter 13, a significant proportion of the businesses that file Chapter 11 are ultimately forced into Chapter 7 and then out of business.

Often, when a partnership files for bankruptcy, its partners end up filing as well. As individuals, though, they're eligible for Chapter 13, depending on the amount of their debt.

Starting with a clean slate: Chapter 7 bankruptcy

Any kind of business can file a *liquidation bankruptcy,* or Chapter 7, which wipes out most of its debts. This action is usually your best option when your business is so debt-ridden and your income so inadequate that there's little chance that you'll be able to repay your debts and stay in business. However, you still have to pay certain kinds of debts, such as taxes. Also, you will lose business property when you file Chapter 7, depending on whether your business is a sole proprietorship, partnership, or corporation.

If your business' financial situation is bad enough, your creditors have the right to force it into bankruptcy by filing an involuntary Chapter 7 bankruptcy.

As soon as serious financial trouble begins, consult with a bankruptcy attorney — the sooner the better. If you have this meeting early enough, the attorney may actually be able to suggest things you can do to address your business' financial woes and avoid bankruptcy. Also, the attorney can tell you what not to do if you're thinking about filing, because certain actions can diminish the potential benefits of bankruptcy. For example, if you pay one of your unsecured creditors but don't pay any of the others within 90 days of filing, the court can void that payment and get your money back.

Although filing bankruptcy no longer carries the stigma it used to, bankruptcy damages your personal and/or your business's credit record and makes it tough to get new credit at competitive terms for at least seven to ten years — the length of time a bankruptcy stays on a credit record. It's tough enough to build a successful business without having to overcome a bankruptcy.

Chapter 10

Credit: Getting It, Using It, Losing It, Rebuilding It

*U*sing credit is the American way. In fact, not having access to it can limit your choices and opportunities in life — it's a necessary evil! For example, without credit, it would probably be close to impossible for you to purchase something as expensive as a new home or car or to pay for your child's college education unless you won the lottery or your rich uncle left you a pile of money. Also, not having credit makes even relatively minor financial transactions like renting a car, reserving a hotel room, or ordering something through the mail or over the Internet much more difficult.

As helpful as credit can be, it can also be dangerous. A wallet full of credit cards or a checking account with overdraft protection can get you in a lot of trouble. They can make it all too easy to spend more than you earn. And if you don't make your debt payments on time, you not only end up paying late fees, penalties, and high rates of interest, but you can also damage your credit record, possibly lose your right to use credit, and in the worst-case scenario, end up in bankruptcy.

Considering the benefits and the dangers of using credit, if you're going to have it, you should know about the federal laws that relate to getting, using, and losing credit. Some of these laws protect you from being discriminated against when you're applying for credit or ensure that you have the information you need to evaluate and compare credit offers. Other laws give you certain rights when you use credit or when you have trouble paying your bills.

Still other laws regulate the powers of credit bureaus — powerful, data-rich companies that collect and sell vast amounts of information on virtually every American consumer — and give you the right to file bankruptcy as a means of gaining protection from your creditors when your debts exceed your ability to pay them.

Call your state attorney general's office of consumer protection to find out about your state's consumer credit laws. They may give you more rights and protections than the federal laws do.

Getting Credit

Two federal laws protect you when you're applying for credit: the Equal Credit Opportunity Act (ECOA) and the Truth in Lending Act (TLA).

The Equal Credit Opportunity Act

This law says that when you apply for credit, you must be evaluated on the basis of your credit-worthiness only, not on factors that have nothing to do with your ability to repay your debt. The law applies to any creditor who regularly extends credit to consumers, including banks, retailers, bankcard companies, finance companies, and credit unions.

The ECOA and creditors

Among other things, the ECOA says that it's illegal for creditors to

- ✔ Discriminate against you because of your race, sex, age, national origin, or marital status, or because you receive public assistance.

- ✔ Ask about your marital status if you're applying for separate, unsecured credit, with one exception: You can be asked about your marital status if you live in a community property state. No matter what state you live in, however, you can be asked about your marital status when you apply for joint credit (credit you and your spouse share) or when the credit is secured or collateralized with property you own.

- ✔ Ask whether you have children or plan to have them.

- ✔ Disallow regular sources of income, such as reliable veteran's benefits, welfare payments, Social Security payments, alimony, child support, and so on. Nor may they refuse to consider or discount any income you earn from a part-time job, pension, annuity, or retirement benefits program.

The ECOA also says that creditors must

- Let you know whether you've been denied or granted credit within 30 days of receiving your completed application.

- Give you a specific reason (or tell you how to get the reason) why you're denied credit or granted less credit than what you applied for. This same rule applies if a creditor closes your account, refuses to increase your line of credit, makes a negative change in the terms of your credit and doesn't make the same change for other consumers, or refuses to give you credit at the same, or approximately the same, terms as were offered when you initially applied for the credit.

Special help for women

When the ECOA was written, it was common for women not to work outside the home and to have little or no credit in their own names. If they became divorced or widowed, they found it very difficult to build a life for themselves on their own because they had no credit history, even though they may have managed their families' finances. Women were credit nonentities in the eyes of banks, credit card companies, and other sources of credit. The ECOA therefore included provisions specifically written to help married women build credit histories in their own names, separate from the credit histories of their husbands. The ECOA is an equal opportunity law, which means that if necessary, men can use the law to help them build credit identities apart from their wives as well.

To help each spouse build his or her own credit history, the law says that you have the right to

- Get credit in your birth name, your first name, and your spouse's last name, or in your first name and a combined last name, such as a hyphenated last name.

- Get credit without a cosigner, assuming you meet the creditor's standards.

- Have a cosigner other than your spouse if you need one.

- Keep your own accounts if your marital status changes or if you change your name, assuming you will be able to continue making payments on those accounts.

A creditor can ask you to update your application for the credit you shared with your spouse before your marital status changed due to a divorce or because of his or her death. After reviewing your updated information, the creditor may ask you to reapply for the credit on your own or it may change the terms of that credit. The credit terms may change because you don't make enough money on your own, you don't have a good credit history, or for some other reason.

✔ Have information on accounts you share with your spouse (joint accounts) reported in both of your names.

The law also requires all creditors to provide their credit reporting agencies with credit record information in the names of both spouses when a husband and wife share an account.

To be sure that information on all your credit accounts is being reported in your name, request a copy of your credit record from the three major credit reporting agencies: Experian (formerly TRW), TransUnion, and Equifax. Instructions for requesting your record appear in the section "Getting in touch with the three credit reporting agencies" later in this chapter.

The Truth in Lending Act

The Truth in Lending Act (TLA) says that before you sign a credit installment agreement (a contract to pay back what you borrow by making monthly payments), the creditor must give you certain information to help you understand the cost and terms of the credit so that you can compare it to alternative credit sources. The TLA applies to banks, retailers, bankcard companies, credit unions, and others.

The TLA says that you must be given written information that states the amount you're financing, the number of payments you're obligated to make, the dollar amount of your monthly payments, the rate of interest you'll pay on the credit, and most importantly, the credit's annual percentage rate or APR — its annualized cost.

Another important provision of the TLA helps protect you when you apply for financing and use your home as collateral. (This provision doesn't apply to a home mortgage loan.) It says that you have three days, not including Saturdays, Sundays, and legal public holidays, after signing an agreement to notify the lender *in writing* that you've changed your mind and want to cancel the loan. This is the *right of rescission.*

Using Credit and Protecting Your Credit Record

After you have credit, it's your responsibility to use it wisely, which means making your payments on time and in full and resolving billing and other credit-related problems as quickly as possible so that they don't damage your credit record.

Wise use of credit also means not having too much of it. Having a lot of credit, even if you've been paying the credit accounts on time, can damage your credit history. Also, if you have too much credit, you risk being late with your payments or not being able to keep up with the payments at all, which harms your credit record, too. You may also begin getting calls from debt collectors, you may lose some of your property to your creditors, and you may even end up in bankruptcy. In short, your life can become full of stress and worry.

Every time you apply for new credit or for an increase in your credit limit, the creditor reviews your credit record. Each review shows up on your credit record as an "inquiry." Creditors do not like to see a lot of inquiries and are less apt to extend new or additional credit to applicants who have "too many."

And now, a few words about credit records and credit reporting agencies

If you have credit, information about who you owe money to, how much you owe, whether or not you pay your bills on time, and a lot more is collected by at least one of the three national credit reporting agencies — Experian, Equifax, and TransUnion.

The Fair Credit Reporting Act (FCRA) is the federal law that regulates the activities of the credit reporting agencies that comprise the powerful, billion-dollar credit reporting industry. It also regulates the businesses that use credit reporting agency information as well as the businesses that supply information to credit reporting agencies.

The FCRA was written in the 1970s, before computerization changed the face of the credit and credit reporting industry. It has been amended twice — once in 1996 with the passage of the Consumer Credit Reporting Reform Act and, most recently, in 2003 when Congress passed the Fair Credit Transactions Act (FACTA). Some of the changes that resulted from the amendments have given consumers more rights and protections, but others have increased the rights of the credit reporting industry.

Credit reporting agencies get their information from three main sources.

- ✔ **Subscribers:** Subscribers are the creditors who provide information to credit reporting agencies on how well the consumers to whom they've extended credit are meeting the terms of their credit agreements. Subscribers include banks, credit card companies, large retailers, and so on.

✔ **Public records:** These records tell credit reporting agencies if you have any tax liens on your property, any court judgments against you, and if you've filed for bankruptcy, among other things.

✔ **You:** When you complete a credit application, you provide basic information about yourself, such as your Social Security number, age, home address, employer, and so on.

How credit record information is used

Credit reporting agencies sell their information to creditors, employers, insurers, investors, loan servicing companies, state and local child enforcement agencies, and to anyone with "a legitimate business need" to know what you owe, how you manage your credit, and other information in your credit record. They also sell your credit score. For example, when you apply for credit, the creditor either orders a copy of your credit record and reviews it as part of the credit-granting process or checks out your credit score. If your credit record contains too much negative information or your credit score is too low, you may be denied credit, be approved for less than the amount you applied for, or be offered credit with terms that aren't as attractive as what someone with a problem–free credit record and a high credit score would qualify for. Also, insurance companies may check your credit record or your credit score to decide whether to insure you or to determine the cost of your existing policy, and an employer may review your credit record or credit score as part of its hiring or promotion decision-making process.

Getting in touch with the three credit reporting agencies

It's a good idea to request a copy of your credit report from each of the three national credit reporting agencies every six months to make sure that your reports are accurate and to correct any problems or errors you may find.

Before applying for a mortgage loan or any other really important credit, request a copy of your report from each of the national credit reporting agencies. You want to be sure that the reports don't contain inaccurate information that can hurt your chances of getting the credit you want.

If you don't understand something in your credit report, call the credit reporting agency that produced it and ask for help. The agency is legally required to have staff available to help you understand the information in your report.

There are three ways to obtain a copy of your credit record: by mail, by phone, or online. Use the following contact information for each credit reporting agency.

- ✔ Equifax
  Disclosure Department
  P.O. Box 740241
  Atlanta, GA 30374
  www.equifax.com
  1-800-685-1111

- ✔ Experian
  National Consumer Assistance Center
  P.O. Box 2002
  Allen, TX 75013-2104
  www.experian.com/consumer/index.html
  1-888-397-3742

- ✔ TransUnion
  Consumer Disclosure Center
  P.O. Box 1000
  Chester, PA 19022
  www.transunion.com
  1-800-888-4213

If you request your credit reports in writing, be sure to provide the following information: your full name (including Jr., Sr., the II, the III, and so on if you use any of these suffixes); your date of birth; your current address and your previous address if you haven't lived at your present residence for at least five years; your Social Security number; your spouse's name and Social Security number if you're married; your daytime and evening phone numbers; and proof of your name and current address (a copy of your driver's license and a utility bill, for example).

An overview of your credit record rights

Given the power and influence that credit reporting agencies can have in your life, it's important to be familiar with your rights when you're dealing with them. For example, you have the right to

- ✔ Know what's in your credit record.

- ✔ Receive a free copy of your credit record if you're denied credit, insurance, or employment due to information in your credit file or if a creditor, insurance company, or employer takes some other adverse action against you because of that information. Other adverse actions include: your credit limit is lowered, you're turned down for a promotion, or the cost of your insurance premium is increased. You must request your free copy within 60 days of being notified of the adverse action.

✔ Receive a free annual copy of your credit report from each of the three national credit reporting agencies. As a result of FACTA, consumers can obtain all three of their free reports simultaneously or one at a time throughout the year by contacting just one Web site (www.annual creditreport.com), phone number (1-877-322-8228), or address (Annual Credit Report Request Service, P. O. Box 105281, Atlanta, GA 30348-5281). Initial eligibility for the free reports is being phased in geographically, starting in the West. The schedule is:

  • Residents of Western states: December 1, 2004

  • Residents of Midwestern states: March 1, 2005

  • Residents of Southern states: June 1, 2005

  • Residents of Eastern states: September 2005

Order a copy of your credit report even if you haven't suffered an adverse action. Expect to pay for any additional copies of your credit report if you've already used up your annual freebie. As this book goes to press, the cost of a credit report is $9 (plus sales tax in some states). However, depending on your state, you may be legally entitled to additional free reports or lower-cost reports. States with this benefit are Colorado, Georgia, Maine, Maryland, Massachusetts, New Jersey, and Vermont.

✔ Get a free copy of your credit report from each of the national credit reporting agencies if you're out of work and plan on applying for work within the next 60 days.

✔ Receive a free copy of your credit report from all three of the national credit reporting agencies if you're the victim of identity theft or if you're receiving public assistance.

✔ Have a credit reporting agency investigate information in your credit record that you believe is wrong. You're also entitled to have the provider of that information investigate the problem.

✔ Have information that you contend is wrong or outdated corrected or deleted from your credit record if the credit reporting agency or the information provider can confirm its inaccuracy or can't verify it.

✔ Have a credit reporting agency that corrects a problem in your credit file report the correction to any employers who reviewed the file during the past two years, or to anyone else who looked at it over the past six months.

✔ Have a written statement included in your credit record explaining any negative information it may contain. For example, you may want potential creditors to know that you were late on your debt payments in the last year because your spouse was hospitalized and the costs of medical care took every penny you had.

Written statements don't carry a lot of value anymore however because more and more creditors and insurance companies make decisions about consumers based on their credit scores, which are derived from the consumers' credit record information rather than by reviewing the actual information in their credit files.

✔ Have most negative information automatically deleted from your credit record after seven years. However, Chapter 7 bankruptcies remain in your record for ten years. (The three national credit reporting agencies report Chapter 13 bankruptcies for seven, not ten, years.) Also, unpaid tax liens can be reported for 15 years, and court judgments can remain in your credit report for as long as 20 years.

✔ Sue a credit reporting agency, information provider, or user of your credit file information when your credit reporting legal rights have been violated. However, your right to sue is limited by the FCRA and its amendments.

Correcting credit record problems

If you discover a problem in your credit report and you ordered the report by phone or through the mail, complete the investigation/research request form that should have come with the report, make a copy for your files, and return it to the address indicated on the form. Send the form via certified mail with a return receipt requested.

If you didn't receive an investigation/research request form, call the phone number provided by the credit reporting agency to initiate an investigation into the problem. If you ordered your credit report online, return to the credit reporting agency's Web site for instructions on how to initiate an investigation.

If you initiate an investigation through the mail, attach to your completed form copies of any information you may have that supports your belief that your credit record is inaccurate. Such information may include cancelled checks, correspondence, and account statements.

After the credit bureau receives your communication, it contacts the creditor or the public agency that reported the information you're disputing so that it can confirm its accuracy. If the creditor or agency says the information is correct, it stays in your credit record. But if the creditor says, "Yes, it's wrong," or if the credit reporting agency can't confirm the accuracy or inaccuracy of the information that you're questioning within 30 days of your letter, then the FCRA says that the information must be deleted from your record.

Credit reporting agency investigations aren't very thorough. More often than not, poorly trained employees conduct thcm. Therefore, if a creditor or public agency says, "I'm right, and the consumer is wrong," the credit reporting agency generally takes it at its word.

A credit bureau must complete its investigation within 30 days unless you provide it with additional information during that time period.

If your credit record problem is corrected, the credit reporting agency must send you

- ✔ A corrected copy of your credit report

- ✔ A notice of your right to have your corrected report sent to any employers who reviewed your report during the previous two years and to anyone else who looked at it in the last six months

If you're not successful at getting your credit record corrected and if you continue to believe that your report is in error, here are some other things to try:

- ✔ Provide the agency with new documentation.

- ✔ Contact the creditor directly about the problem and send it a complete set of supporting documentation. Ask the information provider to send the credit reporting agencies it works with the correct information and to correct its own database so it does not continue reporting inaccurate information.

- ✔ Contact a consumer law attorney who has specific experience dealing with credit reporting agencies for advice about what to do next.

You should also

- ✔ File a complaint with your state attorney general's office of consumer protection if your state has its own credit reporting law.

- ✔ File a complaint with the FTC. You can file your complaint online at www. ftc.gov; by calling 1-800-382-4357; or by mailing your complaint to the FTC at Consumer Response Center, 600 Pennsylvania Avenue, Washington, DC 20580.

- ✔ Prepare a written statement — no more than 100 words — explaining why you think your credit record is wrong. The credit reporting agency must make it a permanent part of your credit record.

What's your score?

Your credit score is a numeric representation of your credit worthiness. It's derived from the information in your credit file. Many creditors, as well as a growing number of employers and insurance companies, use your credit score rather than your actual credit report to make decisions about you.

Fair Isaac Corporation, which develops decision management and analysis programs for lenders, retailers, insurance companies and other businesses to help them make wise decisions in regard to extending credit, issuing policies, and so on and to help them reduce fraud, has developed the FICO score, which most creditors and financial institutions use in their decision-making processes. Your FICO score can range from 300 to 850, and the higher the score, the better. However, other credit scoring programs exist; for example, Fair Isaac has developed credit

scoring software for each of the three national credit reporting agencies. The Equifax credit score is called BEACON; Experian's is the Experian/Fair Isaac Risk Score; and TransUnion's is called EMPERICA. Because each credit reporting agency has slightly different information about you in its database, and because each agency's software assigns different weights to the information in your credit file, expect your credit score to vary from company to company. Therefore, just as you should know what your Equifax, Experian, and TransUnion credit reports say about you, so too you should know what kind of credit score you have with each company, as well as know your FICO score. You can order all of your scores at the FICO Web site, www.myfico.com. You can also go to the Web site of each of the credit reporting agencies to purchase your credit score from them.

Although they may help, written statements are of limited impact. There's no guarantee that anyone will read your statement when you apply for credit, employment, or insurance. Also, a growing number of businesses use computers to review consumers' applications or check out their credit scores. In both cases, your written statement will never be considered.

To help make sure that potential creditors, insurers, or employers read the information in your written statement, it's a good idea to give them a copy of it when you're applying for credit, insurance, or a job.

I don't think I owe this: Correcting billing statement problems

Check your monthly bankcard and charge card statements to make sure that they accurately reflect the payments you've made, that your account balance is correct, and that they don't show any charges to your account that you didn't make or didn't authorize. If you do find problems with a statement, the federal Fair Credit Billing Act (FCBA) spells out the process you need to follow to resolve the problems, and it provides you with special protections while you're pursuing a resolution.

The FCBA also helps if you have problems with overdrafts from your checking account.

If you discover a problem with your credit statement, write the creditor about the problem within 60 days after you receive the first bill with the incorrect information. Succinctly explain the problem and note the dollar amount involved, all relevant dates, your name and address as it appears on your billing statement, and your account number. Include copies of any sales slips or other documentation that provide proof that you're correct. Make a copy of the letter for your files and send the original via certified mail, return receipt requested, to the billing inquiries address listed on your statement.

Calling a creditor about a billing statement problem doesn't activate the protections of the FCBA. And don't send your dispute letter with your account payment. It may not get to the appropriate person.

While you're waiting for a response from your creditor, keep the following in mind:

- ✔ You don't have to pay the amount you're disputing or any related finance charges. The charge may continue to appear on your bill, however.

- ✔ You must continue making payments on the rest of your account.

- ✔ The amount you're disputing can be applied to your total credit limit.

- ✔ Your creditor can't report the amount you're disputing to a credit bureau or threaten to damage your credit record.

- ✔ Your creditor can't close your account or threaten you with legal action.

The creditor must acknowledge your letter in writing within 30 days of receiving it. Within 90 days or two billing cycles, the creditor must either tell you why your bill is accurate or correct it, crediting your account for the amount in dispute and for all related finance charges, late fees, and so on.

If the creditor maintains that your bill is correct, the creditor must provide you with a written statement of exactly how much you owe and why. You may also ask to be provided with supporting documentation.

If you continue to disagree with the creditor, you have ten days after receiving its explanation of what you owe and why to write back that you still refuse to pay the amount in dispute. At this point, however, the creditor can begin reporting you as delinquent to the credit bureaus it reports to and can initiate collection action against you. But as long as you've protested in writing within the ten-day time frame, when the creditor reports you as delinquent, it must also report that you don't believe that you owe the money.

The FTC offers many informative brochures on how to use bankcards and on credit in general. You can view them online at www.ftc.gov, or you can order them by writing to FTC, Consumer Response Center, 600 Pennsylvania Avenue, NW, Washington, DC 20580.

When You Can't Pay Your Bills

If you begin having trouble paying your bills, contact your creditors immediately! Let them know that you're having trouble and ask them if you can make smaller payments or interest-only monthly payments for a certain period of time. Also, tell them what you're doing to get your financial situation stabilized. If you don't contact creditors and just ignore your bills, hoping they'll just go away (fat chance of that!), you can expect to begin receiving calls or letters from debt collectors, and you'll end up doing some serious damage to your credit record.

If you want help negotiating lower monthly debt payments, contact one of the debt counseling offices associated with the nonprofit National Foundation for Consumer Credit. For little or no cost to you, a counselor at one of these offices can help you get your financial situation under control. Among other things, the counselor helps you develop a realistic budget and may negotiate more affordable monthly payments with your unsecured creditors. To locate the office closest to you, call 1-800-388-2227 or go to www.nfcc.org.

Dealing with debt collectors

It's 9 a.m. Monday morning, and the debt collectors have started calling again. Just what you need! It's bad enough that you've lost your job, you're having trouble finding another one, and you're worried about the stack of unpaid bills on your desk. You don't need debt collectors adding to the stress and worry you're feeling — if you could pay them, you would! But right now, you barely have enough money to buy groceries, put gas in your car, and pay your utility bills!

If debt collectors are hounding you, the federal Fair Debt Collection Practices Act (FDCPA) can help you. The law regulates the activities of debt collectors, including attorneys who regularly collect consumer debts, and gives you certain rights when dealing with them. Here are some of the law's most important provisions:

- ✔ A debt collector can only contact you between 8 a.m. and 9 p.m. But you have the right to indicate in writing that you'd prefer to be contacted at another time, and the debt collector must honor your request. Also, if your employer doesn't want you to be contacted during working hours and you tell the debt collector (in writing) to stop calling you at work, the calls must stop.

- ✔ A debt collector can contact you by phone, fax, mail, in person, or by telegram. To protect your privacy, however, a debt collector can't send you a postcard that mentions your debt or send you an envelope that has anything on it that outwardly lets someone know that it came from a debt collector.

- ✔ After a debt collector contacts you for the first time about your debt, you must be sent a written notice within five days telling you how much you owe, who you owe it to, and what you can do if you don't think you owe it.

- ✔ You can send a debt collector a letter saying that you don't want to be contacted anymore except to be informed of any additional steps the debt collector or creditor intends to take to collect from you. The debt collector must honor your request.

- ✔ A debt collector can't contact anyone about your debt except to find out where you live or work.

- ✔ A debt collector can't threaten you with physical harm or harm to your reputation, use profanity, or make false statements as a way to pressure you into paying. Also, you can't be threatened with deductions from your paychecks or with a lawsuit unless the debt collector or your creditor actually intends to take action and is legally entitled to do so.

Although the FDCPA doesn't apply to in-house collection departments, your state may have a law that regulates what they can do.

For step-by-step information and advice about how to deal with debt collectors and your debt collection rights, go to www.stopdebtcollectors cold.com.

If you're having trouble paying off your student loan, don't assume that you get special treatment if you default on it. The lender can use the services of a debt collector to collect from you, sue you for nonpayment, and report your delinquency to credit bureaus. What a way to start life after college!

More extreme measures

If a debt collector doesn't scare you into paying what you owe and serious damage to your credit record doesn't scare you either, your creditor may decide to "turn up the heat." The creditor can sue you and get the court's permission to garnish your wages, if your state allows such action, or it may get permission to seize some of your property and sell it. (Every state exempts certain kinds of property from seizure and sale. Exempt property usually includes your home up to a certain value, household items and apparel up to a certain value, and the car you use for work, unless it's collateralizing a loan.)

✔ If a creditor sues you, all the lawsuit procedures and processes explained in Chapter 1 apply.

✔ If a creditor seizes some of your property, it will probably be auctioned off, and the proceeds will go toward paying your debt. If the property sells for more than the amount of your debt, you get the excess.

✔ If your wages are garnished, your employer must begin paying some portion of your paycheck to your creditor. Federal law, however, limits how much creditors can garnish from each check and the kinds of debts that garnishment can be used for.

If you owe what the debt collector is trying to collect, try to work out a way to pay off the debt over time. You can also try to settle the debt for less than what you owe on it, assuming that doing so doesn't jeopardize your ability to pay your most important living expenses and your most important debts — your home mortgage, home equity loan, any other debts that are secured by your home, and your car loan if you need the car to get to and from your job, for example. If you can't work something out with the debt collector, contact a consumer law attorney right away. The National Association of Consumer Advocates (NACA) or the National Consumer Law Center (NCLC) can refer you to a qualified consumer law attorney in your area. To get in touch with NACA, call 202-452-1989 or visit www.naca.net. To contact the NCLC, call 617-542-8010 or visit www.consumerlaw.org.

If you don't pay the money that a debt collector wants to collect from you, it may decide to pursue more extreme measures — like suing you, for example. Also, the longer you put off paying the debt, the more damage you do to your credit record.

If you don't think you owe the money or if you disagree with how much the debt collector says you owe, write to the debt collector no later than 30 days after being contacted. The debt collector must stop communicating with you. Collection efforts can resume, however, if the debt collector sends you proof of your debt.

If you think your rights have been violated

Here's what to do if you think that your legal rights have been violated:

- ✔ Make sure that you understand your rights. Call the Federal Trade Commission (877-382-4357 or 202-326-2222) and the consumer affairs office of your state attorney general to clarify your rights. Be aware of any deadlines you must meet in order to exercise your legal rights or anything special you may need to do to trigger the protection of the law.

- ✔ After you understand your rights, write the creditor or debt collector you're having a problem with to explain that you feel your legal rights have been violated. Mention the law you believe applies to your problem. Keep a copy of your letter, and send the original by certified mail with a return receipt.

- ✔ If your problem isn't resolved or if you're unhappy with the solution proposed by the creditor or debt collector, contact a consumer law attorney. The attorney you work with should have specific experience dealing with debt collection problems. Depending on the facts of your case, the attorney may advise you to file a lawsuit under the FDCPA or your state's debt collection law, which may offer you more protections and remedies than the federal law. Under the federal law, you can sue for actual, and sometimes punitive, damages. If you win your lawsuit, you can collect attorney's fees and court costs.

- ✔ File a complaint with your state attorney general's office of consumer protection, assuming your state has a law that applies to your problem.

Also, file a formal complaint with the Federal Trade Commission (FTC) by writing to: FTC, Consumer Response Center, 600 Pennsylvania Avenue, NW, Washington, DC 20580. You can also call to complain (877-382-4357), or file your complaint online at www.ftc.gov. Although the FTC will not act on behalf of an individual consumer, if it receives enough complaints about a specific creditor or about a specific industry practice, it may take action. If your complaint is about a financial institution's violation of a credit law, complain directly to the agency that regulates it.

When you believe that a financial institution has violated your rights, you have a few different options for who to contact.

If the creditor is a nationally chartered bank, contact

> Comptroller of the Currency
> Consumer Assistance Group
> 1301 McKinney St., Suite 3710
> Houston, TX 77010
> 1-800-613-6743
> www.occ.treas.gov

If the creditor is a state-chartered bank that is insured by the Federal Deposit Insurance Corporation and is a member of the Federal Reserve System, contact

> Consumer and Community Affairs
> Board of Governors of the Federal Reserve System
> 20th and C streets, NW
> Washington, DC 20551
> 202-452-3693
> www.federalreserve.gov

If the creditor is a state-chartered bank that is insured by the Federal Deposit Insurance Corporation but is *not* a member of the Federal Reserve System, contact

> Federal Deposit Insurance Corporation
> Supervision and Consumer Protection Division
> 550 17th St., NW
> Washington, DC 20429
> 1-877-275-3342
> www.fdic.gov/consumers/index.html

If your complaint is with a federally insured savings and loan or federally chartered state bank, contact

> Office of Thrift Supervision
> Department of the Treasury
> Compliance Policy
> 1770 G St., NW
> Washington. DC 20552
> 1-800-842-6929
> www.ots.treas.gov

If your complaint is with a federally chartered credit union, contact

National Credit Union Administration
Consumer Affairs Division
1775 Duke St.
Alexandria, VA 22314-3428
703-518-6300
www.ncua.gov

Taking the pressure off: Filing for bankruptcy

Sometimes, when you're drowning in debt, hounded by your creditors, and maybe even threatened by the IRS, filing for bankruptcy can be your best option. After you file a bankruptcy petition with the U.S. Bankruptcy Court and pay the appropriate fee, an automatic stay will be issued, requiring all of your creditors to cease their collection actions. No more calls from debt collectors, no more threats and letters. Although your financial troubles aren't over, the automatic stay takes the pressure off.

Before you file for bankruptcy, schedule an appointment with a reputable nonprofit debt counseling office to see if the office can help you work out a debt repayment plan that allows you to avoid filing.

Filing for bankruptcy without the help of a bankruptcy attorney is foolhardy. The bankruptcy process and the federal law that governs it are complicated, and dealing with the court and angry creditors can be frightening. A good bankruptcy attorney can help you avoid costly mistakes, help you keep as much of your property as possible, and make sure that you get rid of as much of your debt as possible, too. The attorney also serves as intermediary between you and your creditors, and answers your questions. Some states certify attorneys in bankruptcy.

The American Bankruptcy Institute's (www.abiworld.org) Consumer Education Center provides basic, straightforward information about the various types of consumer bankruptcy and explains how each one works. You can also search for a certified bankruptcy attorney in your arca.

If you file a Chapter 7 liquidation bankruptcy, most of your debts are erased and you don't have to pay them. If you file a Chapter 13 reorganization bankruptcy, you have the opportunity to pay small, monthly payments —amounts you can afford — so that you can pay off what you owe during a three- to five-year period.

Under the guise of cracking down on consumer abuse of the bankruptcy system, the Bush Administration implemented the Bankruptcy Civil Enforcement Initiative in 2001. The initiative has made the consumer bankruptcy process more difficult, more time-consuming, and more costly by calling into question the honesty of consumers who file for bankruptcy and by making it more difficult for consumers to get rid of debt.

Despite the benefits of bankruptcy, you should always consider it your option of last resort. That's because filing for bankruptcy seriously damages your credit record and because the FCRA says it can stay on your credit record for up to ten years. Remember, most credit problems only stay on your record for seven years. While a bankruptcy is on your record, you will find it difficult to get credit at reasonable terms.

Regardless of what type of bankruptcy you file, the legal process is governed by the federal Bankruptcy Code. There are no state bankruptcy laws.

The two types of bankruptcies for consumers are *Chapter 7* and *Chapter 13*.

The three national credit reporting agencies report Chapter 13 bankruptcies for only seven years. However, they report Chapter 7s for ten years.

Chapter 7 bankruptcy

Chapter 7 is a liquidation bankruptcy. It's an appropriate choice when you have so much debt compared to your income that there's no way you will be able to pay back what you owe. When you file Chapter 7, most, but not all, of your debts are wiped out. You also lose some of your property — your nonexempt assets. These assets are sold, and the proceeds are used to help repay your creditors.

Federal bankruptcy law includes a list of the types of property that you can claim as exempt when you file Chapter 7. Your state has its own list. In some states, you can choose between the federal list of exemptions and your state's and use whichever list is best for you.

In Chapter 7, certain types of debts must be paid off before others. Priority debts must be repaid first. These debts include taxes and the administrative expenses of bankruptcy. In many Chapter 7s, unsecured debts are never repaid because not enough funds are available from the sale of a consumer's nonexempt assets. In fact, often, the only debts that can be paid off are some of the consumer's priority debts.

Chapter 7 doesn't erase (*discharge* is the legal term) all of your debt — no such luck! You still have to pay off some things. Although not a complete list, what follows are some of the types of debt that remain after your bankruptcy is over:

- ✔ Alimony and child support payments
- ✔ Most taxes
- ✔ Some educational loans
- ✔ Fines and penalties that government entities have charged you with
- ✔ Any debts you incur after you file

Chapter 13 bankruptcy

Chapter 13 is a reorganization bankruptcy. You're allowed to lower most of your debt payments to amounts that you can afford to make, and you have three to five years to pay off your debt. Your plan for getting out of debt must be formalized in a reorganization plan and approved by the court. Although you're expected to pay off as much of your debt as possible, some of your *unsecured* debt (debt that is not collateralized) may be wiped out in Chapter 13.

If you owe more than $290,525 in unsecured debt and more than $871,550 in secured debt, you can't reorganize using Chapter 13 and must use Chapter 11 instead. This type of reorganization bankruptcy is more expensive and complicated, and a high percentage of those who use it end up converting to Chapter 7 liquidation. Big businesses most often use Chapter 11.

Life after bankruptcy

After your bankruptcy is behind you, if you're like most consumers, your first thought will probably be "How can I rebuild my credit history?" A positive credit history is key to getting new credit at reasonable terms. The condition of your credit record may also affect your ability to purchase adequate insurance; to get the job, promotion, or security clearance you've applied for; or to get the apartment or home you want to rent. However, because a bankruptcy can remain in your credit record for up to ten years, you won't have a trouble-free credit history for a long time. However, you don't have to wait ten years to begin the credit rebuilding process — you can start 14 to 24 months after your bankruptcy is over. Little by little, you can begin adding positive information to your credit history. Over time, the negative information in your credit record becomes too old to be reported, is dropped from your file, and is replaced with positive information; thus, your credit history improves.

While you're waiting to rebuild your credit, make good use of the time: Review your credit record to make sure that it doesn't include any incorrect information, and correct any problems that may exist. Also, begin saving money.

Things you should never do before filing for bankruptcy

When you're in the middle of a financial crisis, you may be tempted to take the pressure off by doing things that will not be helpful later if you decide to file for bankruptcy. That's why it's always a good idea to consult with a bankruptcy attorney when you're having serious money troubles but may not have decided to file bankruptcy. Here are some of the things the attorney will tell you not to do:

✔ Don't give your creditors postdated checks. If they bounce, you can be charged with a criminal offense, and bankruptcy won't protect you from criminal prosecution.

✔ Don't transfer any of your property to your friends, family, or anyone else one year prior to filing with the hope that you can keep it out of your bankruptcy and then get it back later. If you do, the bankruptcy *trustee* — the court official who supervises

your bankruptcy — may cancel the transfer and take the property back. Also, if you try to conceal any transfers and are discovered, you can be accused of fraud.

✔ Don't use your credit cards to run up more than $1,100 worth of debt for luxury goods or services with a single creditor within 60 days of filing. Also, don't get a cash advance of more than $1,100 within 60 days of filing. Neither debt can be wiped out by your bankruptcy.

✔ Don't pay one creditor at the expense of other creditors within 90 days of filing. If you do, the trustee can void that payment and distribute the money more fairly among your creditors.

✔ Don't voluntarily give up an asset you really need, like your car.

Don't try to hurry the rebuilding process by working with a disreputable credit repair organization. These companies charge exorbitant fees to "clean up" damaged credit records. Some even claim they can make bankruptcies disappear. Don't waste your money! Only time can make negative information go away.

The Credit Repair Organizations Act

In an effort to protect consumers who want help rebuilding or improving their credit histories, the federal Credit Repair Organizations Act (CROA) was signed into law in 1996. The law is enforced by the FTC, but many states have also passed their own legislation restricting the activities of these organizations.

The CROA says that

- **A credit repair organization must provide you with a written contract before it takes any money from you.** The contract must state the credit repair organization's full name and business address and spell out the services the organization will provide to you as well as their total cost. The contract must also specify how long it will take the organization to provide its services and what guarantees if any the firm makes to you.

- **You can cancel your contract for any reason within three business days of signing.** To cancel, you must use the cancellation form the credit repair organization should have provided you with when it gave you a copy of the signed contract.

- **The credit repair organization can't provide you with any of the services listed in its contract until the three-day cancellation period has expired.**

- **The credit repair organization can't take any money from you until it has completed all of the services in its contract.**

- **Before providing you with a written contract or statement, the firm must give you a "Consumer Credit File Rights under State and Federal Law" disclosure statement.** The CROA spells out exactly how the statement must be worded. Among other things, the statement must inform you of your right to dispute inaccurate or out-of-date credit record information on your own and your right to obtain a copy of your credit record from the credit reporting agencies. In addition, the statement must provide you with an overview of your rights when you're working with a credit fix-it firm, including the right to sue if the firm violates the CROA.

- **The credit repair organization can't encourage you to alter your identity in order to get a new, problem-free credit identity, nor may it attempt to mislead or deceive you in any way.**

If the credit repair organization you decide to work with violates the CROA, get in touch with a consumer law attorney. The attorney can help you pursue the remedies the CROA entitles you to. For example, the law says that

- **A contract that doesn't comply with the CROA is void and unenforceable.** Therefore, if a credit repair organization doesn't meet the requirements of the law, you don't owe the organization any money.

- **You can sue a credit repair organization that violates the CROA for actual damages or the amount you paid to it, whichever is greater.** You can also sue for punitive damages, and you may also be able to collect your attorney's fees and court costs.

Chapter 11

Smart Spending

. . . .

In This Chapter

▶ Buying products by mail and online

▶ Dealing with door-to-door salespersons

▶ Avoiding scams of all kinds

▶ Buying products on warranty

▶ Buying new and used cars

▶ Traveling by plane

▶ Understanding your investing legal rights

. . . .

*I*f you're like most people, no matter how hard you work, it seems like there's never enough money to go around! So, it's important that you use your money wisely, do what you can to avoid getting ripped off, and be aware of your legal rights if trouble develops. Wise spending involves

✔ Negotiating contracts for important financial transactions, something discussed in Chapter 1

✔ Understanding your legal rights and responsibilities when you use credit, covered in Chapter 8

✔ Evaluating product and service warranties

✔ Being alert for scams

And much, much more.

Consumer World (www.consumerworld.org) features articles of interest to consumers. The site is also a great source of information and updates regarding laws and regulations that affect consumers and links to a wide variety of other consumer-related Internet resources. You can also subscribe to an online Consumer World newsletter if you want to receive regular updates.

Shopping by Mail or on the Internet

In today's busy world, many of us let "our fingers do the walking" or "our mouse do the clicking" when we shop. What's easier and more fun than looking through the pages of glossy catalogs full of tempting merchandise or browsing colorful Web sites late at night looking for that perfect item — and then finding it, placing your order, and waiting for its arrival? Nothing! And you can do it all from the comfort of your home or office!

When you order by mail, phone, fax, or the Internet, the federal Mail Order or Telephone Rule (MOTR), which is enforced by the FTC, says that your order must be shipped to you when the company says it will be. (If the company doesn't give you a ship date, the MOTR assumes your purchase will be shipped within 30 days.) If the company can't meet that deadline, it must give you an *option notice* that offers you the choice of either canceling your order and receiving a prompt refund or agreeing to the delay.

If you pay for your purchase with a credit card, you're also protected by the Fair Credit Billing Act. For more on this law, flip to Chapter 10.

Knock Knock: Buying from a Door-to-Door Salesperson

If a salesperson who comes to your home or place of business sells you goods or services that are primarily intended for personal, family, or household uses and are worth at least $25, then you're protected by the federal Cooling-Off Rule, which is enforced by the FTC. The rule says that you have until midnight of the third business day after your purchase to cancel the transaction and request a full refund. This right also applies if you purchase goods or services at a temporary location being used by a seller — at a convention, fair, hotel, and so on. You don't have to provide a reason for your cancellation.

The Cooling-Off Rule doesn't apply to home-sale parties (for example, parties to sell kitchen supplies, jewelry, or cosmetics), sales that are the result of prior negotiations made at the seller's permanent business location, purchases made as a result of an emergency (for example, your home is flooded, and you need someone to remove the water), the purchase of a vehicle at a temporary location set up by the seller, or the sale of real estate, insurance, and securities.

The Cooling-Off Rule requires the seller to inform you of your cancellation rights at the time of sale and to give you two copies of a cancellation form — one for you to keep and one for you to send to the seller if you decide to cancel the sale — as well as a receipt or contract. The receipt or contract must be dated, indicate the seller's name and address, and explain your right to cancel. In addition, it must be written in the same language as the salesperson's sales presentation.

To cancel the sale, sign and date one copy of the cancellation form and mail it to the address you were provided for cancellation. The envelope must be postmarked before midnight of the third business day after the contract date. Saturday is considered a business day. Send the form certified mail, return receipt requested.

If you're not given a cancellation form, you can write your own cancellation letter.

After you cancel, the seller is required to do the following within ten days:

- Cancel and return any papers you signed.
- Refund all of your money, and make arrangements to pick up any merchandise that may have been left at your home.
- Return any trade-in.

Also, the seller must either pick up any items within 20 days or reimburse you for your postage costs if you agree to ship the merchandise to the seller.

Any merchandise you're returning to the seller must be in as good condition as it was when you received it from the seller. If the goods aren't in that condition, or if you fail to return the merchandise, the contract you signed remains in effect.

Avoiding Scams: Do I Have a Deal for You!

Susan and her husband Mark are having money troubles. She's been laid off from her well-paying job, and now she and her husband are having difficulty making ends meet. Their creditors are demanding to be paid, and at least one bankcard company has canceled their credit card. Susan is worried about how their financial woes will affect their credit histories. Then one day, she gets an e-mail from a legitimate-sounding business telling her about an incredible investment opportunity that she needs to act on right away. If everything in the e-mail is true, Susan and Mark's financial troubles will soon be over!

Susan is like many consumers who are down on their luck. In desperation, they begin looking for a quick way to make lots of money. Often, they fall prey to wealth-building scams. These scams may be marketed through the Internet, by phone, through the mail or personal sales, or on TV as *infomercials* — program-length ads that seem like real TV shows, not advertising. These scams promise

- **Investments with big payoffs:** So-called easy ways to make a lot of money through investments of all kinds include real estate, gems, stock offerings, land deals, even ostrich farming! If it were this easy, we'd all be rich!

- **"Guaranteed" jobs:** At most, you'll receive a list of companies to write to.

- **"Guaranteed" loans or credit cards:** These offers are made regardless of your credit history or income — always a sign of something fishy.

- **Business opportunities:** The only business that makes money from these "opportunities" is the company selling them.

- **Work-at-home "opportunities" with promises of big money:** Yeah, maybe you can make the thousands you're promised — if you work day and night!

- **Travel deals:** That dream vacation is never as cheap or as glamorous as it sounds.

- **Prize offers:** These "free" prizes actually cost you a lot of money, and you may end up with nothing to show for the expense.

- **Magazine offers:** You don't buy just the magazine you want; you buy multiple subscriptions to magazines you'll never read, sometimes for hundreds of dollars!

In a sad twist on the adage, "you can't get something for nothing," you generally get nothing for something if you respond to a wealth-building ad! Usually, after paying money (often a good deal of it) up front to purchase supplies, computer equipment and software, and videotapes, or after attending a sales pitch in the guise of a seminar, you end up with little of real value or nothing more than empty promises.

Sure signs of scams

Every year, Americans lose billions of dollars because they're victimized by scams. For example, the FTC reported that in 2003, it received close to 302,000 complaints from consumers about fraud, and the median loss for each victim was $228. The consumers who complained were victimized over the Internet, by phone, and through the mail.

To help you avoid becoming a victim yourself, here are some surefire signs of a scam. Beware if:

- The offer sounds too good to be true. It probably is!
- The caller is very friendly and seems to know a lot about you.
- The e-mail containing the offer is unsolicited.
- The company or individual making the offer refuses to send you written information about the offer.
- You're told that you have to ACT NOW.
- You have never heard of the company or the organization.
- You must pay an upfront fee to take advantage of the offer.
- The investment you're offered is described as "risk free." Don't kid yourself: There's no such thing as a risk-free investment. If there were, we'd all be millionaires!
- You're congratulated for being chosen for this "special offer" or for "being a winner." Yeah, right!
- You're told that having bad credit or low income is "no problem."
- As a condition of getting your discounted or free gift, you must attend a sales presentation or meeting.
- You're instructed to send money right away, by courier or overnight delivery, not by mail.
- You're told to call an 800 or 900 number for more information.
- You're pressured to complete all business transactions by phone or over the Internet, and you're offered nothing in writing — no contract, no guarantee, nada!

Believe it or not, consumers actually responded to a scam promising them that if they helped a Nigerian astronaut who was lost in space, they would share in the $15 million bonus he would receive upon reentry! Some people will believe anything.

Protect yourself from being duped by getting smart about scams and rip-offs. Two good places to get information are the

- Federal Citizen Information Center (`www.pueblo.gsa.gov/crh/cahform.htm`)
- National Fraud Information Center/Internet Fraud Watch (`www.fraud.org`), supported by the National Consumers League

The Telemarketing Sales Rule

The federal Telemarketing Sales Rule spells out some basic ground rules for telemarketers who make interstate calls and gives consumers the power to stop unwanted calls. It also provides states with the powers they need to crack down on fraudulent telemarketers. It applies to calls made to sell something to consumers as well as to solicitations for charitable donations, sweepstakes, prize promotions, and investment opportunities. The rule says the following:

- ✔ You have the right to tell a telemarketer not to call you again. If the calls continue, the company is breaking the law.

- ✔ Telemarketers can't call before 8 a.m. or after 9 p.m.

- ✔ Telemarketers must tell you upfront that they're trying to sell you something and must give you the name of the company they're calling for and what they're selling. If they're calling you about a prize promotion, they must tell you that you don't have to pay anything or purchase anything to win.

- ✔ The telemarketer is barred from trying to mislead you about the earnings potential, profitability, or risk of an investment, product, or service that he or she is calling you about.

- ✔ You must be given all of an offer's costs, restrictions, and conditions before spending any money on what the telemarketer is selling.

- ✔ Telemarketers can't process any billing information for your payment without first obtaining your specific informed consent.

- ✔ Telemarketers must fully disclose the terms of any free trial period after which your account will be automatically billed unless you take a specific action to cancel.

- ✔ Telemarketers soliciting charitable donations must promptly disclose to you the name of the organization they're calling for and why they're calling.

- ✔ Telemarketers are required to transmit their phone number to your Caller ID service as well as their name, when possible.

You can limit the number of telemarketing calls you receive by signing up with the National Do Not Call Registry. To register, go to www.donotcall.gov or call 1-888-382-1222 from the phone you want to register. You will receive fewer telemarketing calls within three months of registering your number. Your number stays in the registry for five years, and you can renew your registration at that time.

If you're the victim of a fraud, you can also file an online complaint form at these sites so that the FTC and other appropriate local and state government offices will know about how you were ripped off. Your complaint can help protect other consumers from being duped in the same way.

Consumer Sentinel (www.consumer.gov/sentinel) is a one-stop, secure investigative cyber tool and complaint database that provides hundreds of law enforcement agencies in the United States, Canada, and Australia with immediate access to Internet cons, telemarketing scams, and other consumer

fraud-related complaints. It also gives you the opportunity to let law enforcement officials worldwide know if you have been defrauded by a scam. The
FTC maintains the Consumer Sentinel database.

Hazards on the Internet

According to the National Consumers League, Internet fraud cost consumers
close to $15 million in 2002. In part, this loss is because the Internet is a virtu-
ally unregulated information and marketing media, which makes cyberspace
a gold mine for scam artists.

Cyberspace ads for scams generally fall into two categories: classified advertising and disguised advertising. Bogus classified ads are easiest to spot
because they include the usual hype and too-good-to-be-true promises that
characterize consumer scams.

As the name implies, disguised ads are harder to spot. Because this kind of
advertising is most commonly found on online bulletin boards and in chat
groups, it's not always clear whether the ad is an innocent comment by
another visitor to cyberspace or the assertion of a scam artist laying the bait
to snare another unsuspecting consumer. If you take the bait or if you suspect a scam, contact your commercial online provider as well as the other
local, state, and federal offices and nonprofit organizations mentioned in this
chapter.

Charitable scams

Americans are suckers for a heart-wrenching plea from a "good cause." But
not all good causes are legit. In fact, some bogus charities select names that
sound almost identical to the real thing in order to trick you into parting with
your money. Here are some tips on how to avoid getting duped.

  ✔ When a nonprofit organization asks you for money, unless you're very
    familiar with the organization or with the person who's calling and you
    know that it's a reputable organization, ask for written information,
    including a statement of its mission, a review of its current projects, a
    list of its board of directors, a balance sheet, a summary of its sources
    and uses of funds, an explanation of how your donation is used, the per-
    centage that goes to support the organization's mission, and the per-
    centage that goes toward its overhead. Also, find out if the IRS has
    approved the organization by asking the nonprofit to send you verifica-
    tion of its 501(c)(3) status.

- ✔ Watch out for organizations that try to dupe you into donating to them by using names that sound like well-known, well-respected charities.

- ✔ Call the charity directly. Find out if the organization is aware of the solicitation and has authorized the use of its name. If not, you may be dealing with a scam artist.

- ✔ Check out a charity's financial information. For many organizations, this information can be found online at www.guidestar.org or by calling GuideStar at 757-229-4631. (GuideStar is the national database of nonprofit organizations.)

- ✔ Most states regulate charities, so when a charity asks you for a donation, check it out by contacting your state attorney general's office or the office of your secretary of state. Go to the National Association of State Charity Officials Web site at www.nasconet.org to find out exactly what office to contact in your state.

- ✔ Never give the representative of a charitable organization your credit card number over the phone.

- ✔ Don't make your gifts in cash.

- ✔ Before you give to a charity, check it out with the Better Business Bureau's Wise Giving Alliance at www.give.org or call 703-276-0100.

- ✔ Resist high-pressure appeals to give.

Making yourself scam proof

Common sense and a healthy dose of skepticism can help you avoid becoming the victim of a scam. Many con artists use the phone to target unsuspecting consumers, so the following advice can make it easier for you to deal with them.

- ✔ Assume that if an opportunity is good today, it will be just as good tomorrow, next week, or maybe even a month from now. Don't be pressured into making an on-the-spot decision, especially when money is involved.

- ✔ Tell telemarketers that you're not interested and hang up. The longer a good con artist can keep you on the phone, the more vulnerable you may be to the pitch; con artists can be skilled, convincing liars. Maybe that's why they're in the business they're in!

- ✔ Don't be lured into trusting a telemarketer just because he or she seems to know a lot about you. Con artists often develop their target list from databases that provide them with personal information about you, including your age and income, whether or not you're a homeowner, your occupation, the magazines you read, and so on.

✔ Don't agree to or sign anything without first seeing the details of an offer in writing. You should understand exactly what you're agreeing to. Get all your questions answered. If the offer involves a considerable amount of money, ask your financial advisor, CPA, or attorney to review it.

✔ Check out the company and the offer with your state attorney general's office or state consumer protection office, as well as with your local Better Business Bureau. Don't wait until after you've been ripped off to contact these offices; it may be too late at that point for them to be of much help.

✔ Contact the National Fraud Information Center at www.fraud.org or 1-800-876-7060 to find out if the company that contacted you is in the center's database of fraudulent telemarketers.

✔ Ask about your recourse should you be unhappy with the offer after you've paid for it. Get this information in writing and read the fine print!

✔ Don't give the caller any information about your finances, including bankcard numbers and bank account information.

✔ Know what the FTC's Telemarketing Sales Rule says a telemarketer can and can't do. See the sidebar, "The Telemarketing Sales Rule," earlier in this chapter.

✔ Assume that unsolicited e-mails are selling fraudulent products or services. More often than not, that's the case.

✔ Only download programs from Web sites you're very familiar with and know to be reputable. Otherwise your downloads may contain dangerous computer viruses, or even worse, they may connect your modem to foreign phone numbers, and you won't be aware of what has happened until you get your phone bill for an astronomic amount.

✔ Make your online purchases using a credit card or by using substitute technology that allows you to charge to your credit card account without using your actual account number. Ask your credit card company if it has this technology.

✔ Only shop at secure Internet sites. A secure site should feature a closed padlock symbol or an unbroken key, and when you're making your purchase at the site, the "http" on the address bar should change to "https" or "shttp."

✔ Don't provide any more information about yourself than is absolutely necessary to complete your online purchase.

If you become a victim of a scam

It's such a blow to the ego when we realize we've been duped, especially when there's money involved! But if you've been conned by a scam, it may make you feel a little better to know that there are things you can do to try to recover your money and to help prevent other consumers from becoming victims. You can

- ✔ Report the company and scam to your local Better Business Bureau.

- ✔ Register a complaint with the National Fraud Information Center by calling 1-800-876-7060. The center logs your complaint onto its national fraud database and also contacts the appropriate federal, state and local agencies. Law enforcement organizations around the country use this database.

- ✔ Contact your state attorney general's office. If it gets enough complaints about a particular company, it may take action.

- ✔ Complain to the FTC by calling 1-877-382-4357or by going to www.ftc. gov and filling out an online complaint form. If it receives enough complaints, the FTC will take action. It can seek fines of up to $10,000 per violation against companies that violate its Telemarketing Sales Rule and can even go to court to get refunds for fraud victims.

- ✔ Talk with an attorney about the possibility of filing a lawsuit against the company that ripped you off. Be aware, however, that these lawsuits are difficult to win because companies that peddle scams are often difficult to locate. After they've worn out their welcome in one area, they often relocate and change names.

Buying a Product on Warranty

Many of the products or services you buy come with a *warranty,* which is the seller's or manufacturer's promise to stand behind its product. It's a kind of contract. Having a warranty gives you an extra measure of protection in case something goes wrong with what you've bought.

Warranties aren't mandated by law; however, the federal Magnuson-Moss Act says that if a product comes with a written warranty, you must be given an opportunity to see the warranty information before you make your purchase. The law also says that the warranty must clearly indicate exactly what it covers, its duration, who pays for any repairs under the warranty, your obligations, and so on.

All warranties are not equal

When you're making an important purchase, compare the warranties of the makes and models you're considering as well as their prices. Read each warranty thoroughly, paying special attention to the fine print — the devil is often in the details! Make special note of the following:

- ✔ What parts and repairs does the warranty cover or not cover?
- ✔ What expenses do you have to pay for when you use the warranty?
- ✔ How long does the warranty last?
- ✔ Does the warranty cover *consequential damages?* Probably not. Consequential damages are such things as the time and expense you may incur getting the product repaired and having to take off work.
- ✔ What limitations or conditions does the warranty come with?
- ✔ What do you have to do to get warranty service?
- ✔ What will the company do if the product fails?

Don't rely on a salesperson's oral promise about what can be done if there's a problem with a product. The promise may be nothing more than a sales pitch. Get all promises in writing.

Implied warranties

When we think warranty, we usually think written warranty. If a product doesn't come with a written warranty, however, it usually comes with an implied warranty that can last as long as four years. Implied warranties are created by state law (and all states have these laws), so check with your state attorney general's office or state consumer protection office to learn the specifics of its law on implied warranties.

Of the two kinds of implied warranties, the most common is a *warranty of merchantability,* the seller's promise that a product does what it's supposed to do — that a refrigerator keeps food from spoiling, that a vacuum picks up dirt, that detergent cleans, and so on.

The other kind of warranty is a *warranty of fitness.* It applies when you've purchased a product because the seller tells you it's suitable for a particular purpose. For example, the seller tells you that the tent you've bought will keep you dry and warm even in hurricane conditions.

Products sold "as is" don't come with implied warranties, nor do products that the seller says in writing come with no warranty.

Some states don't allow some types of products to be sold "as is."

Resolving warranty problems

If you try to use your warranty and are told it doesn't cover your particular problem, reread the warranty to confirm what it promises. It's back to the fine print! If you still believe you're right, try to resolve the problem with the business from which you bought the product. If necessary, send a certified letter to the manufacturer, return receipt requested. The manufacturer's address should be included on the warranty.

If you get no satisfaction, here are some other things to try:

- Contact your state attorney general's office or state consumer protection office.
- Try using mediation or arbitration to resolve your problem. Some warranties require that you try mediation or arbitration before suing a company over a warranty problem. See Chapter 2 for mediation and arbitration advice and resources.
- File a claim in small claims court.
- Sue under the Magnuson-Moss Act. At a minimum, you can sue for damages and legal fees.
- Report your problem to the FTC.

Chapter 12

Buying and Selling a Home

*A*fter years of saving and sacrifice, you finally have enough money for a down payment on your dream house! Or maybe you already own a home but want to sell it because your dreams have grown bigger or your family is expanding. For most of us, buying and selling a home are the two most important and most complex financial and legal transactions we ever make. If you want to get the most for your money and avoid the potential legal pitfalls and problems that both buyers and sellers can face, you need to understand the home-buying and -selling processes, including how to work with a real estate broker or agent. This chapter explains all that stuff.

Finding a Home to Buy

Most people begin the house-hunting process by driving through the neighborhoods where they'd like to live, looking for *For Sale* signs, and reading newspaper real estate ads. They may also tour open houses and visit real estate Web sites. And sooner or later, most home buyers begin working with a local real estate agent or broker.

The Internet is a great house-hunting resource especially if you're relocating to a new community or a new state. Many Web sites not only offer listings of homes for sale, but they also offer information about the communities where the homes are located as well as links to home inspectors, appraisers, mortgage brokers, realtor associations, agents, and more. One Web site that offers this sort of information is www.realtylocator.com.

Working with an Agent or Broker

When you schedule an appointment to view a property with a real estate agent or broker, it's important for you to realize that no matter how helpful that person may be, he or she usually works for the seller, not for you. In fact, an agent can't work for you and the seller of a home that you're interested in at the same time.

Sellers list their homes with real estate companies that employ agents who attempt to find home buyers. When a house is sold, the agent receives a *commission,* or percentage of the sales price, paid by the seller. So, agents have a financial incentive to get the highest price possible for the home, not to help you, the buyer, receive a good deal! Furthermore, it's unlikely that an agent will voluntarily offer information about any problems with a home in which you're interested because doing so may discourage you from buying the home or help you negotiate a reduced price.

You should know, however, that some agents work just for buyers, although they're fewer in number than the traditional real estate agent. If you work with a *buyer's agent* (sometimes called a *buyer's broker*), be sure to get a written contract from the agent. The contract should address the following:

- ✔ **How the agent will be paid.** Some agents charge a flat fee for their services or bill by the hour, while others take a percentage of your purchase price.

- ✔ **The specific services the agent will provide to you.**

- ✔ **The contract's duration.** Most buyer's agent contracts last for either six or twelve months. Depending on the market where you're buying a home, it may take you this long to find a home to buy.

- ✔ **How the contract can be cancelled.** The contract should spell out the cancellation process and the amount of the cancellation penalty.

Steer clear of so-called buyer's agents whose fees are based on a home's sales price, which means that they don't have a financial incentive to get the best deal for you.

Contact the National Association of Exclusive Buyer Agents to locate a buyer's broker in your area. The association's members represent buyers only. To reach the association, call 1-800-986-2322 or go to www.naeba.org.

If you don't want to work with a buyer's agent, hire a real estate attorney to help ensure that your interests are protected. The attorney reviews the purchase agreement before you seal the deal on the house you want to buy. Don't assume that the real estate agent handling the sale will do that for you. Remember, the agent is working for the seller, not you.

If You're the Seller

As a seller, you will probably contract with a real estate agent to help you find a qualified buyer for your home. This agent can also help you set a realistic asking price, advise you about the things you can do to help your home sell quickly, and help you close the deal. One of the key benefits of working with an agent, assuming he or she is a member of the Multiple Listing Service (MLS), is that information about your home will be in the MLS, exposing your home to countless other brokers and agents as well as to buyers who may otherwise never know about your home.

Listing your home: What to expect

When you list your home, you're expected to sign a legally binding contract, or *listing agreement.* This document gives the listing agent certain rights and defines the terms of your relationship, including the amount and conditions of the sales commission — usually between 5 and 6 percent of your home's selling price, although it can be more or less depending on the agent and what part of the country you're in. The three basic types of listings are:

- **Exclusive Right to Sell listing:** If an agent other than the one you listed your home with sells the property during the time that your listing agreement is in effect, then the listing agent splits the commission with the other agent. The listing agent also gets paid if you sell your home yourself. Listing agents like this type of listing best.

- **Exclusive listing:** The listing agent gets a commission if he or she sells your home, but if you find your own buyer, you may not have to pay the listing agent a sales commission.

- **Open listing:** You can list your house with any number of agents, and the first one to sell it gets the commission. Also, if *you* find a buyer for your home, you don't owe anyone a commission.

The listing agent may suggest that both of you sign the standard listing agreement used by the real estate firm for which he or she sells. If you want the agreement to include special provisions, consider hiring an attorney to draft a listing agreement for you. If you do use the standard agreement, you can have an attorney review it before you sign and suggest possible changes so that you can be assured that it's fair to you. The attorney can even negotiate the changes. For example, the standard agreement usually entitles an agent to a commission if he or she locates a "ready, willing, and able" buyer for a home, regardless of whether or not the sale actually takes place. You may want to try negotiating an agreement that says that the agent will be paid only if the sale goes through.

Real estate broker, realtor, listing agent, real estate agent: Who are these people?

When you're in the market for a home, you may find yourself dealing with a number of different real estate professionals. To help you understand who's who, here's a list of the roles of the various brokers and agents.

✔ A **real estate broker** is a real estate professional who is licensed by your state to run a real estate business and is paid a fee for negotiating real estate transactions. A broker can have other real estate agents working for him or her and can sell homes, too.

✔ A **realtor** is a real estate agent or broker who is a member of the National Association of Realtors. A consumer with a complaint against a realtor can file it with the local chapter of NAR as well as with the real estate commission in the consumer's state.

✔ A **listing agent** formally puts a seller's home "on the market" and also tries to sell the house.

✔ A **real estate agent** sells real estate for a real estate firm, often as an independent contractor. Real estate agents must work under the supervision of a broker.

Regardless of the type of listing agreement you use and whether or not you hire an attorney, the agreement should include the following:

✔ **Its duration.** You may not want to sign an agreement that lasts for a long period of time — more than 90 days — or that automatically renews. If you don't believe that the agent is doing enough to sell your home, you want the freedom to list it with someone else.

✔ **Your asking price.**

✔ **How the agent's commission is calculated.** Commission is usually a percentage of the selling price.

✔ **Conditions related to the payment of the commission.** Particular attention should be paid to whether you have to pay a commission to the agent if you, not the agent, sell your home.

✔ **The agent's rights and responsibilities to you.**

✔ **Your obligations to the agent.**

✔ **Who pays to advertise your home.**

✔ **How any disputes between you and the agent will be resolved.** Most agreements include a binding arbitration provision for resolving problems that may lead to lawsuits.

A home typically receives the most attention from agents and potential buyers just after it goes on the market. So, be sure your place is priced to sell. When a home stays on the market for an extended period of time, people assume that something is wrong with it, and you're more likely to be forced to drop the price.

Selling your home on your own

An estimated 15 percent of homeowners sell their own homes rather than working with real estate professionals. If you choose the do-it-yourself approach, you have to:

- **Identify the things that need to be done to your home to make it attractive to potential buyers.** Do all you can to make sure your home makes a good first impression, both inside and out. It should be clean and free of clutter. Before you show it, address problems like water stained ceilings, missing knobs, leaky faucets, and so on. Consider asking a friend or relative to walk through your home and point out problems that need your attention.

- **Decide how much to ask for your home.** Some good ways to decide on a realistic asking price for your home include finding out how much comparable homes in your neighborhood have sold for, looking in your local paper's real estate listing section for homes in your neighborhood that are like yours, and reading the marketing fliers that may be attached to *For Sale* signs in front of homes on the market in your neighborhood. Another option is to hire a professional appraiser to value your home; the appraiser tells you how much your home is worth in the current market. The assistance of an appraiser will probably cost you between $200 and $500 depending on what part of the country you live in.

- **Market your home.** The cheapest and easiest way to market your home is to put a *For Sale* sign in front of it. If your home is in an attractive neighborhood where people want to live and your street gets a fair amount of traffic, posting the sign may be all the marketing you need to do. However, you should also let your friends, relatives, and neighbors know that your home is for sale, and you can list it in your local newspaper's real estate section. You may also want to produce a simple flier that provides information about your home, the school district, and your property taxes as well as a couple of photos of your home's interior. Another option is to list your home on a real estate Web site such as www.owners.com or www.4salebyowner.com.

✔ **Show your home to prospective buyers.** On the day of your open house, your home should look clean and neat inside and out. First impressions count! To create a nice atmosphere, consider decorating your home with some fresh-cut flowers, burning a scented candle, and having some quiet music playing in the background. If you have young children and dogs that bark, find a place for them to go during the open house. Prepare a fact sheet for your home that potential buyers can take with them. Include an attractive photo of your home and information about its age and construction, number and type of rooms, and whether it has central air and heat. Additional highlights to include are special features such as a hot tub, sprinkler system, pool, intercom, built-in sound system, security system, and so on. Indicate what public schools children in your neighborhood attend and the amount of your property taxes.

Don't take offense if potential buyers make unflattering comments about some aspect of your home. Consider it constructive criticism. Visitors' comments may point out something that you need to address in your home if your want to sell it for close to your asking price.

✔ **Negotiate with a buyer and go to the real estate closing.** To ensure that everything goes smoothly, consult with a real estate attorney about how the selling process works in your area, your legal responsibilities as a seller, and how to protect your interests in the purchase agreement. You may also want to hire the attorney to help you negotiate an agreement with a buyer and to represent you at the real estate closing.

MetLife's *Life Advice About Selling a Home* offers a good overview of the issues you should consider and plan for as a seller. The guide is located online at `www.pueblo.gsa.gov/cic_text/housing/sellhome/sellhome.htm`, on the Federal Citizen Information Center's Web site.

Truth is on your side

You probably know your home inside and out, warts and all. You may know that its heating system is faulty, that it's foundation is cracked, that it has a termite problem, or that it has some other problem that may affect both its ability to sell quickly and the price you can get for it.

When you're selling a home with structural defects or other problems, you have several options. If you have enough money and time, you can fix the problem before you put your home on the market. Otherwise, you can be up-front about the problem with potential buyers and offer to reduce your asking price if necessary; or you can opt not to volunteer any information about the problem, hoping that the buyer won't discover it until the sale has been consummated and the problem isn't yours anymore. However, failing to disclose such information isn't recommended because you could end up being sued by the buyer of your home.

If your home has serious structural or other problems that may not turn up in an inspection and that would most likely lower the value of your home, most states require that you tell a potential buyer about them. Specifically, you may have to complete a state-required disclosure form and provide it to potential buyers. Also, federal law requires that if your home was built before 1972, you must inform a buyer about all lead-based paint and other hazards in the home that you know about; you must give the buyer an opportunity to test your home for lead, provide an Environmental Protection Agency (EPA) brochure titled *Protect Your Family from Lead in Your Home,* and include specific language in your sales contract. Also, you and the buyer must both sign statements affirming that all of the law's requirements were complied with. You're required to hold on to those statements for three years after the date of sale. To learn more about your lead paint disclosure requirements, visit the EPA's National Lead Information Center Web site at www.epa.gov/lead/ nlic.htm or call 1-800-424-5323.

If the buyer of your home is injured because you didn't comply with EPA disclosure requirements, then the buyer is entitled to sue you for triple the amount of damages he or she actually suffers.

The best way to find out about all of your disclosure obligations and to ensure that you comply with them is to call your state department of real estate or state real estate commission.

A growing number of states require sellers to provide buyers with written statements disclosing the condition of their home — the good *and* the bad.

If your state has no laws requiring that you voluntarily disclose any defects or other problems your home may have, from a legal (not to mention a moral) perspective, it's best to be forthcoming about them because your dishonesty may come back to haunt you. The buyer may have the right to sue you because you weren't forthright about the condition of your home and in essence sold the buyer *damaged goods.* Be aware that the law tends to favor buyers in these situations.

Your real estate agent should be aware of your state's disclosure requirements and should help ensure that you comply with them. In fact, if the buyer sues you over a problem with your home after the closing, your realtor may be sued, too, and may be held liable for nondisclosure.

Filling in the contract blanks

Naturally, if you're the seller, when you're negotiating a purchase and sale agreement, some of your interests are different from the buyer's. The most obvious difference is that you want to get the highest price possible for your home, and the buyer wants just the opposite. But if you're concerned about selling your home as quickly as you can, you may be more open to giving the buyer a good deal.

As the seller, be certain that the contract you sign adequately protects you. This issue is something that your agent should help ensure, assuming you're working with one. Include some (or all) of these provisions in your contract:

- The earnest money will not be returned to the buyer if he or she fails to live up to the terms of the contract; you get to keep it.

- You and the seller set a reasonable time period for the fulfillment of any contingency clauses in the contract — the buyer obtaining adequate financing or selling his or her current home, for example.

- You specify any serious problems or defects that you're aware your home has. Spelling them out helps protect you from the possibility of being sued later by the buyer. For the same reason, if your home is in mint condition, you may also want to include a clause stating that, to the best of your knowledge, your home has no serious problems or defects.

If you want to remain in your home after closing (for example, you're building or renovating a new home, and it may not be ready for you by the date of closing), then you should include a provision in your contract allowing you to continue living in your home for a specific period of time in exchange for paying the buyer rent and possibly other expenses as well.

If You're the Buyer

After you've found your dream home, or something close to it, and you want to buy it, you have to make the seller a formal offer. Usually the offer is for something less than the asking price, although if you're buying in a very competitive market, you may offer more than the asking price if you really want the home. Present your offer and all of its terms in a written contract or *purchase and sale agreement.*

Although the seller's agent can help you draw up the contract and will probably have a standard form you can use, the agent has a financial motivation to draft a contract that benefits the seller. So, unless you're working with a buyer's agent, you may want to get legal help in preparing a purchase and sale agreement. If you don't, you should hire a real estate attorney to at least review the proposed contract before you sign it.

In some areas of the country, when you agree to buy a home, you and the seller sign a *binder* in addition to a purchase contract. When you sign the binder you must also pay a small deposit on the house, also referred to as *earnest money*. A binder includes much of the same information as a purchase contract, but it's not an enforceable contract. It gives you the right to purchase the real estate you're interested in according to the terms you have agreed on for a limited period of time. The buyer loses the earnest money if he or she is unable to obtain the necessary financing by the deadline or changes his or her mind, unless the binder specifically states that the earnest money will be refunded.

At the very least, your purchase and sale agreement should include the following:

- ✔ A legal description of the property you're buying

- ✔ The home's purchase price, including the size of your down payment

- ✔ The amount you're paying in earnest money

    Don't sign a contract that doesn't require that the earnest money be held in a trust account or given to a title company, escrow company, or an attorney.

- ✔ A provision for the return of any deposit or earnest money you've paid if the contract is canceled. The provision should also specify how quickly you get that money back.

- ✔ A statement that the seller must provide you with an unencumbered deed and clear title to the property

- ✔ An itemization of all other documents that you want the seller to provide at closing, such as a survey of the property or title insurance

- ✔ Who is responsible for risk of loss due to fire, water damage, and so on until the title to the property has been transferred into your name or until you've taken possession

- ✔ Whether the property is being sold *as is* or whether the seller is making any promises about the condition of the property

- ✔ Whether the seller must make certain repairs prior to closing

- ✔ The appliances, fixtures, air conditioning units, hot tubs, furniture, and so on that the seller conveys with the house

- ✔ A closing date and the date you take possession of the house — they don't have to be the same. The agreement should also have a provision requiring the seller to pay you rent if he or she can't vacate the property by the date of possession.

- ✔ A provision discussing how expenses, such as the taxes, utility bills, and insurance that the seller may have prepaid, will be prorated or apportioned between you and the seller at closing

- ✔ A financing contingency clause, assuming you need financing to buy the house. At a minimum, this clause should state the general terms of the financing you will try to find and indicate a deadline by which you must find it. If the clause is worded properly, you should be able to cancel the contract if you're unable to secure the financing.

- ✔ A home sale and closing contingency clause. In short, this clause says that you can cancel the contract if you need to sell your current home to buy the new one but you're unable to.

- ✔ An inspection contingency clause. Be sure to include this clause if you want the house to be inspected by a professional for termites, as well as for mechanical, structural, and environmental problems, including the presence of radon, lead paint, or asbestos in the house. Include this clause so that you can cancel the contract if the house doesn't pass muster. This clause is absolutely essential, in my opinion.

- ✔ The date after which the agreement is no longer valid

Including a walk-through provision in your purchase and sale agreement is a good idea because it gives you the right to literally walk through the house you're buying just prior to closing (often 24 hours prior) so that you can inspect the house. During the walk-through, you can make sure that any repairs that the seller agreed to make have been completed to your satisfaction and that nothing expected to convey with the house has been removed.

Depending on the reasonableness of your offer and how badly the seller wants to sell, the seller can accept your offer, reject it, or make a counter offer. If the seller counters, the ball is in your court. You can agree to the seller's counter, respond with a new offer, or you can keep house-hunting.

If you live in a state where it's customary for buyers and sellers to sign a purchase and sale agreement before it's been reviewed by attorneys, protect yourself by including the following phrase on the document: "Subject to the approval of the attorneys for the parties within [a certain number of] days."

After both you and the seller have signed the agreement, you're expected to cement the deal with some earnest money — a tangible symbol of your intention to live up to the terms of the contract. Later, when you close on the house, the amount you paid in earnest money is deducted from your down payment.

If your purchase doesn't go through, you can usually get back your earnest money, plus interest. If you fail to live up to the terms of your contract, however, you may forfeit that money.

Never make your earnest money check payable to the seller. Make it payable to the title company, the real estate agent, or to the real estate firm handling the deal. To prevent the check from being cashed and used for the wrong purpose, write the words *fiduciary agent* or *escrow agent* after the name of the payee.

Finding a Mortgage

If you're like most people, after you've signed a purchase and sale agreement, your shopping has just begun. Now you have to find a lender willing to finance your purchase. Depending on your income and credit history, that may be harder than finding a house to buy.

The best place to start your search is with your current bank or credit union. But don't stop there. Other banks as well as mortgage companies and savings and loans may offer you a better deal. The real estate agent you're working with may also be able to recommend lenders to contact.

Dealing with lenders

Although all lenders tend to have two basic categories of mortgage loans — *fixed rate* and *adjustable rate* — they often differ in regard to the specific types of fixed and adjustable rate loans they offer. Also, they may offer different interest rates and may have different down payment requirements.

Most mortgage loans, regardless of whether they're fixed rate or adjustable rate, are made for 15 or 30 years. Usually, the longer the term of the loan and the bigger the down payment you make, the smaller your monthly payments will be. Also, the larger your down payment, the better your interest rate, which also translates into smaller payments.

Some lenders offer federal guaranteed mortgages. These loans, which are backed by a federal agency like the Federal Housing Administration (FHA) or the Department of Veteran's Affairs (VA), require lower-than-average down payments, so they tend to be attractive to buyers who may not qualify for a conventional loan. Guaranteed mortgage loans may only be available, however, for certain categories of home buyers, certain types of housing, or only for property that falls within a certain price range. Loans that aren't backed by an agency are called *conventional loans.*

If you're a first-time home buyer, or if you meet certain income criteria, your local or state government may sponsor a home-buying program in which you can participate.

Some sellers offer their own financing. If you go this route, the seller essentially loans you money to buy his house. You make direct payments with interest to the seller.

Demystifying loans

Many types of mortgage loans are available. What follows are brief descriptions of some of the most common.

Fixed rate mortgage

The fixed rate mortgage is the traditional type of mortgage loan. Its interest rate and your monthly payment are determined at the start of your loan and usually remain the same throughout its duration.

Graduated payment mortgage

This is a type of fixed rate mortgage. At the start of the loan, your payments are relatively low, but they will rise at a set rate over a specified period of time — five to ten years usually. Then they remain fixed for the remainder of the loan. You may want this kind of mortgage loan if you expect that your income will be rising in coming years.

Adjustable rate mortgages

The adjustable rate mortgage usually starts out at an interest rate that is somewhat lower than what comes with a fixed rate mortgage. However, the rate is tied to a predetermined index, and as the index changes, your interest rate changes, too. Usually, the rate is adjusted annually at a predetermined date. Look for an adjustable rate mortgage that allows your monthly payment to decrease as well as increase. Also, find one that limits both the amount your monthly payment can change at any one time and the amount your payment can increase or decrease over the life of your loan. Most adjustable rate mortgages come with such limits or caps.

Balloon mortgages

This kind of mortgage loan requires you to make a series of equal monthly payments, often for interest only, followed by a large final payment — the *balloon* — which is usually due just three to five years after the loan begins. If you're unable to make the balloon payment when it comes due, you have to refinance your home or sell it.

Assumable mortgages

Sometimes the seller's mortgage loan can be assumed or taken over by the buyer at the seller's interest rate, which may be lower than the current prevailing rate. But when interest rates are high, lenders don't like to make this kind of loan because they usually make more money writing a new one. If a seller's mortgage loan is assumable, read the mortgage agreement carefully to make sure that it doesn't include a *due on sale* clause that gives the lender the right to raise the interest rate to the existing rate if you take the loan over.

Applying for a loan

Brace yourself if you hate paperwork! You see a lot of it when you apply for a mortgage loan.

Most loan applications ask you for information about

- ✔ Your debts and assets.
- ✔ Your credit history, including a list of the account numbers and outstanding balances for all of your bankcards, retail charge cards, and for any other loans you may have.
- ✔ Your employment history. You may be asked to provide proof of your income, including IRS W-2 forms and copies of recent federal tax returns.
- ✔ Information about where your down payment will come from.
- ✔ Information about the home you want to buy.

The lender also reviews your credit record to see if you currently have or have ever had any debt problems.

Before you begin the mortgage loan application process, order a copy of your credit report from each of the three national credit reporting agencies: Equifax, Experian (Formerly TRW), and TransUnion. Review the reports to make sure they don't contain any erroneous information that can prevent you from getting a loan or getting one with good terms.

After you've provided the lender with all the information it needs to process your loan application, it can take as much as 30 days to find out whether or not you've been approved. If you apply for an FHA or VA mortgage, you may have to wait a little longer.

According to the federal Real Estate Settlement Procedures Act (RESPA), which applies to most real estate lenders, the lender must provide you with an estimate of your closing costs when you apply for a mortgage loan or must send you an estimate within three days after you file your application. You must also be given a copy of *Settlement Costs and You,* a brochure produced by the U.S. Department of Housing and Urban Development (HUD).

The federal Fair Housing Act

The federal Fair Housing Act (FHA) protects you from being denied the opportunity to buy the home you want or get the mortgage you need because of discrimination. It prohibits discrimination in housing sales and mortgage loans on the basis of race, religion, color, national origin, and sex. The FHA also protects you from discrimination based on familial status which means that you can't be discriminated against because you have children under the age of 18 living with you, because you're working to get custody of children under the age of 18, or because you're pregnant. (The law also protects prospective tenants from discrimination practiced by landlords.) The FHA also bars real estate brokers and agents from steering certain categories of buyers to particular neighborhoods.

Your state and local governments may have their own anti-discrimination laws related to housing. For example, some localities bar discrimination on the basis of sexual orientation.

If a mortgage lender denies you a loan or a seller refuses to sell to you and you believe you're being discriminated against, you can do the following:

- Call the federal Department of Housing and Urban Development (HUD) at 1-800-669-9777 to file a formal complaint, or go to HUD's Web site to file an electronic complaint at www.hud.gov/offices/fheo/index.cfm. You must file your complaint within one year of the incident. HUD will look into your allegation. If it feels that there has been a violation of the FHA, it will try to negotiate a conciliation agreement with the violator. (If HUD determines that your local or state agency has the same powers that it has to address your complaint, your complaint is turned over to that agency and HUD's involvement ends.) If negotiations are unsuccessful, an administrative hearing will be held before a judge — you'll be represented by a HUD attorney. If the judge finds that discrimination did occur, then the defendant can be ordered to do the following: compensate you for actual damages, including pain, suffering, and humiliation; provide injunctive or other equitable relief (injunctive relief stops someone from doing something); and/or pay the federal government a civil penalty on behalf of the public interest. The defendant can also be ordered to pay "reasonable" attorney fees and expenses.

- File a formal complaint directly with your state or local agency if it has the same housing powers as HUD.

- File a lawsuit at your own expense in federal district or state court within two years of the incident.

If you're approved for a mortgage loan, you have to formally promise the lender to repay it by signing a promissory note. You also have to sign a mortgage or deed of trust giving your lender a security interest in the home you're buying. If you fall behind on your payments, your lender can repossess your home. You may also be required to purchase mortgage insurance if you're considered somewhat of a financial risk.

In addition, you may be expected to buy *title insurance*. This insurance helps protect the lender against the existence of any liens or other encumbrances on the property you're buying that could take priority over its loan to you. Typically, you pay for this insurance in a lump sum at the time of closing. Sometimes, a purchase and sale agreement requires the seller to pay for this insurance.

If your loan is denied

If a mortgage lender turns you down, federal law requires that the lender tell you why in writing. Common reasons include the following:

- ✔ You have a bad credit history.
- ✔ Your income is not large enough to support the mortgage for which you've applied.
- ✔ You can't come up with a big enough down payment.
- ✔ The house you want to buy didn't appraise high enough to justify the size of the mortgage for which you applied.

The federal Equal Credit Opportunity Act (ECOA) bars lenders from rejecting your loan application or treating you differently from other loan applicants because of your race, color, national origin, religion, sex, marital status, age, or disability. In addition, when evaluating your loan application, a lender can't disallow any public assistance funds you may receive or any alimony, child support, or maintenance payments you may receive regularly.

Closing the Deal as the Buyer

The end is in sight! You've gotten your mortgage loan, and now it's time for the closing, also called the *settlement*. But before you close, sit down with your lawyer and review all of the documents that you have to sign and exchange with the seller at the closing. Make sure that they've been properly prepared and accurately reflect the terms of your purchase and sale agreement.

The Real Estate Settlement Procedures Act (RESPA) gives you the right to review a settlement sheet, prepared by your lender or by your attorney, that details all of your closing costs the day before the closing. You'll see another copy at the closing.

At closing, all the final legal formalities required to transfer title from the seller to you take place. You have to sign so many documents that you may feel as though you're literally signing your life away, especially if you're a first-time buyer!

Checks with a lot of zeros are required at closing. The biggest one is your payment to the seller for the price you both agreed less the earnest money you've already put up. Checks may also have to be written to pay for the following:

- ✔ Your lender's title insurance

- ✔ House-related taxes that the seller may have prepaid

- ✔ Certain other house-related expenses that the seller may have already paid for that you will benefit from, such as insurance and utility bills

- ✔ Other expenses that the purchase and sale agreement obligates you to pay

Sometimes there is no formal closing. Instead, an escrow agent handles the closing after the buyer and the seller have provided the agent with the necessary documents and funds.

Closing and the Seller

If you're the seller, don't expect to sit idly by at closing while the buyer does all the work. You have to sign documents, too, including a document transferring title to the home from you to the buyer, an affidavit of title, and a bill of sale transferring any personal property that conveys with the home you're selling.

You have to write a few checks, too. Here are some of the things you have to pay for:

- ✔ Your agent's commission

- ✔ Any taxes owed on the property you're selling

- ✔ The outstanding balance on your mortgage loan

- ✔ Any other outstanding liens on your property

- ✔ Other expenses you agreed to pay in the purchase and sale agreement

As a result of a 1997 change in the federal tax code, if you make $250,000 or less on the sale of your home ($500,000 or less if you're married) and you have lived in the house for at least two out of the past five years (they don't have to be sequential years), you don't have to pay a capital gains tax on your profit. The change in the law also reduced the capital gains tax rate.

Jargon that you should be familiar with

When you buy or sell a home, you may hear some unfamiliar real estate lingo. Not knowing what these words and phrases mean can be stressful. To reduce your anxiety, here are definitions of some of the most common terms:

✔ **Buyer's affidavit:** When a buyer signs this document, he or she is swearing to a lender that there are no pending or existing lawsuits of any sort against the buyer. The buyer is also swearing that there are no tax liens or judgments against him or her that attach to the property after the buyer purchases it.

✔ **Deed:** A written legal document that transfers title to a property from one owner to another. The two most common types of deeds are *warranty deeds* and *quit claim deeds.* A warranty deed guarantees that no one else has a legal claim to the property you're buying. This is the best kind of deed. A quit claim deed makes no such guarantees.

✔ **Encumbrance:** A claim or restriction on the title to a piece of property.

✔ **Lien:** A financial claim against a piece of property.

✔ **Mortgage deed or deed of trust:** When you sign this document, you give the mortgage holder or lender a lien on your home.

✔ **Seller's affidavit:** When a seller signs this statement, he or she swears that no liens or encumbrances are on the property for sale.

✔ **Title:** Title equals ownership. If you have clear title to a piece of property, you own it and have the legal right to use it, control it, and sell it without any restrictions or encumbrances.

✔ **Title insurance:** Insurance protecting you and the lender against losses that may result from any title-related problems that didn't show up during the title search.

✔ **Title search:** Research into a piece of property to find out if there are any liens on the property, unpaid taxes, restrictive covenants or easements, and so on that can affect your right and ability to use the property as you would want. The title search is conducted by a title company, abstract company, or attorney. Although it's not legally required, if you're a buyer, a title search helps protect you from buying a property that has other owners, liens, and encumbrances. You should require the seller to correct any title defects as a condition of sale.

Buying or Building a New Home

New home buyers including those who build a home from the ground up — a *custom* home — must deal with issues that buyers of older homes don't have to consider. You should pay close attention to the reputation of the builder you hire to build your home or the builder who built the home you're thinking about buying. Check out the builder's references, inspect other homes the builder has constructed, and evaluate the builder's warranty. If you're building from the ground up, you also need to consider the terms of the builder's contract and how willing the builder is to negotiate. Here are a few more things to consider:

- ✔ **The warranty:** Many home builders offer insured ten-year warranties that protect home buyers from faulty materials, structural defects, and shoddy workmanship in a home's electrical and heating systems, plumbing, and roof, among other things. (Most states and many local governments have laws requiring a warranty to last for a minimum of a year after purchase. To enforce them, you may have to sue the builder.) Read the warranty carefully so that you understand exactly what it does and doesn't cover, what you must do to activate it, and whether the warranty conveys if you sell your home while the warranty is still in effect. Be aware that warranties tend to protect builders more than buyers.

- ✔ **The contract:** Although most builders use a standard contract, consider it negotiable. A contract should include the following:

  - The price you're paying the builder and any other charges.

  - The amount of your deposit, whether it's refundable, and under what conditions. Most deposits are about 5 percent of the purchase price.

  - The times you can inspect the house during the building process and what the builder must do when you find problems. You should have the right to visit the house periodically while it's being built and just before closing.

  - The date your home will be completed, including a financial penalty clause that costs the builder money for every day after that date that the home is not finished.

  - All of the provisions in your builder's warranty.

Part IV
Tough Stuff: Being Sick, Getting Older, Dying

The 5th Wave   By Rich Tennant

"As you know, your uncle died intestate, and in this State we have our own way of distributing assets to the heirs. Now, do you all know what a piñata is?"

In this part . . .

The chapters in this part cover some pretty tough issues, stuff you may find difficult to deal with, but stuff that all people face at some point in their lives. I'm talking about health care, estate planning, and other legal issues related to growing old. The purpose of the chapters in this part is to help you plan for the future so that you and your loved ones can avoid legal and financial troubles down the road.

Chapter 13

Your Health Care Rights

*W*hy is something so fundamentally important so frustrating and difficult? I'm talking about dealing with the health care system — doctors, hospitals, health insurance companies, and managed care organizations such as HMOs (Health Maintenance Organizations) and PPOs (Preferred Provider Organizations). Doctors often discourage us from playing an active role in our own health care. Medical terminology sounds like gobbledygook and seems designed to keep us in the dark. Rules, restrictions, and delays commonly associated with insurance providers and managed care organizations would test even Job's patience! Also, with their bottom lines under pressure due to ever-increasing health coverage costs, fewer and fewer employers provide coverage to their employees, and if they do, a growing number pass more and more of the cost on to their employees.

Although this country's health care system is in crisis and how best to reform it is a hot topic with about which there is a lot of disagreement, very little has happened to resolve the problem. Lack of consensus about the best way to reform our health care system combined with powerful lobbying on the part of the health insurance/managed care industry are at least partially to blame for the lack of action. Therefore, it's up to you to do what you can to ensure that you get both the health and medical care you need and your health care money's worth. You do that by becoming actively involved in all aspects of your health care, asking questions, understanding your legal rights, and asserting them when you feel you or a family member are not being treated fairly by a medical provider or health plan. If you're pushed, push back. If your questions go unanswered, keep asking. If you don't get what you think is fair, complain. Doing this stuff may not be easy. In fact, you may feel like David did when he fought Goliath. But remember, David won!

HealthCareCoach.com, www.healthcarecoach.com, is a project of the National Health Law Program (NHeLP), a nonprofit legal organization. The Web site educates consumers about managed care and health insurance and features do-it-yourself tips on a wide range of health care topics. It also contains an Action Center where you can find resources to improve the health care you and your family receive.

Having no insurance or lacking adequate insurance not only puts consumers at greater risk for serious illness and even death, but such circumstances are also among the leading causes of consumer bankruptcy.

Power to Patients!

Here's a rundown on your basic legal rights when dealing with doctors, hospitals, and other health care providers.

Informed consent

You have a right to a "plain English" explanation of any medical treatment or surgery your doctor suggests, and you also have the right to agree to or refuse the recommended treatment. Exactly what you must be told varies by state, but at a minimum, you should expect explanations of

- Your health problem
- The risks and benefits of the treatment or procedure your doctor recommends
- The pros and cons of the risks and benefits of any alternative treatments or procedures
- The risks and benefits of foregoing a treatment or procedure

Informed consent also gives you the right to refuse to participate in any medical research projects you may be asked to be part of.

If you agree to the action your doctor recommends, you're asked to sign a *consent form.* Read it carefully before you sign, because it may contain something you weren't told about. Be sure to ask any questions you may have. If the form lists anything that you don't want to agree to, cross that point out and initial the change.

A doctor who fails to get your consent can be charged with a criminal offense.

Generally speaking, you don't have to sign a consent form for a simple, routine treatment or procedure such as getting an inoculation or having your blood drawn. It's usually implied that when you roll up your sleeve or stick out your finger, you're giving your consent. In many states, however, if the blood is being drawn for an HIV test, implied consent is not enough.

If your condition is life threatening, or if you're in the middle of a medical emergency, the doctor responsible for your care doesn't need your permission, or anyone else's, to do what's necessary to save your life or end the emergency.

Generally, parents have the right to consent to medical treatment for their minor children.

You can't give your informed consent if you're drunk, high on drugs, or emotionally out of control and beyond reason. In these situations, the law assumes that your judgment is impaired. Also, you may not be able to give your informed consent when you're mentally incapacitated. But a close relative is usually allowed to give or withhold his or her consent on your behalf.

Nearly every state has passed a law banning so-called *gag clauses* in the contracts that managed care organizations require doctors in their networks to sign. This kind of clause limits the amount of information that a doctor in a managed care network can provide a patient about his or her treatment options. In other words, without the ban on gag clauses, a network may require a doctor to tell his or her patient about some but not all treatment options available to the patient. Doctors have been highly critical of these clauses, arguing that the clauses restricted their abilities to give their patients everything the patients needed to make informed decisions about the best course of action for treating their medical problems. Many doctors also argue that the clauses restricted their abilities to recommend specialists to their patients and to allow their patients to get second opinions. In essence, doctors claim that gag clauses undermined their patients' rights to informed consent.

The right to medical treatment

If you're one of the more than 45 million Americans who are *uninsured* (according to a 2004 Census Bureau report) and the millions more and growing-every-day number who are *underinsured,* you may live with a gnawing fear that some day you or a dependent will need hospital emergency care and will be turned away because you can't pay for it.

You should sleep a little better knowing that federal law and most state laws require that all public and private hospitals treat anyone with a medical

When you can't speak for yourself

Life is full of surprises, both good and bad. Sometimes, even if you're the healthiest person, you can suddenly become seriously ill with no hope of recovery or you can be critically injured and literally lose the ability to speak for yourself and make your own decisions. Unless you've planned for this possibility, you may be kept alive indefinitely, hooked up to expensive life support systems that could quickly deplete your assets and take an emotional toll on your family members and close friends. Also, someone else you may or may not trust may be appointed by the court to handle your legal and financial affairs.

You should draft a number of different legal tools to prepare for the possibility that you may become physically or mentally incapacitated and unable to manage your own affairs: a *durable power of attorney for finances,* a *durable power of attorney for health care,* and a *living will.* Each of these tools is legally recognized in every state, but each state has its own criteria for what makes each tool legally enforceable. Chapter 15 covers these important tools in much more detail.

You can purchase a fill-in-the-blanks durable power of attorney for finances form at an office supply store, download one off of the Internet, or have an attorney prepare the form for you.

You can prepare a durable power of attorney for health care or a living will using standard fill-in-the-blanks forms available on the Internet. You can also obtain the standardized forms from your local hospital, health care provider, or your local or state Agency on Aging. You can also hire an estate planning attorney to customize the documents for you. Also, some states allow you to combine the instructions contained in each document into a single document called an advance health care directive.

If you use a standardized form, be sure that it's considered legally valid in your state because each state has its own requirements for what makes the three legal documents legally enforceable. Also, review your completed documents each year to make sure that they continue to reflect your wishes, and if you want to amend or cancel them, do so in accordance with your state's law.

Review each of your documents with whomever you're giving the decision-making power to so that you can be certain that he or she understands your wishes. Also, review your living will with your doctor so that you can be sure that he or she will help get it activated when the time comes.

If you spend a lot of time in more than one state, prepare a legally valid durable power of attorney for health care and a living will for each state. You may also need to prepare multiple durable power of attorney documents for your legal and financial affairs.

Contact the nonprofit organization Partnership for Caring, Inc. to obtain free fill-in-the-blanks durable power of attorney for health care and living will forms that are valid for your state. To order the forms, contact Partnership for Caring at 1620 Eye Street, NW, Suite 202, Washington, DC 20006 or at 202-296-8071. You can also download the forms at www.partnershipfor caring.org.

emergency, including women in labor, regardless of their ability to pay. Hospitals as well as individual doctors who turn emergency patients away can be accused of "patient dumping" and risk government fines, lawsuits, and the loss of their accreditations.

Uninsured and underinsured Americans put increasing pressure on already overcrowded hospital emergency rooms. As a result, emergency room personnel may redirect the emergency vehicle you're in to another hospital, creating obstacles to your receiving timely and possibly life-saving medical care.

Emergency patients can't be turned away, but it can be a different story if you need routine medical care and you don't have any way to pay for it. For example, a private hospital has the right to turn you away if you're not an emergency case. But you can probably receive care if you go to a public hospital, because federal law requires most public health facilities receiving government grants and loans to care for anyone regardless of the patient's ability to pay.

If you schedule a doctor's appointment for a non-emergency medical problem, in most states, you can be refused treatment if you have no insurance or any other means of paying for your care. If, however, you have an established relationship with a doctor, he or she can't legally "abandon" you or refuse to continue treating you because of your financial situation without giving you sufficient time to locate a new doctor.

Hospitals and doctors can't refuse to treat you because of your race, ethnic origin, sexual orientation, and so on. That's called *discrimination,* and if they discriminate, they can be sued.

The right not to be released before you're ready

Today's hospitals feel a lot of pressure to minimize their costs by releasing patients as soon as possible. Utilization review companies set standards for hospitals, insurance companies, and managed health care organizations regarding when it's necessary for someone to be hospitalized as well as what an appropriate length of stay is for a particular medical problem. If you stay longer than the "appropriate length of stay," it's usually at your expense.

Most states require that you be given a 24-hour advance notice of your pending discharge from the hospital.

If you're told that the time has come for you to vacate your hospital room and you don't feel that you're well enough to leave, you can appeal your discharge. Start by talking with the hospital's patient representative who can fill you in on the appeal process. Try to get your doctor involved too, because doctors typically have more clout than patients in the hospital hierarchy.

After your appeal has been filed, the utilization review company should respond within two working days. If your appeal is denied, and especially if you become much sicker or are injured after you leave and you can attribute it to a premature discharge, you may be able to sue the hospital, your doctor, your insurance company, and the utilization review firm, depending on the circumstances.

The right to refuse medical treatment

Although your decision may be misguided, you have the right to refuse any medical treatment or surgery you don't want. You also have the right to leave a hospital at any time, assuming you're mentally competent. Before you leave, however, the hospital can ask you to sign a form releasing it of any legal responsibility should your medical condition take a turn for the worse after you leave.

The right to see what's in your medical records

In less enlightened times, your medical records were considered your doctor's property. In other words, no federal law gave you the right to that information, although close to one-half of the states had laws governing medical record access. However, the federal Health Insurance Portability and Accountability Act (HIPAA) has changed things by establishing a national minimum standard for consumers' access to medical records. Although states can still have their own medical record access laws, their laws can't take away consumers' HIPAA rights.

HIPAA applies to health care providers — doctors, pharmacies, hospitals, medical staff involved in your care, laboratories, dentists and so on — health plans, and health clearinghouses (medical billing services, for example), assuming they transmit consumer medical information electronically, which means virtually all providers given the computerization of today's society. HIPAA also establishes national privacy standards for your medical information. Those standards are discussed in Chapter 8.

You can find out if your state has its own law related to medical record access and the privacy of your medical records by visiting the Health Privacy Project's Web site at www.healthprivacy.org and clicking on the "State law" button. Another option is to contact your state's medical society.

HIPAA gives you the right not only to read the information in your medical records but also to obtain copies of those records. After you ask for copies, the medical provider must provide them to you within 30 days of receiving your request. However, the provider can have an additional 30 days to comply with your request if it provides you with a written explanation of why the additional time is needed. The medical provider is entitled to charge you

a reasonable fee for copying the records and mailing them to you if you don't
want to receive the requested information via e-mail.

Your doctor has the right to withhold from you certain information in your
medical records if he or she believes that seeing the information may endanger you or someone else emotionally, psychologically, or physically. However,
you have the right to appeal your doctor's decision.

You have the right to have any errors in your medical records corrected and
to have missing information added, assuming your medical provider agrees
with you about the error or the missing information. In most instances, an
error must be corrected (or missing information added) within 60 days of the
medical provider receiving your request. However, if a provider gives you a
written explanation of the need for more time, it can have an additional 30
days to make the required change.

If a medical provider violates your HIPAA rights, you have the right to file a
complaint with the provider's Privacy Officer (HIPAA requires every provider
to have one). Since the passage of HIPAA, the first time that you visit a health
care provider or use a provider's services, it is required to provide you with a
privacy notice explaining, among other things, how to file a complaint against
the provider. The notice should also explain how to file a complaint with the
Office of Civil Rights (OCR) of the Department of Health and Human Services
(DHHS). You may file a complaint with the OCR if you don't get satisfaction by
complaining to the provider's privacy officer. You can also obtain information
about the complaint process by visiting www.hhs.gov/ocr/hipaa or by calling 1-866-627-7748. You must file your initial HIPAA complaint within 180 days
of the alleged HIPAA violation. Also, you can't be denied medical treatment
for having filed a complaint.

If you file a complaint with the DHHS, the department may investigate your
complaint and try to resolve it on an informal basis. If the department
decides that a medical provider violated your HIPAA rights, the provider
could be fined as much as $25,000 and could even face criminal prosecution if
the Department of Justice gets involved.

If the complaint process doesn't resolve your problem, you may want to consult with a consumer law attorney who has HIPAA experience, although you
don't have the right to sue under HIPAA. However, your attorney may be able
to sue your health care provider using your state's law.

Prescription for problem solving

If you've read the preceding sections, you have a basic understanding of your
rights when dealing with your doctor and other medical providers. If you
think that your rights have been violated and you don't believe that the

violation applies to HIPAA, your first step should be to express your concerns directly to your doctor. (If the violation applies to HIPAA, follow the instructions in the previous section of this chapter.) If you get no satisfaction, try the following:

- ✔ File a complaint with your local and/or state medical association, either of which may be willing to help you resolve your problem, perhaps through mediation.

- ✔ Contact the board that licenses doctors in your state — your state health department can give you the phone number. Depending on the nature of your problem, the number of complaints already registered against the doctor, and the results of any investigation that the board initiates, among other things, the doctor's license to practice medicine may be suspended or even revoked.

- ✔ Speak with a consumer law attorney about your options.

Find out about organizations that can provide you with emotional support as well as information when you're dealing with a particular health or medical problem by going to the list of Patient Advocacy Groups at `www.aeiveos.com/resource/advocacy.html`.

The American Hospital Association's Patient's Bill of Rights

The Patient's Bill of Rights, drafted by the American Hospital Association, has been adopted by most hospitals. It sets out your basic rights when you're hospitalized. They include the right to

- ✔ "Considerate and respectful care."

- ✔ Be provided understandable information about your medical condition and proposed treatment as well as the outlook for your recovery from your doctor and others involved in your care. You also have the right to review the pros and cons of your treatment options, including the risks.

- ✔ Refuse a certain medical treatment, surgery, or plan of care assuming your refusal is not in conflict with your state's law or the policies of the hospital.

- ✔ Expect that the hospital will honor the directives in your durable power of attorney for health care and your living will, assuming that your requests are not in conflict with the laws of your state or hospital policies.

- ✔ Expect that the information in your medical records be treated as private, confidential information by your hospital except when your state law requires or allows certain information to be reported.

- ✔ Review your medical records and have anything you don't understand explained to you.

Your Rights If You're HIV-Positive or Have AIDS

Acquired Immune Deficiency Syndrome (AIDS) is caused by the virus known as HIV. If you carry the virus, you're HIV-positive and can give the virus to others.

Although people with HIV and AIDS are still discriminated against, governments at all levels have defined and codified the legal rights of men and women afflicted with this disease in order to help protect them from discrimination and provide them with the means of addressing any discrimination they may encounter. I've compiled a summary of the rights of individuals with HIV and AIDS as defined by federal law. They have the right:

- To use public accommodations, including restaurants, retail establishments, hotels, and government buildings

- To have their communications with their doctors be kept confidential under most circumstances

- To equal access to educational opportunities, assuming they meet all eligibility standards

- To not be discriminated against in the workplace — both on the job and during the employment process — because of their health problems (For example, you can't be denied a job, demoted, or denied a promotion simply because you have HIV/AIDS.)

- To not to be discriminated against when shopping for and financing a home or when renting a place to live (Also, a person with HIV/AIDS can't be evicted if he or she is living up to the terms of the lease.)

Presently all states have laws relating to the confidentiality of someone who tests positive for HIV or who is diagnosed with AIDS. In the case of an AIDS diagnosis, all states require that the individual's name be reported to the state's health department. However, states prohibit all health department personnel from identifying the name of the person with AIDS. That information is *supposed* to remain confidential. Realistically, however, there are no guarantees.

When it comes to new cases of HIV, rules about how that information should be reported vary from one state to the next. Whether or not to report names is a particularly important issue now that powerful new drugs have been developed that make it no longer inevitable that someone who is HIV-positive will develop AIDS. Many HIV/AIDS advocates and policymakers argue, therefore, that reporting names is unfair to people who are HIV-positive because that information may get out even if state laws require that it be kept confidential. They further argue that if the information were to be disclosed, the person whose name is exposed may be subject to discrimination. HIV/AIDS advocates and policymakers also worry that this risk may deter some people from getting tested for HIV. Even so, about 70 percent of states require that identified cases of HIV be reported by name to state health departments; the remaining states use codes or some other reporting system to better protect the privacy of some HIV-positive citizens.

It's illegal to discriminate against an adult or child with AIDS. If your child's school is reluctant to let your infected child come to class, the federal All Handicapped Children Act may help. It says that if a child doesn't pose a health threat to other children, he or she must be allowed to attend regular classes. If your child's school refuses, you can sue it. Given the history of such lawsuits, you have a good chance of winning your case.

Ryan White Comprehensive AIDS Resources Emergency (CARE) Act

When the federal Ryan White Comprehensive AIDS Resources Emergency (CARE) Act was reauthorized in 2000, it created incentives for states to move toward HIV name reporting and partner notification programs when someone tests positive for HIV. The law funds primary health care and support services for persons living with HIV/AIDS. It's named after an Indiana teenager whose struggle with HIV/AIDS helped educate Americans about many aspects of the disease.

Privacy rights when you're HIV-positive or have AIDS

Presently, all states have laws relating to the confidentiality of a person who is HIV-positive or has AIDS. However, the laws vary somewhat from state to state. Here are the general rules:

✔ Twenty-seven states have laws that specifically criminalize the act of exposing someone to HIV or transmitting the virus to someone else via a specific behavior. Also, all states have criminal laws that can be used to prosecute someone who commits such crimes knowingly.

✔ A majority of states require that after your state's health department is notified of your health problem, the department must try to locate and notify your sexual partners as well as anyone you may have shared needles with if you're an IV drug user. Obviously, your cooperation is essential. Again, your anonymity is supposed to be maintained, but in many instances, it may not be very difficult for someone to figure out that you're the one with the health problem.

✔ Health care providers may be permitted to notify blood banks and organ transplantation companies that you're HIV-positive without your permission. This communication is a matter of protecting the public health.

✔ If you're applying for insurance, you can be asked if you have HIV/AIDS, and the insurer has the right to deny you coverage based on your answer. However, if you're already insured, you probably can't be denied coverage of problems relating to your medical problem unless HIV/AIDS is specifically excluded from your policy as a pre-existing condition. As with other pre-existing conditions, however, you don't have to offer up information unless you're specifically asked to do so.

✔ If you're a health care worker, you may have an obligation to notify your employer of your HIV-positive health status.

If you want to learn your state's policies regarding HIV and AIDS, call the National AIDS Hotline at 1-800-342-2437. The hotline provides callers with free information and referrals about HIV and AIDS — no questions asked.

If you're HIV-positive or have AIDS, you have a moral obligation, if not a legal one, to inform your current and past sexual partners about your health problem. If you use drugs and have shared needles with others, let them know too. If you refuse to do so, depending on your state, your doctor may have a legal obligation to do the notifying for you.

Organizations you should know about

If you're HIV-positive or have AIDS, these organizations may be able to help you with legal problems related to your diagnosis:

✔ Lambda Legal: www.lambdalegal.org

✔ American Civil Liberties Union (ACLU): www.aclu.org

✔ National Association of People With AIDS: www.napwa.org

Fighting Medical Malpractice

Although modern medicine often seems miraculous, doctors are not miracle workers. You can't sue your doctor for medical malpractice just because a prescribed treatment or surgery doesn't cure what ails you. But if you believe that your doctor failed to follow accepted medical practices in diagnosing and/or treating you, and if you suffered serious harm as a result, you may have the basis for a malpractice lawsuit in your state's civil court.

HIPAA places significant limits on the circumstances under which patients who are members of a managed care plan can sue their doctors. Also, in 2004, the U.S. Supreme Court ruled that patients can't sue their managed care plans for improper denial of health services even if the denial has tragic consequences. In so doing, the court struck down patient protection laws in at least ten states, including Arizona, California, Georgia, Maine, New Jersey, North Carolina, Oklahoma, Texas, Washington, and West Virginia.

Most states have a one- to three-year statute of limitations for medical malpractice lawsuits. However, the length of the statute may be longer if the alleged violation involves a minor or a sexual act.

If your case is strong enough, you may be able to find an attorney willing to take your case on contingency; however, medical malpractice is a very specialized area of the law, so not just any attorney can take your case.

Medical malpractice cases tend to be tough to win. If you lose, depending on the terms of your contingency agreement, you may be liable for your attorney's expenses, which can run well over $50,000. Also, some states have capped the amount you can win in a malpractice lawsuit or require that you try arbitration before suing, so things may not turn out as you hope they do.

Paying for Your Medical Expenses

No federal law governs the activities of health insurance companies or managed care organizations. What they can and can't do is completely up to the states to decide.

To find out your state's laws regarding health insurance companies or managed care organizations, call your state insurance commission or your state attorney general's office.

Taking advantage of employer-supplied coverage

Employers usually aren't required to provide health insurance to their employees, although a handful of states require coverage under certain circumstances. Those private sector employers that do provide insurance are expected to comply with the provisions of the federal Employee Retirement

Income Security Act (ERISA). In addition, if employers have at least 25 employees, they must offer their employees the option of enrolling in a managed care plan instead of a traditional health insurance plan.

According to a study conducted by the Center for Studying Health System Change, between 2001 and 2003, the number of Americans receiving health coverage through their employers dropped by 9 million. Furthermore, many employers who continue to offer health coverage are passing on a larger share of the cost of that coverage to their employees and/or are offering lesser-quality coverage than they previously offered. These trends are largely due to a slowed economy and rising health care costs.

Some states require employers who offer their employees health insurance to include certain kinds of coverage. For example, treatment for substance abuse is the kind of coverage most often mandated. However, other states also require coverage for newborns, coverage of mental health problems, and hospice care.

When you're interviewing for a new job, you can't be asked whether you have a pre-existing medical condition.

If you're covered by the insurance plan of your spouse's employer and you get divorced, the employer must allow you to remain on the plan at the group rate for up to three years.

Generally, health insurance companies and managed care organizations can establish their own criteria for determining who they cover and the kinds of medical treatments, procedures, and medications they pay for. So, if you have a pre-existing health condition, they can refuse to cover that problem for a specified period of time, or even forever. And if your health is really bad, they can refuse to cover you at all.

If you're "uninsurable," don't lose heart. You may be able to purchase coverage through a state insurance pool for high-risk people. The coverage is limited and expensive, but it's better than nothing! Also, in many states, Blue Cross/Blue Shield offers *open enrollment* periods during which anyone who applies, regardless of their health status, can obtain coverage.

If you're getting on in years and you're shopping for health insurance, make sure that the policy you're considering doesn't include a clause stating that it won't be renewed after you turn 65 or some other age.

If you have health coverage, you can breathe a big sigh of relief because you can't lose your insurance if you file a lot of claims or develop a serious health problem that costs the insurer a lot of money. You can be dropped from coverage, however, if you don't keep up with the payments for your coverage or if your insurer discovers that you lied on your application.

Maintain your employer-provided health coverage through COBRA

If your employer has more than 20 employees and you quit your job or are fired, the federal Consolidated Omnibus Budget Reconciliation Act, also known as COBRA, allows you to continue receiving COBRA coverage for up to 18 months assuming you sign up for the coverage within 60 days of your employer informing you of your right to it. Also, to be eligible for COBRA coverage, you can't have lost your job due to gross misconduct and you must have been covered by your employer's health plan for at least 18 months. Your dependents can receive COBRA coverage too if they were on your employer's health plan during your employment. The only hitch with COBRA is that you have to pay the full cost of your insurance — no more employer subsidies.

Signing on for government-sponsored health programs

Medicare and Medicaid are large government-sponsored insurance programs. Medicare covers elderly people, certain disabled people, and those with permanent kidney failure. Medicaid provides coverage for low-income people with few assets.

As soon as you turn 65, you're automatically eligible for Medicare, regardless of your income. Chapter 14 discusses Medicare in detail.

Medicaid is a federal-state program. People receiving public assistance like Aid For Dependent Children (AFDC) and Supplemental Security Income (SSI) are automatically entitled to receive Medicaid benefits. So is anyone else who meets the income and asset eligibility criteria of his or her state.

Apply for Medicaid at your local social services or welfare office. Depending on your state, you may be able to apply for Medicaid at other locations. Be prepared for the usual inefficiencies and red tape of government bureaucracy — lots of paperwork and long delays. You have to provide proof of your financial status. For details about the Medicaid program in your state, go to the State Programs section of the Web site of the Centers for Medicare and Medicaid Services at www.cms.hhs.gov/Medicaid/whoiseligible.asp.

If you're approved, at a minimum you're entitled to the basic package of benefits and services that the federal government requires all states to offer Medicaid recipients if the states want to receive federal matching funds.

Some states can offer more coverage if they want. Basic Medicaid benefits and services include the following:

- Doctor care
- Medical and surgical dental services
- Nursing facility services for persons age 21 and older
- Home health care for persons eligible for nursing facility services
- Pediatric and family nurse practitioner services
- Family planning services and supplies
- Prenatal care
- Hospital services (inpatient and outpatient)
- Certain rural health clinic services
- X-rays and other diagnostic tests
- Federally qualified health center services
- Nurse-midwife services
- Early and periodic screening, diagnosis, and treatment services for children under age 21

A crash course in managing managed care

Presently, approximately 90 percent of all Americans receive their health care coverage through some sort of managed care health plan. These plans integrate the financing and delivery of health care services to consumers via contractual arrangements with health care providers, and they require plan members to use certain doctors, hospitals, and other health care providers. Consumers who participate in a managed care plan are given financial incentives to use the services of the plan's providers. The two most popular types of managed care organizations are HMOs (health maintenance organizations) and PPOs (preferred provider organizations).

HMOs require consumers who enroll in their plans to use doctors and other health care providers who are a part of their provider network and dramatically discount the cost of that care. HMO members make a very small co-payment when they use the services of a network provider, and typically, if a member uses the services of a non-network provider, the HMO will not pay him or her for the cost of those services.

All HMOs are state-licensed. HMOs participating in the federal Medicare or Medicaid programs must also be federally licensed.

PPOs are groups of doctors and other medical providers who negotiate with employers, insurance companies, or other sponsoring groups to provide their employees or members with discounted medical services. PPO members can also use providers who are not part of the PPO, but the members aren't reimbursed at the same rate as they would be if the providers were within the PPO's network.

Back in the 1990s, when managed care first became popular, it was touted as the panacea for rising health care costs, but it has had mixed success in keeping medical costs down. Also, compared to traditional fee-for-service health care plans, managed care has had some additional benefits for consumers, including:

- ✔ **Lower out-of-pocket costs**

    When you visit a doctor, have a diagnostic test, go to the hospital, have a prescription filled, and so on, you usually pay just a small co-payment.

- ✔ **Less paperwork for consumers to deal with**

- ✔ **Better coverage for preventative health care**

On the downside however, especially if you're a member of an HMO, your choice of doctors and other medical providers is limited. Also, your access to specialists is restricted because to get to them you must go through a "gatekeeper" or your primary care physician who makes a referral.

Increasingly, patients, consumer groups, nurses, and doctors are decrying certain policies of some HMOs. They're critical of the following:

- ✔ HMOs can jeopardize a patient's health by limiting that person's access to the specialists, treatments, and procedures that he or she may need — all in the name of cost-cutting.

- ✔ HMOs impose lots of rules and restrictions on participation.

- ✔ Some HMOs aren't 100-percent forthcoming with consumers about the rules of their plans.

- ✔ Some HMOs use financial incentives or the threat of penalties, including dismissal, to pressure doctors into not providing their patients with complete information about all their medical care options. However, most states have passed laws prohibiting the "gagging" of doctors. The practice of pressuring doctors to withhold information from their patients is in direct conflict with the concept of informed consent and puts doctors in an uncomfortable position: Should they be loyal to the HMO they're working for in order to assure their financial well-being, even if it means not providing their patients with the best possible care, or should they risk antagonizing the HMO by being honest and open with their patients, even if what they recommend is expensive and is going to cost the HMO more money?

✔ HMOs interfere with the ability of doctors to provide their patients with the care they need. For example, some HMOs require doctors to prescribe generic drugs for their patients rather than brand name products, even if the doctors believe that the generic versions are inferior.

As a consequence of the criticism that many have leveled against some HMOs and the federal government's failure to regulate the managed care industry, some states have enacted regulations to control managed care organizations and have passed legislation to protect consumers from certain industry practices. These practices include dramatically limiting the length of hospital stays (including requiring that new mothers leave the hospital within 48 hours of giving birth) and restricting what doctors can tell their patients about their medical care options. Some of these state laws also require that doctors tell patients about any HMO financial incentives or penalties that may affect the care the patients receive.

If you're in a managed care plan and you require emergency care, your plan must pay for that care even if you don't get a referral to the emergency room from your primary care provider.

Getting a handle on health savings accounts

Included in the Medicare prescription drug coverage legislation President Bush signed into law at the end of 2003 is a new vehicle for financing the cost of your health care — the Health Savings Account (HSA). An HSA pairs an IRA-like savings account with a qualified low-cost, high-deductible health insurance plan (a "qualified plan" is one with a deductible of at least $1,000 for an individual and a deductible of at least $2,000 for a family). An HSA is available to employees through their employers, to the self-employed, and to other health care consumers.

Here is how an HSA works: You, or you and your employer, contribute pre-tax dollars to your health savings account to pay your routine medical expenses. (Your employer's contributions aren't treated as income for tax purposes.) Each year, you and/or your employer can contribute up to the amount of your health plan annual deductible, but no more than $2,600 for individuals and $5,150 for families. In other words, even if you have a deductible greater than either of these amounts, $2,600 or $5,150 is the most that can be deposited in your account in a given year.

Some of the specific features and benefits of an HSA include:

- ✔ If you already have a Medical Savings Account, you can roll the funds into an HSA.

- ✔ The interest and investment earnings generated by your HSA are tax-free while they're in the account, assuming you use them to pay qualified medical expenses such as your health insurance deductible and co-payments for medical services, prescriptions, medical products, and so on. In addition, the funds can be used to purchase over-the-counter drugs and long-term care insurance and to pay your health insurance premiums if you become unemployed. (You're taxed on any money that you withdraw from your health savings account and spend on items and services that are *not* qualified medical expenses. You're also charged a 10-percent penalty.)

- ✔ You can use the funds in your account for preventive care such as physical exams and screenings, routine prenatal and well-child care, immunizations, tobacco cessation programs, and obesity weight-loss programs.

- ✔ You, not your managed care plan, decide which doctors and specialists you see, what tests and procedures you want, and so on.

- ✔ You don't lose the funds in the account if you change employers.

- ✔ If you don't use up all of the funds in your HSA in a particular year, you don't lose them — they roll over to the next year.

- ✔ You can let the funds in your HSA accumulate for years tax-free and use them for your retirement. Then after you reach age 65, you can begin drawing money out of the account for non-medical purposes without paying a penalty.

HSAs aren't for everyone, however. For example, if your family has a lot of routine medical expenses, or if someone in your family has a chronic disease, then the maximum amount you can stash away in your HSA each year may not be enough to pay for everything, and you will have to come up a way to pay for the rest of your medical expenses.

If you have problems with your claims

If you file a claim with your health plan and the company refuses to pay it, or if you think your reimbursement is too small, you have a right to challenge the company's decision. Insurers do make mistakes, and surveys show that claim reimbursement calculations are frequently wrong!

Here's how to challenge your health plan's decision:

1. First, reread your policy to make certain that you're not confused about your coverage; however, reading your policy may leave you thoroughly confused because policies don't tend to be written in straightforward English.

2. Then call your health plan's customer service office for an explanation. The company probably provides an 800 number for such inquiries.

If you're not satisfied with what you learn and you're not covered by your employer's health plan, check the information you received from the plan regarding how to begin the appeals process. Most likely you must make a phone call or write a letter. In your phone call or letter, ask for written clarification of the company's policy regarding your claim. Compare the company's explanation to what's stated in your policy. If you still can't get any satisfaction, write to your state's insurance commission or to the office that regulates managed care organizations in your state. In your letter, copy both the CEO of your health plan as well as the head of its claims department.

Depending on your state, if your state office can't help you resolve your claim, it may suggest that you take your problem to an outside review board. Alternatively, you may want to hire a consumer law attorney, assuming the amount of money in dispute is substantial. You can sue for actual and punitive damages, attorney fees, and pain and suffering.

If your insurance plan is regulated by ERISA, you have to follow ERISA's appeal process. This process should be described in the information booklet you received when you enrolled in the plan. If you have questions about the process, talk to the person at your place of work in charge of the plan.

Good news for folks with pre-existing conditions

It used to be that if you or someone in your family had a pre-existing health condition that was covered by your employer's health plan, you felt compelled to stay with that employer even if you hated working there or needed to make more money; you were afraid that a new employer's health plan may not cover the condition. However, the federal Health Insurance Portability and Accountability Act (HIPAA) gives you the freedom to change jobs by requiring that your new employer's plan cover any medical conditions that were covered by your previous employer's plan. However, the new health plan is entitled to require that you wait up to a year before the problem is covered.

If you follow the appeals process and your appeal is denied, ERISA gives you the right to sue for actual damages and attorney fees.

Whenever you're dealing with an insurance company or managed care organization, it's important to keep detailed notes of all conversations you have with the company's personnel, including the date of each conversation, the name and title of the person you spoke with, and a summary of the comments and/or promises made by the person/s you spoke with. This information may be helpful to your efforts to resolve your problem, and it could be very useful if you end up filing a lawsuit.

Chapter 14

Getting Older: We All Do It

- -

In This Chapter

▶ Financing your retirement

▶ Winding your way through the Medicare maze

▶ Obtaining nursing home care

▶ Finding good home health care

- -

*Y*ou're getting older, like it or not. Sooner or later, you need to begin planning for your golden years if you want them to be truly golden. Or maybe you've already begun the planning process. At a minimum, it should include the following:

✔ Laying the groundwork for financing your retirement — no small feat given that financial experts estimate that to sustain a retirement lifestyle comparable to the one you may be enjoying now, you'll need 70 to 90 percent of your gross pre-retirement income.

✔ Knowing your options should your health or physical condition necessitate home health care.

✔ Familiarizing yourself with the residential options available to older adults should your health fail and you need to move out of your home or apartment into a different sort of residence. This planning includes considering how you're going to pay for the care if it becomes necessary. Depending on the type of residence you select, adequate planning and good health insurance can mean the difference between being able to pay for the cost of living there with your own resources or having to deplete your life savings in order for Medicaid to help pay for it.

Those of you with older parents in failing health may already be dealing with some of these issues. If you are, you understand the kinds of financial and emotional challenges older adults often face even when they've made solid plans. You also understand that pension plans, Medicare, and Medicaid are governed by complex, confusing webs of rules and regulations that can quickly overwhelm older people and prevent them from getting what they're entitled to receive.

Don't count on Social Security to provide you with a comfortable retirement lifestyle. At best, your monthly checks will fund a subsistent living.

The federal Web portal FirstGov for Seniors, at `www.firstgov.gov/Topics/Seniors.shtml`, is your entryway to a wide range of information and resources related to older adults, including consumer protection, important federal and state agencies and offices, key laws and regulations, retirement, money, and health. This site is worth book-marking on your Internet browser.

Financing Your Retirement

How our expectations have changed! We used to expect that after 40 plus years of working, we'd retire to enjoy hobbies, travel, family, and friends and live comfortably on a pension plan funded by our employer — a *defined-benefit* pension plan — and Social Security, augmented by whatever personal savings and other investments we'd been able to accumulate during our working years.

Although that carefree vision of our golden years may still be attainable, increasingly, it's up to us to make it a reality, At best, Social Security only covers your most basic expenses, and defined-benefit pension plans are pretty much perks of the past, replaced by *defined-contribution* pension plans. This type of pension places much (if not all) the burden for building a retirement nest egg on you, not on your employer.

The retirement nest egg you're able to amass may have to finance as much as 30 or more years of living if you retire at age 65. So if you have a pension, it's critical that you make sure its funds are managed wisely and, when pension problems develop, that you know your legal rights. Doing so can mean the difference between a relaxed, comfortable retirement and one full of worry, stress, and even poverty. These days, nothing is guaranteed, not even a financially secure old age!

A growing number of retirement-age adults are delaying retirement in order to remain in the workplace. Some of them begin second careers or work part time. Although part of their motivation for not retiring may be financial, many older adults are healthy and intellectually vital and want to stay fully engaged in the world around them as long as possible.

Defined-benefit and defined-contribution pension plans — what's the difference?

If you're lucky, you have a defined-benefit pension plan. If you do, your employer automatically enrolled you in it after you met certain eligibility requirements. Your employer also guaranteed you either a specific amount of retirement income, $3,000 per month for example, or more likely, a monthly pension based on a formula that usually takes into account the number of years you work for your employer, your age, and the size of your salary. Your employer is legally obligated to contribute enough money to its pension fund each year and to manage and invest the money in that fund in a manner that will guarantee that you and other participating employees receive the income you were promised when you retire.

A key advantage to participating in a defined-benefit pension plan is that it's probably insured and protected by the Pension Benefit Guaranty Corporation, or PBGC. The PBGC requires an employer who wants to terminate its pension plan to have enough money to pay its employees all of the pension benefits they're entitled to, both vested and not, before the employer can end the plans. The employer can pay its employees the pension benefits they're entitled to in a lump sum or through an annuity. When an employer with a defined-benefit pension plan wants to end the plans because of serious financial difficulty, perhaps because continuing the plan may force the businesses to shut down, the PBGC will pay guaranteed benefits, usually covering a large part of whatever earned benefits employees are entitled to, up to a certain dollar limit which is set by law and changes annually. The PBGC also attempts to recover funds from the employer.

To find out if your defined-benefit plan is PBGC-insured, ask your employer or your plan administrator. If you have questions about the PBGC or about your pension plan should it be taken over by the PBGC, write to the agency: Pension Benefit Guaranty Corporation, 1200 K Street, NW, Washington, DC 20005-4026; or call 202-326-4000. If you're hearing impaired, call 1-800-877-8339. For more information about the PBGC, visit its Web site at www.pbgc.gov.

The opposite of a defined-benefit plan is a *defined-contribution* plan. Examples of defined-contribution plans, also known as *retirement plans,* include employee stock ownership plans (ESOP), profit-sharing plans, 401(k), and 403(b) plans. Of the three, the most popular is the 401(k).

There are several important distinctions between these two types of pension plans.

- Participation in a defined-contribution plan is not automatic — it's voluntary, and you have to enroll.

- Your active involvement is required if you want your defined-contribution pension plan to be a success. Although your employer may or may not contribute to it, *you* decide how to invest the money in your retirement account. (In defined-benefit plans, your employer makes this decision.)

- Your employer makes no promises regarding how much retirement income your defined-contribution pension will provide you. The amount will depend on a variety of factors, including how much is in your plan and what the funds are invested in.

The experience of many Enron employees highlights the risk you may be taking if you invest a high percentage of your 401(k) funds in your employer's stock. When the value of Enron's stock plummeted, the retirement accounts of those employees took a dive as well, ultimately leaving them not only without jobs but also without the funds they thought would help provide them with a comfortable retirement. Investment diversification helps protect you from big losses in your 401(k).

If your employer deducts money from your paychecks and deposits those funds in your 401(k) account, federal law requires the employer to deposit the money into your account as soon as it's administratively feasible, or no later than the 15th business day of the month following the month in which the deduction occurred. This legal loophole can tempt cash-strapped employers who need some extra operating capital. However, some of the employers who take advantage of the loophole are unable to replace the money in time to deposit it by the required deadline. When they can't, they are in essence defrauding their employees. Because the sooner your money is deposited in your 401(k) account the sooner it can begin growing, it's important to monitor how quickly your employer makes such deposits. If you find that your employer isn't making deposits on a timely basis, write a letter to your employer's plan administrator; send it certified mail with a return receipt requested. If this approach gets you nowhere, use the appeals process every pension plan is legally required to establish, and if you strike out there, contact the federal Employee Benefits Security Administration (EBSA) at 1-866-444-3272. The office protects employee benefits, including their retirement benefits.

The failures of Enron, WorldCom, and other companies and the staggering losses employees working for these companies experienced illustrate the sad fact that a pension doesn't guarantee a comfortable retirement.

How 401(k) plans work

About 70 percent of all workers participate in 401(k) plans or 403(b) plans — the nonprofit equivalent of a 401(k) for those of you working in the public or nonprofit sectors.

Here's a brief overview of how a 401(k) plan works. When you're eligible to begin participating in your employer's 401(k) plan, instead of getting the full amount of your salary, you defer some of it for deposit into your 401(k) retirement account. When it comes to the limit on how much you can defer each year, the Economic Growth and Tax Relief Reconciliation Act of 2001 set a maximum contribution amount of $13,000 for the year 2004, $14,000 for 2005, and $15,000 in 2006. After that the law provides for increases in $500 increments each year to account for inflation. Also, your employer's plan may have its own limits.

You aren't taxed on the amount you defer or on any interest your retirement account may earn until you withdraw it. Therefore, it's best to contribute as much as possible to your 401(k) or 403 (b) each year, especially if your employer matches all or some of your contributions. Keep in mind that you may have to work for your employer a minimum number of years before the matches begin.

Your employer provides you with a number of different options for the funds in your account. The options offer you the opportunity to be more or less conservative with your money. If you're unhappy with the performance of the option you choose, you can select another option whenever you want or at periodic points throughout the year, depending on how your plan works.

As a result of the Sarbanes-Oxley Act passed by Congress in 2002, your employer must give you at least 30 days' written notice prior to a black-out period — a period when you can't make any trades in your 401(k) or any other changes. The notice must be written in plain English so you can understand it. Although most employers have provided notice of blackouts in the past, scandals associated with the top executives of Enron, WorldCom, and a handful of other companies made it necessary to put this requirement into law.

Being "vested" is not a fashion statement

Whether your plan is a defined-contribution or a defined-benefit plan, if you're *vested* in your pension plan, you won't lose what money you've accumulated if you decide to leave your current employer before you've reached retirement age. When you're vested, you've been participating in a plan long enough to have a non-forfeitable right to your pension benefits no matter where you work. If you're not vested, you're still entitled to 100 percent of whatever you have contributed to the plan and to whatever interest your contributions have earned. But you aren't entitled to whatever your employer has contributed.

If you're vested and you leave your current employer, you can either keep your retirement dollars in your current pension plan or take them out. If you decide to cash out, you receive your money in a lump sum payment. If you decide to leave your retirement dollars where they are and your former employer was contributing to your plan, those contributions stop.

The federal government has established two schedules that employers can use to determine the rate at which their employees become vested. But employers are free to use a more generous schedule if they choose.

Employers are prohibited from changing their vesting schedule in order to deny their vested employees the retirement benefits they've accumulated when they retire.

Following the Employee Retirement Income Security Act (ERISA)

Although your employer isn't legally required to establish a pension plan for you, if it does and you work in the private sector, your employer's plan must meet the requirements of the federal Employee Retirement Income Security Act (ERISA). This law was enacted in 1974 to address some of the key abuses occurring in the private employer pension system by creating minimum standards for pension plans and by giving both plan participants and their beneficiaries certain rights. For example, ERISA requires that the administrator of your employer's plan, who may or may not be an employee, must do the following:

✔ Provide you with written information about your pension plan and your pension benefits. Some of this information is free and should come to you automatically on a periodic basis. It includes the following:

- A free summary plan explaining the basic facts about your employer's pension plan — its benefits and how they're calculated, eligibility requirements, when you can begin receiving retirement benefits, what you must do to begin collecting them, and so on. You should get this information within 90 days of enrolling in a plan. Also, if your plan changes, the plan administrator must notify you of the change either by providing you with a revised summary plan, or with a separate document called a *summary of material modifications*. This information is also free.

- A free summary annual report telling you where the money in your pension fund has been invested and how well it has done. This report is a condensed version of the report that most pensions must file with the U.S. Department of Labor each year. You should receive your summary report no later than 90 days after the end of each plan year.

Annual reports and summary annual reports don't make for exciting reading; even so, read them carefully! They can reveal important information about the health of your pension fund and can highlight potential problems that may have a direct bearing on how much retirement income you end up with.

- Other pension-related information that your employer must provide to you, for free or for a charge depending on what you ask for. (Your request should be made in writing.) This information includes an individual benefit summary giving you the total value of the retirement benefits that you've accrued so far and details on whether those benefits are vested.

✔ Abide by certain rules in establishing a process that you can use when you retire and want to begin collecting your pension benefits.

✔ Establish an appeals process that you can use when you have problems with your pension. For example, you may have trouble collecting your benefits or the amount of your monthly benefit may be wrong. ERISA also gives you the right to sue your pension plan in state or federal court if you exhaust your plan's claims and appeals processes.

✔ Provide survivor's benefits to your surviving spouse if you have a vested right to your pension, no matter whether you die before or after you retire.

If your employer doesn't provide you with the plan information you're entitled to, contact the federal Employee Benefits Security Administration by mail or by phone. The address is U.S. Department of Labor, Employee Benefits Security Administration, Public Disclosure Room, 200 Constitution Avenue, NW, Room N-1513, Washington, DC 20210. Call the office at 866-444-3272. You will be sent an invoice for the cost of copying the materials you request.

ERISA also does the following:

✔ Sets standards of conduct for pension plan fiduciaries (a *fiduciary* manages a pension plan and is responsible for investing its assets) and establishes penalties for those who don't meet the standards. For example, fiduciaries generally can't use money earmarked for a pension plan for any other purpose, and they can't mix pension funds with other funds. Also, fiduciaries can't put pension fund dollars in high-risk investments or in only one or just a very few investments. Although you can sue your plan's fiduciaries for mismanagement or misuse of funds, the fund, not you, gets the monetary award if you win.

If you — and only you — make all investment decisions for your employer-sponsored pension plan, the plan's administrators and others with responsibility for it don't have fiduciary responsibility for the consequences of your decisions.

✔ Prohibits employers from firing you or laying you off just to avoid paying you pension benefits.

✔ Gives you the right to sue your pension plan to get the benefits you're due and to enforce your pension rights in general. The Secretary of Labor can also sue a plan if there's sufficient cause.

Getting what you've earned

ERISA's rules regarding when you can begin receiving retirement benefits vary depending on the specific type of plan you're enrolled in.

✔ **If your plan is a defined-benefit plan,** it specifies a retirement age, which is generally when you will be eligible to begin receiving your vested accrued benefits. However, the plan may also provide for early retirement with benefits.

✔ **If your plan is a 401(k) plan,** you may be able to take some or all of your vested accrued benefits if you terminate employment, retire, die, become disabled, reach age 59, or suffer a hardship.

✔ **If your plan is a profit-sharing plan or a stock bonus plan,** you may be able to receive your vested accrued benefits after you terminate employment, become disabled, die, reach a specific age, or after a specific number of years have elapsed.

Read your plan's summary to find out all of the rules that apply to you. If you have any questions, contact the plan administrator.

How you receive your pension benefits depends on what kind of pension you have. If you have a defined-benefit plan, you will probably receive payments over time in the form of an annuity. If you have a defined-contribution plan, you may get your funds in a lump sum, or your plan may make some other provision for payment.

Although you may be eligible to begin receiving your pension benefits, you may not receive them immediately because your pension plan may need time to value your account balance, liquidate your investments, calculate your monthly payment, and so on.

After you file a claim to begin collecting your pension benefits, your plan must respond to your claim in writing within 90 days. If your claim is denied, the pension plan administrator must send you a written notice explaining why. (If you don't get a response to your claim by the deadline, ERISA says that you should assume that your claim has been denied.) You have the right to appeal your denial by requesting a formal review. Again, put your request in writing. You have 60 days to file your appeal, and if you don't file within that time period, you're out of luck.

Ordinarily, the plan administrator must respond in writing to your appeal within 60 days of receiving it. However, if your plan provides for a special hearing and one is held, the plan administrator gets another 60 days to respond. In the response, the plan administrator must spell out the exact reasons for his or her final decision, specifically referencing the rules of your pension plan. If you're unsatisfied with the outcome, you can sue in state or federal court. Hire an attorney who specializes in pension problems to help you. If your case is strong, the attorney may take your case on contingency.

Handling problems with pension benefits and claims

The nonprofit Pension Rights Center in Washington, D.C., is a source of assistance for pension problems. If you live in certain areas of the country, its Pension Information and Counseling Project may be able to help you. Those areas are: Michigan; Ohio; the mid-Atlantic area; Missouri; Kansas; Illinois; New England, including Connecticut, Maine, Massachusetts, New Hampshire, Rhode Island, and Vermont; Minnesota; Wisconsin; and Arizona. For more information about the Pension Rights Center, call 202-296-3776 or go to www.pensionrights.org.

When an employee sues his or her pension plan, precedent indicates that the courts are more likely to decide for the plan.

It's estimated that more than half of the approximately 60 million Americans covered by retirement plans are not getting the benefits they've earned. The highest error rates are associated with 401(k) and profit-sharing plans. If left uncorrected, even a small error in calculating a pension can add up to a substantial amount of lost retirement income, which is a good reason to stay on top of your pension benefits as they're accrued by reading and understanding the reports you receive.

Although certainly a percentage of the errors in pension benefit determinations can be attributed to the deliberate effort of some employers to cheat their workers out of money, most of the mistakes are caused by the sheer complexity of the law and by the fact that ERISA gets amended nearly every year. Small business employers have an especially difficult time keeping up with the law and incorporating its ever-changing provisions into their pension plan administration systems. Mathematical errors and mistakes in data entry also contribute to the errors.

The best and cheapest way to ensure that you get what you deserve is to keep tabs on your pension benefits as they accumulate: Read your summary plan description, check your yearly benefit statements, match pension contributions through the year with your year-end statement, and ask the plan administrator about anything you don't understand.

If you think someone made an error in the calculation of your pension benefits, contact your employer's plan administrator in writing and ask for a detailed explanation of how your benefits were calculated. The administrator must respond in writing within 90 days. If you don't agree with the response, use the appeals process as you would use for appealing a pension claim denial (Read "Getting what you've earned," earlier in this chapter).

The National Center for Retirement Benefits (NCRB) can act as your pension detective — for a price. It can determine what your pension should be and can help you get what you may be missing, on contingency. In most instances, it takes 20 percent of what it collects. Although a 20 percent cut may sound excessive, it can be worth the price if an error is significant. Contact NCRB by phone, 1-800-666-1000; or via its Web site, www.ncrb.com.

Other things you should know about pensions

Pensions can be tricky and complicated, so here are a handful of facts to keep in mind:

- ✔ Your employer can limit its pension program to certain categories of workers, or it can offer different options to different employee categories. All employees within a particular category must be treated the same, however.

- ✔ Your employer can establish requirements for how long you must work before you can begin participating in its pension plan and accruing pension benefits and for when you can become vested in your retirement plan. Generally, assuming your employer's plan covers your position, you must be allowed to participate in it as soon as you've reached age 21 and have put in one year of service with your employer. This rule applies whether you are a full-time, part-time, or seasonal worker.

- ✔ Your employer isn't required to continue offering a pension plan.

- ✔ Depending on your plan, your monthly pension benefit may be reduced if you're receiving Social Security benefits.

- ✔ Depending on the laws of your state, if you divorce, your ex-spouse may be entitled to a share of your pension benefits.

✔ If your employer is acquired by or merges with another company and your current pension plan is continued, your new employer can't set new "years of service" standards for becoming vested. However, this restriction doesn't apply if your plan is discontinued and replaced with another.

✔ Under certain conditions, your pension plan can be suspended if you return to work after retiring.

✔ If your employer files for bankruptcy, whether or not your 401(k) is affected depends on the type of bankruptcy your employer files. If it files a Chapter 11 reorganization bankruptcy, the employer continues to operate, and your 401(k) may not be affected. However, if it files a liquidation bankruptcy or Chapter 7, your employer shuts down, and it's likely that your retirement plan ends as well. As soon as you hear that your employer (or former employer) may or is going to file for bankruptcy, get in touch with the plan administrator for your 401(k) to determine how your plan is likely to be affected. You should also find out who will administer the plan during a bankruptcy and how accrued benefits will be paid if the plan is terminated.

Managing Medicare

Medicare is a federal health insurance program available to nearly everyone age 65 or over, regardless of income. The federal Centers for Medicare & Medicaid Services (CMS) administer the program, establishing its benefits, rules, and conditions. But CMS contracts with private health insurance companies to process claims and make payments. The money to fund the Medicare program comes from your paychecks in the form of payroll deductions as well as from the premiums and coinsurance payments that Medicare participants pay.

As long as you meet the program's age requirement, you can enroll in the Medicare program even if you continue working.

Like the Social Security program, Medicare is in financial trouble because, while the number of Medicare beneficiaries is increasing, the number of workers per retiree to fund Medicare is decreasing. On top of that imbalance, the cost of medical care has escalated. Although the Balanced Budget Act of 1997 ensured that Medicare Part A will be solvent until 2007, it is estimated that Medicare will go bankrupt in 2008 unless Congress reforms the program. For example, Congress may decide to increase the amount that program participants must pay and to reduce the amount that Medicare pays its medical providers.

Help! I'm lost in the Medicare maze

The Medicare program is extremely complex, full of confusing rules, exceptions, procedures, and processes that make the program difficult to understand and use effectively. In fact, having a Ph.D. in bureaucracy would be a real asset when dealing with Medicare! Adding insult to injury, the program doesn't cover many basic types of medical care, and its long-term care benefits are very limited. Therefore, you may need to buy additional medical insurance if you can afford it.

Medicare actually consists of two separate programs. One program is the original fee-for-service plan — *Parts A and B*. With this plan, you pay for your health care services and products as you receive them and use a red, white, and blue Medicare card to verify your enrollment in the Medicare original fee-for-service plan.

The other program is *Part C* Medicare — the Medicare Advantage plan, which used to be known as the Medicare + Choice plan. This second program allows you to receive your Medicare benefits through private companies that offer managed care plans, private fee-for-service plans, preferred provider organization plans, and medical savings accounts. The advantage of Part C is that the private company plans offer more options than the original Medicare program and sometimes more benefits too. However, you may have to pay an additional monthly premium for those extra benefits. Depending on your area of the country, all of the Medicare Advantage plans may not be available to you. For information about which ones are offered in your area, go to www.medicare.gov and select "Medicare Personal Plan Finder," or call 1-800-633-4227.

In this chapter, most of my discussion of Medicare focuses on the original Medicare program, Parts A and B. Although it can't fill you in on all of the program's twists and turns, the discussion should give you at least a hint of what a challenge the program can be. For much more information on many aspects of Medicare, go to www.medicare.gov and select "Publications." You can read the information booklets online, print them off, or order them through the mail.

Medicare Part A

The original Medicare program has two parts: Part A, Hospital Insurance, and Part B, Medical Insurance. If you or your spouse is eligible for Social Security or Railroad Retirement benefits, you're automatically eligible to receive Part A benefits free of charge; however, "free" isn't really free because you still have to pay a deductible and coinsurance payments.

Not sure if you're automatically eligible for Part A benefits? Look on your Medicare card. Does "Hospital Part A" appear on the lower left corner of the card? If so, you're covered by Part A.

If you're 65 but not automatically eligible to receive Part A benefits, you may still be able to get them by paying a monthly premium. Also, if you're under 65 but you've been receiving Social Security or Railroad Retirement program disability benefits for more than 24 months, or if you've been on dialysis for permanent kidney failure or had a kidney transplant, you may be eligible for Medicare. Call 1-800-772-1213 or visit your local Social Security Administration to find out if you're eligible for Medicare, and if you're not, whether you can purchase the program's benefits. If you receive benefits from the Railroad Retirement Board, call your local RRB office or 1-800-808-0772.

Part A covers the cost of "medically necessary" inpatient care at a hospital, critical access hospital (a small hospital that provides limited outpatient and inpatient care to residents of rural areas), psychiatric hospital, or skilled nursing facility participating in Medicare. Part A also covers the cost of medically necessary home health care and hospice care. The following is a partial list of the kinds of medical care and services Part A covers. When you receive these services, Medicare pays its share of their cost, and you pay your share, also called your *co-payment*. The amount of your co-payment depends on the particular Part A service you receive.

- A semiprivate room and all your meals
- Regular nursing services and the drugs you receive
- The cost of special care including intensive care and coronary care
- All but the first three pints of blood unless you or someone you know donates blood to replace what you use
- Lab tests, X-rays, and other radiology services billed by the hospital
- Medical supplies such as casts, splints, and so on
- The use of a wheelchair and other appliances
- The cost of operating and recovery rooms
- Rehabilitation services such as physical, occupational, and speech therapy
- Mental health services provided by a doctor or a qualified medical health professional
- Skilled nursing facility benefits

  Medicare pays the cost of skilled nursing care if you enter a skilled nursing facility within 30 days of leaving the hospital, you were hospitalized for at least three days prior to your admittance, the care that you receive at the facility is related to your hospital stay, and if you have days left to use in your benefit period. Also, for Medicare to pay, the care you receive must be something that only a skilled nursing facility can provide and must be ordered by your doctor. Exactly how much of the cost of your stay Medicare pays depends on how long you stay at the skilled nursing facility. For example, if you stay for one to twenty days, Medicare picks up the entire cost, but if you stay more than 100 days, you're responsible for 100 percent of the cost beginning on day 101.

✔ Home health care benefits

Medicare pays the full cost of covered home health services if you're confined to your home and need intermittent skilled nursing care, physical therapy, or speech therapy, or if you need ongoing occupational therapy. If you need durable medical equipment, you must make a 20-percent coinsurance payment. To be covered by Medicare, a doctor must order your home health care, and the care provider must be a Medicare participant.

✔ Hospice care

If your doctor and the hospice director certify that you're terminally ill and probably have less than six months to live, and if you sign a form stating that you prefer to receive hospice care rather than the routine Plan A benefits you would receive for your terminal illness, Medicare pays for the care, regardless of whether it's provided at your home or in a hospice facility (as long as it's provided by a Medicare-participating provider). Doctor and nursing care, individual and family psychological help, prescriptions, respite care, and social services are among the hospice-related services paid for by Medicare. Medicare also pays for "appropriate" custodial care, including homemaker services. Although you don't have to pay any deductibles for this benefit, you're responsible for a co-payment of up to $5 for each prescription drug you receive during outpatient hospice care. Also, if you're in a hospice facility, you have to pay 5 percent of the Medicare-allowed rate, which varies in different parts of the country.

Medicare Part B

When you turn 65, you also become eligible to participate in Medicare Part B, but it costs you. You have to pay a monthly premium that changes annually. Usually, after you enroll in Part B, your premiums are deducted automatically from your Social Security checks.

Medicare Part B typically covers about 80 percent of the cost of the "medically necessary," Medicare-covered services you receive from your doctor.

It also covers outpatient hospital care and some medical services that Part A does not cover, including the services of physical and occupational therapists, some home health care and supplies, physical and speech therapy, diagnostic tests, durable medical equipment, lab services, and blood transfusions. You must pay the remaining 20 percent — that's your coinsurance payment.

At first glance, the preceding list of covered services may seem pretty comprehensive. You may change your mind, however, when you see what Part B doesn't pay for:

- ✔ Most routine physical exams
- ✔ Most prescription drugs
- ✔ Most immunizations
- ✔ Exams for prescribing and fitting eyeglasses or hearing aids
- ✔ Dentures
- ✔ Most routine foot care and dental care

Enrolling in Medicare

You can enroll in Medicare during one of two enrollment periods — the initial period or the general period. The initial period begins three months prior to your 65th birthday and continues for three months. The general period occurs every January 1 through March 31.

Although you can enroll in Medicare Part B when you're older than 65, you pay a 10-percent premium penalty for every year you delay enrolling, with one exception — if you're still working and are covered by your employer's group health insurance plan. As soon as you retire, you have seven months to enroll without penalty.

If you try to enroll in Medicare and are denied participation, you have the right to appeal to the Social Security Administration. Depending on how far you take your appeal, you can request a hearing before an administrative law judge and even file a lawsuit in federal court. The appeals process is described in greater detail in the "What to do if your Medicare claim is denied" section, later in this chapter.

The devil is in the details

It's time for just a small taste of how confusing and complicated the original Medicare program can be. Brace yourself!

Benefit periods

Medicare measures your use of Part A services in terms of *benefit periods.* Your *first* benefit period begins the first time you receive inpatient hospital care under the Medicare program, and it ends after you've been out of the hospital or a skilled nursing or rehabilitative facility for 60 days in a row. Your *second* benefit period begins when you receive inpatient hospital care again, and so on. There's no limit on the number of benefit periods you can have for hospital care, skilled nursing facility care, and rehabilitative care.

Within each benefit period, Medicare pays for up to 90 days of all medically necessary inpatient hospital care covered by Part A. For example, in 2004, from the first day through the 60th day of your hospital stay during a benefit period, Part A pays for all covered services after you've paid your inpatient hospital deductible of $875. From the 61st day through the 90th day of a hospital stay during the same benefit period, Part A pays the full cost of all covered services except for your coinsurance payment of $219 per day, which you pay. Your coinsurance payment is $438 per day if you stay in a hospital from the 91st to the 150th day. If you stay beyond 150 days, you pay nothing.

If you need to be hospitalized for more than 90 days and want Medicare to pay for it, you can use some of your *lifetime reserve days.* Medicare gives you 60 extra, or reserve, days to use during your lifetime if necessary to help pay for Medicare Part A services. Reserve days carry a coinsurance payment, and you can tap your reserve days only once.

Medicare-approved charges and Medicare providers

Medicare sets approved charges for each medical service it covers. These charges represent the most it's willing to pay for a service. If you're charged more than the Medicare-approved amount, you have to pay the difference. And doing so can get expensive because Medicare's approved charges often fall far short of actual costs.

To minimize your medical costs, try to use medical providers who accept the Medicare-approved amount as full payment. Doing so is called *taking on assignment.* You can find out which medical care providers in your area take on assignment by reviewing the *Medicare-Participating Physician Directory* available free from your local Social Security office, your local or state office on aging, and from most hospitals.

Although doctors aren't required to treat Medicare patients, they can't charge Medicare patients more than other patients. Also, if a doctor doesn't take on assignment, Medicare generally limits how much he or she can charge to about 15 percent more than the Medicare-approved amount. Doctors who charge more than this amount can be fined. Medicare also places similar limits on some suppliers.

If you feel that you've been overcharged, ask for a reduction in your bill or a refund if you've already paid. If you don't get either, call your Medicare carrier for help.

Some states, including Connecticut, Massachusetts, Minnesota, New York, Ohio, Pennsylvania, Rhode Island, and Vermont, have laws limiting your out-of-pocket charges to less than 15 percent of the Medicare-approved amount.

If you can't afford the original Medicare program

You have a couple options if the costs of Medicare are beyond your financial means and you can't afford the cost of a Medigap policy or supplemental insurance (see the section "Purchasing Medigap insurance"). One option is to apply for one of three *Medicare Savings* programs. However, to qualify for these programs you must meet certain income guidelines and you're limited in the value of the assets you can own, excluding your house and car. (For example, in 2004 in most states, you could not own more than $4,000 worth of assets if you were single or more than $6,000 if you were married. Some states set higher limits.) If you qualify for one of these programs, depending on the particular savings program you enroll in, your Part B premiums are paid for you, or your premiums, deductibles, and coinsurance are paid. Your state may also have its own program to help you pay your Medicare premiums and maybe your deductibles and coinsurance, too. For more information about these programs, call Medicare at 1-800-633-4227.

Medicaid is another option for reining in the costs of Medicare, assuming your financial resources are very limited. Call your State Health Insurance Assistance Program to find out if you're eligible for Medicaid. You can find more information on the program in Chapter 13.

Filing Medicare claims

If you're enrolled in the original Medicare plan, the providers and suppliers you use submit claims for reimbursement to the appropriate insurance company. In other words, you don't have to file any claims yourself. However, if the providers and suppliers accept Medicare assignment, they will charge you for any coinsurance payments or deductibles you may owe. If they don't accept assignment, they may require that you pay the full amount of your medical bill and then Medicare will reimburse you. However, the providers and suppliers will still file the claims on your behalf.

Your medical provider may decide not to submit a claim to Medicare if it believes that the service it provided will not be covered; however, you can request that it file a claim regardless. If Medicare refuses to pay, you can appeal. The appeals process is described in the next section of this chapter.

When you use Part B of the program (see the section "Medicare Part B" for details), your medical provider usually submits a Medicare claim to the appropriate insurance company if it takes on assignment. Medicare pays you 80 percent of the approved amount after subtracting any part of the deductible you've not already met. Your medical provider can charge you for that amount plus your coinsurance payment — the remaining 20 percent of the approved amount; otherwise, you're responsible for paying the full amount of your bill and for submitting your own claim to Medicare.

After your Part B claim has been filed, you're notified of its status via a notice called an *Explanation of Medicare Part B Benefits*. This notice tells you what your co-payment is and how much Medicare is paying. It also gives you a toll-free number for getting in touch with the insurance company that processed your claim if you have any questions.

If you receive your Medicare benefits through the Medicare Advantage program, you don't have to file any claims. That's because Medicare pays such plans a set amount of money each month to provide medical services to their plan participants rather than operating on a fee-for-service basis.

What to do if your Medicare claim is denied

If your Medicare claim is denied, if the amount of your reimbursement is less than what you think is fair, or if you're refused the medical care or service you believe that you need, you can appeal Medicare's decision. You have this right whether you're enrolled in the original Medicare program or in the Medicare Advantage program.

If you're enrolled in the original Medicare plan, information about how to appeal accompanies each Summary Notice related to a service or product you received from Medicare. Follow the instructions for appealing. Be sure, however, that you file your appeal within 120 days of the notice related to whatever it is you're unhappy about.

If you are unsatisfied with the outcome of your appeal and the issue you appealed meets certain criteria, you can ask to have your problem decided by an administrative law judge. You may also be eligible to sue in federal district court.

The Medicare appeals process is cumbersome, slow, and inadequate. Take heart, however. If you can wait for the wheels of government justice to turn, ever so slowly, and especially if you can get your doctor actively involved in your appeal, your chances of winning are good.

While your appeal is being processed, you're liable for the medical bills relating to it.

Temporary relief: Medicare's prescription drug card

Starting in 2006, Medicare will provide prescription drug coverage. Until then however, Medicare-eligible seniors can reduce their out-of-pocket drug costs by using the new drug card authorized by the Medicare Prescription Drug Improvement and Modernization Act of 2003. The card entitles these seniors to discounts on most brand name prescription and generic drugs. Eligible seniors include individuals who are at least 65 and who are already enrolled in Medicare. Also, some drug companies offer their own Medicare-approved discount cards just for their own drugs.

If you're already receiving prescription drugs through Medicaid or through another prescription drug program that is Medicare-funded, you're not eligible for Medicare's drug card.

If you are eligible for the prescription drug card, you must choose which Medicare-approved drug card you want by going to www.medicare.gov or by calling 1-800-633-4227. Insurance companies, pharmacies, and other groups are offering a confusing array of drug cards. To help you determine if any of the cards meets your needs, ask the following questions:

- ✔ Which card offers the drugs you need at a discount?
- ✔ How much can you save?
- ✔ Are the savings greater than any other discounts you already receive?
- ✔ Can any of the cards be used at a pharmacy near you? (Some drug cards can only be used at certain pharmacies.)

Even after doing your research and finding answers to these questions, you may not find a card that's right for you.

Although some of the cards are free others cost as much as $30 annually. However, you're entitled to a free drug card if you're poor or disabled and have no drug coverage. In addition, Medicare will pay you $600 per year to help defray the costs of your prescription drugs.

Prior to contacting Medicare or visiting its Web site to learn about your prescription drug card options, make a list of all of your prescription drugs.

After you choose a prescription drug card, you're not allowed to change to a different card if you become unhappy with the one you selected. Also, the companies that sponsor the cards can change the list of drugs they cover and the prices they charge for those drugs at any time. In other words, it's possible that before the prescription drug card program ends and Medicare's drug coverage begins in 2006, your card may not provide you with discounts on the drugs you need.

Be sure that the card you purchase has the official Medicare-approved symbol on it. Some unscrupulous businesses may try to sell you a card that looks like it's legit, but is not part of the program.

Purchasing Medigap insurance

Because the original Medicare program does not cover so many essential medical services (see the sections "Medicare Part A" and "Medicare Part B" for information), those with the financial resources to do so often purchase Medicare supplemental insurance or *Medigap* insurance. You don't need this kind of insurance if you're in a Medicare managed care plan, and in fact, it may be illegal for an insurance company to sell you Medigap insurance if it's aware that you're enrolled in such a plan. Also, you do not need Medigap insurance if you're enrolled in the Medicaid program, and you probably don't need it if you're a retired federal employee or if you receive insurance coverage through your union or former employer (because their plans probably provide supplemental coverage). Check with your plan administrator to make sure you're covered.

The best time to buy this extra insurance coverage is during your Medigap open enrollment period, which occurs during the first six months that you're 65 or over and enrolled in Medicare Part B. During this period, you can't be turned down for Medigap insurance because of any health problems you may have, nor may a Medigap insurer place special conditions on your policy or increase the cost of your insurance because of your health or claims history. This open enrollment period is a one-time opportunity — use it or lose it!

If you have a pre-existing condition, no matter when you buy Medigap insurance, an insurer can impose a waiting period of up to six months before coverage of that condition kicks in.

Federal law has established ten standardized Medigap plans — Plans A-J. Each of these plans differs from the others in terms of its coverage and cost, with Plan J being the most comprehensive and the most expensive. Insurance companies that sell Medigap policies must adhere to the coverage standards for each of the ten plans. However, they can set their own prices for each plan. When you're shopping for a Medigap policy, take into consideration the kinds of supplemental coverage you need and how much you can afford to spend. You should also take into account the quality of the service each insurance company offers, the particular conditions they place on pre-existing health problems, what sort of renewal guarantee they offer, and the strength and reliability of the insurance company.

Some businesses prey on seniors who are in the market for a Medigap policy, so be sure that both the insurance agent who sells you a policy and the insurance company that offers the policy are licensed to sell Medigap insurance. Verify that the front of the policy you purchase says "Medicare Supplement Insurance" — those words are required by law. If you don't see this phrase, it's not a Medigap policy. If you think that you've been scammed, contact your state insurance office. You may also want to contact a consumer law attorney. A good resource for locating an attorney who can help you with this problem is the National Association of Consumer Advocates (NACA). Contact NACA by calling 202-452-1989.

Federal and state laws regulate the sale of Medigap insurance. Insurance companies and agents who violate these laws may be subject to criminal and/or civil penalties.

If your doctor offers you a *retainer agreement* that provides you with certain non-Medicare-covered services and that waives your Medicare coinsurance and deductible payments, beware. The agreement may violate federal Medigap laws. Also, if a doctor refuses to see you as a Medicare patient unless you pay him or her an annual fee and sign a retainer agreement, report the doctor to your State Department of Health. You can also report the doctor to the federal government by calling 1-800-638-6833.

Although Medigap can certainly help you pay your medical bills, it doesn't take care of everything. For example, Medigap insurance does not pay for long-term care; you need to purchase yet more insurance for that. Also, if Medicare refuses to pay the costs of a medical service or item because it's "unreasonable and unnecessary," your Medigap insurance probably won't pay for it either.

If you're participating in the Medicare Advantage program, you may not need to purchase Medigap insurance. Many of the companies that offer Medicare coverage through this program also provide many of the services not covered by Medicare for little or no extra cost.

For additional information about Medigap insurance and your policy options, read Medicare's *Choosing a Medigap Policy: A Guide To Health Insurance For People With Medicare.* You can read this publication online at `www.medicare.gov/Publications/Pubs/pdf/02110.pdf`, or you can order it by calling 1-800-633-4227. You can also get your Medigap insurance questions answered by calling this same number and speaking with a Medicare customer representative or by calling your State Health Insurance Assistance program.

Nursing Home Care

As the elderly population grows, the private sector's involvement in providing nursing home care also grows — today, about 65 percent of all nursing homes are privately owned. The nursing home industry has become a big and profitable business fueled in part by the fact that the federal and state governments pay about 70 percent of the bills and demand relatively little in return from nursing home providers. As a result, the quality of care being provided by nursing homes in the United States ranges widely, from excellent to abysmal.

The sooner you begin planning for the possibility of nursing home care, the better chance you have of locating a good facility. Too often people end up selecting a nursing home in the middle of a medical crisis when they may have little or no time to comparison-shop. Furthermore, if you wait to look for a good nursing home until you need one, you may find that no beds are available in the better facilities. You may have avoided this problem by looking around earlier and putting your name on the waiting lists of the nursing homes you were interested in.

When looking for a nursing home that provides quality care, you can do the following:

- ✔ **Contact the U.S. Administration on Aging (AOA).** Among other things, this office maintains an online Eldercare Locator service that links you up with information and referral services in your state as well as with the Agency on Aging in your area. You can call the Eldercare Locator directly at 1-800-677-1116, visit its Web site at `www.aoa.dhhs.gov`, or call the AOA at 202-619-0724.

- ✔ **Contact your state's long-term care ombudsman.** If he or she is unwilling to come right out and say which homes are especially good, you may at least be steered away from the really bad ones you may be considering with phrases like "There are better ones," or "We've gotten a few complaints about them recently," or "I wouldn't want my mother there." You can obtain the number for the Ombudsman program by calling your local or state Agency on Aging, by visiting the Web site of the National Long Term Care Ombudsman Resource Center at `www.ltcombudsman.org`, or by calling the Resource Center at 202-332-2275.

✔ **Shop around by visiting some nursing homes in your area.** Make a couple of unannounced visits at different periods of the day, and keep your eyes open. If possible, stay for at least an hour so that you begin to blend into the woodwork, and just observe.

✔ **Ask to see a home's *Statement of Deficiencies and Plan of Correction* from its most recent state or federal inspection.** The report should be on file at the nursing home, and you have a legal right to look at it. Don't expect a perfect report, but you may want to eliminate a home from your list if it was cited for some serious problems that could affect your health, safety, or quality of life, and if it appears as though the problems have not been corrected.

✔ **Pay careful attention to the physical appearance as well as the ambiance of the nursing home.** Is it clean, well-lit, well-maintained, and attractively decorated? Does it smell bad? Are television sets blaring? Is it too cold or too hot? Do people seem friendly? Is there laughter?

✔ **Take note of the residents.** Are they clean, neatly dressed, and is their hair combed? Are residents interacting positively with one another and with the staff?

✔ **Evaluate the safety and availability of exits.** Are the exits in the home clearly marked? Are there unobstructed paths to the exits?

✔ **Eat the food if possible.**

✔ **Find out what kind of regularly scheduled activities are available for residents.** Are daily activities offered? Are there regular outings for ambulatory residents as well as opportunities for them to attend religious services?

✔ **Ask for a copy of the contract residents have to sign and read it carefully.** Sometimes it's called a *financial* or *admissions agreement.* It should clearly state all costs and services the nursing home provides as well as the facility's legal responsibilities.

It's illegal for nursing homes to use *duration of stay* contracts. These contracts require residents to continue paying out of their own funds even if they've used up all of their personal resources and have become eligible for Medicaid.

Avoid contracts that let a nursing home off the hook with waivers of responsibility for a resident's lost possessions, injury at the home, and so on. Also avoid those that include clauses giving the home blanket approval for certain treatments. Both types of clauses are illegal.

✔ **Talk with the staff.** Are they friendly and courteous?

✔ **Talk with residents and with their family members if possible.**

✔ **Investigate the nursing home's compliance history.** For this information, contact your state's Department of Health or whatever agency is responsible for licensing nursing homes in your area.

> ✔ **Find out if Medicaid, Medicare, Medigap, or your long-term care insurance will pay for any of your care.**
>
> ✔ **Ask how many full time doctors, nurses, and staff work at the nursing home each day.** Avoid nursing homes that employ a lot of part time staff. They may not be able to provide residents with consistent day-to-day care, and a part-time staff has less opportunity to get to know residents.

All nursing homes must be licensed by the state in which they're located and must meet certain state standards. Homes participating in the Medicare and Medicaid programs must also meet federal standards and must comply with the Nursing Home Reform Act (which is covered in the next section).

The increase in the number of elderly has helped create a new profession — *geriatric care managers.* For a fee, these professionals assess an older person's needs and even arrange necessary care. Although many geriatric care managers provide invaluable help to older people and their families, the profession is unregulated. So, shop carefully for a geriatric care manager, check all references, and get all agreements in writing.

If you plan to place an elderly loved one in a nursing home, try to find one located relatively close to where you live or work. You can visit often and make certain that your loved one is being treated well and receiving the appropriate care. Being vigilant is particularly important if Medicaid is helping to pay for your loved one's nursing home care because studies show that, compared to private care patients in nursing homes, patients who rely on Medicaid tend to receive lower quality services, even within the same nursing home. For example, they may reside in a special wing where they receive poorer quality food and medical care compared to residents who reside in the private pay wing of the facility.

The Nursing Home Reform Act

The federal Nursing Home Reform Act was enacted in the late 1980s to help raise the standards of nursing homes participating in the Medicare and Medicaid programs. States are required to monitor the compliance of nursing homes with this law.

States frequently drag their feet when it comes to carrying their Nursing Home Reform Act monitoring responsibilities, and the federal government has been lax in enforcing the law. To be fair, lack of sufficient resources also contributes to these enforcement problems. Making matters worse, the process for resolving problems when they are identified can take months.

Nursing home residents' bill of rights

When you enter a nursing home, you don't check your rights at the door. You're still entitled to vote, enter into contracts, marry, practice your religion, control your own health care, and more. To help underscore your rights, the Nursing Home Reform Act guarantees residents the right to

- Participate in developing an individualized plan of care for their nursing home stay
- Select their own doctors
- Have their personal preferences and needs respected
- Pursue the facility's grievance process without fear of reprisal and make recommendations for improvement
- Privacy in their medical treatments and their medical and personal records
- Be informed about their medical conditions, problems, and medications and to see their doctors as needed
- Be free of abuse and physical restraints, tranquilizers, and other mind-bending drugs, except when such treatments are doctor-ordered
- Refuse treatment and medications they do not want
- Receive their mail unopened
- Manage their own finances or have a full accounting of their finances if the nursing home is managing them
- Participate in resident councils
- Associate freely with the people and groups they choose
- Visit privately with their spouses and have family visits
- Share a room with a resident spouse and be informed in advance of any change in room or roommate

Your state may have its own laws regarding nursing homes. If so, state requirements must be at least as tough as the federal law, but some state laws are more stringent.

Despite its shortcomings, the provisions of the Nursing Home Reform Act represent an important step in the right direction. Although the list that follows is by no means a comprehensive overview of the law, it highlights some of the most important provisions:

- Sets minimum standards for nursing home construction, safety, nutrition, recreation, and medical services, among other things.
- Requires that nursing homes have a registered nurse on duty at least eight hours per day, every day of the week, and a licensed nurse on duty at all times.

✔ Requires that nursing homes be open and honest about their costs. You have a right to know the basic costs of staying at a nursing home and what services cost extra.

✔ Mandates periodic state nursing home inspections. The law requires that these inspections focus on the quality of life that the nursing home is providing its residents. So that the inspections involve more than just a review of a home's records, inspectors must also talk to and observe residents. A nursing home that doesn't pass muster can lose its license and the right to continued participation in the Medicare and Medicaid programs.

✔ Requires that nursing homes conduct an initial assessment of a new patient's needs and develop a plan of care based on that assessment. Also, if the condition of the patient changes, the nursing home must conduct a new assessment to determine if a change to the current plan of treatment is necessary.

✔ Establishes a Bill of Rights for nursing home residents. (See the sidebar, "Nursing home residents' bill of rights.")

Getting help through ombudsman programs

The Federal Older Americans Act requires all states to run an ombudsman program for residents of long-term care facilities, including nursing homes and skilled nursing facilities. You can get information about this program from your local or state Agency on Aging. You should also receive information about the ombudsman program when you move into a nursing home or skilled nursing facility.

Ombudsmen advocate for nursing home residents and investigate and try to resolve problems. They have the legal power to inspect nursing home records, talk with residents, and do what's necessary to respond to complaints. If you're shopping for a nursing home, the ombudsman in your area can also provide you with advice and guidance.

If you need an ombudsman's help but you're concerned about possible reprisals, the ombudsman must maintain your anonymity at your request.

Protecting your rights

If you're having a problem with your nursing home, try resolving it on an informal basis by bringing the problem to the attention of the person who is causing it or someone in a position to fix it, such as a nurse, nurse's aid, or doctor. Don't be confrontational or act angry. If your conversation gets you nowhere, talk with the person who supervises the problematic individual or with the administrator of the facility.

If informal methods don't work and your problem is serious enough to continue pursuing, use the facility's formal grievance process — every nursing home must have one. Another option is to talk with the home's residents' council or family council. (Most nursing homes have one or both types of councils to help deal with issues and complaints.)

You may also want to take advantage of sources of assistance outside the nursing home, including

- ✔ Your state's ombudsman program
- ✔ The agency that licenses and certifies nursing homes in your state. It may send someone out to investigate your complaint, order that the problem be corrected, and impose penalties.
- ✔ An attorney who specializes in elder law. Depending on the nature and seriousness of your problem, you may have the basis for a lawsuit.

Paying for nursing home care

At today's prices, the average annual cost of a nursing home stay is $57,500, according to a GE Financial survey. However, depending on your state and the nursing home, you could spend more than $100,000 a year! If you're not a math whiz, these averages mean the monthly cost of your nursing home care could range from nearly $5,000 to more than $8,000 per month. Ouch! Obviously, without adequate insurance, time in a nursing home can wipe out your life savings in no time, leaving little for the loved ones who survive you.

Medicare pays for relatively little of your nursing home care, which means that you may need Medicaid's help unless you have significant financial resources and/or a good long-term care policy. Even if you have the bucks to pay for your care out of your own pocket, you may eventually need Medicaid's help if your stay is long.

Medicaid cannot be of help unless your income and the value of your assets are extremely low, because it's a health insurance program for indigent people. If you're not Medicaid-eligible when you enter a nursing home, to become eligible, you have to spend most of your income and other assets paying for your care until you've become poor enough. This process is called *spending down.*

When you apply for Medicaid, don't try to hide any of your assets and income. If you do and the government discovers it, you can be denied coverage and forced to repay anything Medicaid's already paid for you; you may even be liable for civil and criminal penalties.

If you plan far enough in advance, there are legal ways to have your cake and eat it too. In other words, you can preserve much of your wealth and also become eligible for Medicaid. Although planning to become eligible for Medicaid is something you should discuss with an attorney who understands the rules of Medicaid inside and out, some of the things you can do to protect your assets include the following:

- Transferring them to others
- Placing them in an irrevocable trust
- Investing in your home

If you transfer any assets from your name within 36 months of applying for Medicaid, Medicaid will deny your application for as long as 30 months. Exactly how long your application is rejected depends on the value of the assets and the cost of the nursing home care. There are exceptions, however.

Purchasing long-term care insurance is one way to preserve your assets and pay for much of your nursing home care, but it's quite expensive. Also, the long-term care insurance industry has a history of abuse because long-term care insurance is not as well-regulated as other types of insurance: Agents have misrepresented the policies they sell, and consumers have had trouble collecting benefits and getting refunds when they cancel their policies. The industry is cleaning up its act, though. About 35 states have passed laws regulating long-term care insurance policies, so you should be able to find a number of good ones.

Don't wait until you're elderly to buy a long-term care policy. It may be unaffordable at that point.

To ensure that the long-term care policy you buy pays for the care you may need, educate yourself about possible features of such policies, work with a trusted insurance broker, and consider several different policies before selecting one. Be sure the one you choose offers broad coverage.

Need help finding a good long-term care insurance plan? Get in touch with the Eldercare Locator by visiting www.eldercare.gov or by calling 1-800-677-1116. Another resource is *Planning for Long Term Care,* published by the National Council on the Aging. The book is available at NCOA's Web site, www.ncoa.org, for $15.

Many long-term care insurance policies pay little or none of the costs of less-skilled care like assistance with daily living. Shop for a policy that provides the broadest possible coverage.

There are other ways to pay for nursing home care besides long-term care insurance and Medicaid. They include a *viatical settlement* and a *reverse mortgage.* Viatical settlement companies purchase your life insurance policy for a lump sum and continue paying on the policy until your death. Although viaticals have been used traditionally to help finance the cost of AIDS treatments, they're now being used to help finance the cost of long-term stays in nursing homes because of Alzheimer's. (You can find an explanation of how viaticals work in Chapter 16.) The other option, a reverse mortgage, gives people who are at least 62 the opportunity to convert the equity in their home into a source of monthly income. The downside is that, as a result, someone with a reverse mortgage ends up with less and less equity in his home over time, and if he lives long enough, he may have no equity left at all when he dies. In that case, the bank owns 100 percent of his home.

Home Health Care

Home health care services can often help you avoid or delay nursing home care. Depending on the agency you work with, you can receive basic medical care or skilled nursing care, assistance with dressing, and even house cleaning and shopping.

Although technically they are regulated, the federal standards that apply to home health care agencies are pretty minimal, and especially if these agencies are not Medicare-certified, they operate with little government oversight. Given that their services are provided behind closed doors, older people using home health care agencies can be easily victimized. This isn't to say that there aren't good home health care agencies, but before hiring one, you should thoroughly check it out. To locate a reputable agency, get referrals from your doctor, other elderly people, your local or state Agency on Aging, or a social worker at a senior center. After you have some names, ask the following questions:

- ✔ **Are you licensed?** Most states require licensing, although a license doesn't guarantee quality care.

- ✔ **Are you accredited?** The Community Health Accreditation Program (www.chapinc.org; 1-800-669-9656), the Joint Commission on Accreditation of Healthcare Organizations (www.jcaho.org; 630-792-5000), the Accreditation Commission for Health Care, Inc.

(www.achc.org; 919-785-1214), and Home Care University
(www.nahc.org/HCU/home.html; 202-547-3576) all provide
accreditation.

✔ **How long have you been in business?**

✔ **Will Medicare, Medicaid, or my private insurance provider pay for
your services?** Find out exactly what they do and don't cover.

✔ **Will you provide me with written information about the services you
offer and their costs, together with your billing procedures?**

✔ **What are your charges?** Get estimates for the costs of a medical professional's and nonprofessional's time and for drugs, equipment, and
supplies.

✔ **Do you prepare a written plan of care for each of your patients? Do
you involve your patients and their caregivers in the development of
such plans? Do you educate them about how the plan will be implemented?**

✔ **Will your agency provide services day or night depending on what my
doctor requires?**

✔ **Are you bonded?** Bonding is required in some states. If you sue a
bonded agency and win, you stand a better chance of seeing some
money.

✔ **Are your nurses, dietitians, therapists, and so on licensed or certified?
How much training do your nonprofessionals have?**

✔ **How often will your supervisor visit my home?**

✔ **Whom do I contact if there's a problem?** The agency should have a
number that you can call 24 hours a day, seven days a week.

✔ **Do your caregivers work directly for your agency? Do you run background checks on them?**

✔ **Will you provide me with references from other patients or caregivers
who have used your agency?**

Around-the-clock home health care can cost twice as much as a nursing
home, and in most instances, Medicare doesn't help pay that cost.

Get in touch with the National Association for Home Care & Hospice (www.
nahc.org; 202-547-7424) or the National Council on the Aging (www.ncoa.
org; 202-479-1200) for information on how to choose a home health care
agency and for a list of such agencies in your area.

Other Residential Options for Seniors

An increasing number of living options are available to seniors who can't or don't want to continue living in their own homes. Depending on the status of your health, your personal preferences, and the size of your pocketbook, one of these other residential options may be of interest to you.

- ✔ **Residential care homes:** Also referred to as *group homes* or *board and care homes,* these residences provide a small number of seniors with a place to live in a home-like setting. Residents receive meals and care at these homes from live-in caregivers. Although residential care homes are not medical facilities, residents typically are provided assistance with day-to-day tasks such as dressing and taking medication, and their housekeeping and laundry are taken care of. Some group homes may also provide more specialized care and services. Not all states license these types of homes, and in states where they're licensed, many receive relatively little monitoring by the state. Therefore, it's important to choose a residential care home carefully and pay frequent unannounced visits to the home if you have a loved one staying in such a facility.

- ✔ **Assisted living residences:** These residences provide a place to live for seniors who need assistance with day-to-day activities but don't need 24-hour nursing care. Such facilities are usually larger and more institutional than residential care homes. Many of them offer residents their own apartments with small kitchens, but assisted living residences usually also offer a common dining room as well as activities, transportation, housekeeping services, and assistance with dressing and medications as needed. They may offer limited nursing supervision.

- ✔ **Retirement communities:** These communities are for active seniors with minimal health problems who want to live among other people their own age. The communities may offer a wide range of activities and services, including meals, transportation, excursions, and housekeeping assistance.

- ✔ **Continuing care retirement communities:** These communities offer a range of living options on a single "campus," including residential units for older people who are still healthy and active, assisted living, and nursing home care. Some even offer special accommodations for Alzheimer's patients. As your needs change, you can transition from one living arrangement to another without moving far from your spouse or friends. You have to pay a one-time fee to live in a continuing care retirement community, the amount of which ranges widely from a low of about $20,000 to a high of as much as $300,000! Plus, you're responsible for a monthly fee. Often a continuing care retirement community offers several different types of contractual arrangements.

If you're interested in learning more about the rights of older people, I recommend you check out the SeniorLaw Home Page, located at www.seniorlaw.com. It helps you access information about elder law, Medicare, Medicaid, estate planning, and more. If you're interested in information on issues related to aging, including getting help and support, dementia, Alzheimer's, and senior housing and residential care, this noncommercial Web site is for you.

Chapter 15

Estate Planning

*E*state planning. Isn't that just for rich people or really old people? No. It's for anyone, old or young, who owns property — a home, vehicles, retirement benefits, stocks, bonds, mutual funds, life insurance, and so on — and cares about who will get it when he or she dies.

Estate planning is for people who work hard for what they own, who want to protect their assets while they're alive, and who want to be sure that, when they die, after-death expenses like probate costs, creditor claims, legal fees, and taxes won't eat up their estate and leave next to nothing for the people they care about.

Estate planning is for business owners who need to plan what will happen to their business or business interests after they die. It's for parents with young children who want to choose the person who will raise their children if they both die.

Estate planning is also for anyone who wants to help ensure that if they're near death with no hope of recovery, their estate will not be depleted by unwanted and expensive life-sustaining measures.

You can find a wealth of information about all aspects of estate planning by going to go the FINDLaw Web site, www.findlaw.com, and clicking on "Estate Planning." Among other things, you can read helpful articles and FAQs, download forms, and link up with other estate planning resources on the Web.

What Does Estate Planning Involve and How Do I Do It?

Planning your estate involves preserving and protecting your assets while you're alive with adequate insurance, durable powers of attorney, and a living will. (I cover all of these terms later in the chapter.) It also involves planning for your death by taking inventory of and valuing the property you own, deciding who you want to have your property after you die, and at a minimum, writing a will. Depending on the size and complexity of your estate (which simply encompasses all of the property you own), estate planning can include (in addition to a will) the use of *inter vivos* gifts, testamentary and living trusts, beneficiary designations, joint ownership, and other legal mechanisms for conveying your property to others. You should also reduce the number of assets in your estate that have to go through the probate process because that process will reduce the value of your estate. If your estate is worth so much that it will have to pay federal estate taxes at your death, to properly plan your estate and preserve your assets, you need to make strategic decisions about how to minimize your estate's federal tax liability.

If you die without having prepared an estate plan, you will have died *intestate*. Therefore, the laws of your state determine who receives your assets.

Set up a *living trust* if you want to be able to place conditions and controls on when your estate planning beneficiaries can receive the assets that you leave to them and what they can do with those assets. You have no control over such things if your estate plan is based on a will. For example, your spouse goes through money like water, and you're afraid that if you die first and leave your spouse everything you own in your will, he will use up his inheritance and eventually may not have anything left. If you want to base your estate plan on a living trust, work with an estate planning attorney who has a lot of living trust experience.

The Importance of an Estate Planning Attorney

Complex federal and state laws govern much of estate planning, making it a potentially complicated undertaking for all but the smallest, simplest estates. Unless you know the rules and are familiar with the range of estate planning tools you can use, you may not accomplish what you intended, waste money, and create legal and financial headaches for the people you leave behind. So when it comes to estate planning, my advice is this: Call an estate planning attorney.

The help of an estate planning attorney can be particularly valuable if you have a small to modest estate. When your assets are limited, it's especially important to plan your estate correctly because even minor expenses can have a relatively larger negative impact on the value of your estate than if your estate were substantial.

Even if you're confident about your estate planning knowledge and know-how, it's a good idea to meet with an estate planning attorney before you begin preparing your plan. The attorney can provide the following services:

- ✔ Reassure you that you're on the right track with your estate plan or suggest a better approach. For example, the attorney may recommend that you and your spouse set up living trusts rather than create will-based estate plans.

- ✔ Familiarize you with the estate planning laws you need to know about and tell you how to address them through your plan.

- ✔ Suggest ways you can reduce your estate planning expenses with helpful hints about how to limit your probate costs or avoid probate all together, and how to minimize your federal estate taxes and your state's estate taxes as well, if your state imposes such a tax.

- ✔ Point out issues and concerns you may not have considered.

- ✔ Warn you about potential problems you may need your estate plan to address. For example, if your estate is worth a lot, you can use your estate plan to reduce the amount of federal taxes your estate will owe after your death, and if your spouse is a spendthrift, your plan can prevent him or her from having unrestricted access to the assets you want him or her to have if you die first.

Many people procrastinate writing a will. Hiring an estate attorney to do it for you means that you'll actually have one! Expect to pay $250 to $1,200 for a simple will — one that does not include a testamentary trust — and possibly more depending on where you live. For example, attorneys in large urban areas tend to charge more than those located in rural areas.

Before I get into some of the specifics of estate planning, here's a final note about estate planning in general: Always think of it as a "work in progress." Your estate planning needs will evolve over time as your wealth grows and as the circumstances in your life change. For example, you have another child; your wife becomes incapacitated; you become estranged from one of your children; you have grandchildren; and so on. In fact, it's a good idea to review your estate plan annually. Another reason to review your estate plan regularly is to make sure that it continues to reflect your wishes.

Starting with a Will

According to *Consumer Reports,* an estimated 66 percent of all Americans do not have a legally valid will! Yet writing one is the single most important thing most people can do to control who will get their property after they die. The cornerstone of all estate planning, a will gives you a voice after death.

Specifically, a will lets you name your beneficiaries and specify exactly what you're giving to each person. Married couples often leave most of their property to one another, but you can also designate as your beneficiaries your children, other family members, your unmarried partner, favorite charities, your college alma mater, or whomever. It's your call.

You also name an estate *executor* in your will; this is the person who shepherds your estate through the probate process, including paying your creditors and distributing your assets to your beneficiaries. (See "Going through the probate process" later in this chapter if you're unfamiliar with the term *probate.*) And you can use your will to designate personal and property guardians for your minor children. In fact, in some states, the only way you can legally designate a personal guardian for a young child is by naming that person in your will.

The perils of dying without a will (apart from being dead)

Knowing what can happen if you die without a will, which is called dying *intestate,* helps underscore the importance of having one. What follows are some examples of the kinds of problems you may unwittingly create by dying intestate.

- ✔ **Your state probate court decides who will inherit your property.** The court distributes it to your legal heirs based on the laws of your state. As a result, your spouse may not get all of the property you intended that he or she have when you died, and people you don't like or don't even know — your long-lost cousin Johnny whom you haven't seen since you were both 2 years old — may end up with some of what you own. The court gives nothing to your close friends or favorite charities. If you live with someone in an unmarried relationship, your partner will receive none of your estate unless your family decides to share some of it with him or her.

Your *heirs* are the relatives who are legally entitled to inherit from you. Your *beneficiaries* are the people you choose to leave your property to; they may or may not be your heirs.

✔ **Your heirs won't be able to sell or borrow against your assets (real estate, stocks, vehicles, and so on) without first initiating the legal processes necessary to have ownership transferred to them.** These processes may be time-consuming and costly. Here's a real-life example: After you die, your spouse needs to cash in some stock to help pay for some unexpected expenses. But because you never transferred ownership of the stock to your spouse, you still own it even though you're dead! Your spouse can't sell the stock until the ownership is legally transferred, even if he or she needs money right away.

To really drive this point home, here's another example: You and your unmarried partner shared a home for many years. Although you always thought of your home as belonging to both of you, only your name is on the title. Because you died without a will, your partner has no legal claim to the home and therefore will probably lose the home.

✔ **Unless one of your legal heirs offers to act as executor of your estate and that person is approved by your area's probate court, the court, not you, will appoint an administrator to serve in that role.** The administrator is paid for his or her services by your estate, leaving less for your heirs.

✔ **If you leave minor children behind without another parent, the children may end up being raised by someone you don't like or who doesn't share your values — even by someone you don't know — if no relative or close friend offers to raise them.**

✔ **If your minor children inherit from your estate and if the value of their inheritance exceeds the amount your state allows a minor to own without active adult supervision, the court will appoint a property guardian to manage the inheritance until the children reach age 18 (or age 21 in some states).** The cost of the property guardian's services is deducted from your children's inheritance.

Making a will legal

Every state has its own laws regarding what makes a will legally valid. If your will doesn't meet your state's standards, it may be dead on arrival in probate court because it isn't recognized as a legal will. Here are some of the requirements you may have to meet to make your will legally valid:

✔ You must be a legal adult — at least 18 years old in most states — when you write your will or when your attorney prepares it for you.

✔ You must be "of sound mind," which means that you must understand what you're doing. You understand your relationships to the people in your will; you know the nature of the property you own; you realize the significance of a will.

> ✔ You must be preparing your will because you want to, not because anyone is forcing you to or threatening you if you don't.
>
> ✔ Your will must be written, signed by you, dated, and witnessed, usually by two people.

Giving away property

As important as a will is, you can only use it to give away certain kinds of property: property that you own by yourself and your share of property that you own with others as a *tenant in common.*

The list of property that you *can't* give away in your will is a lot longer. It includes the following:

> ✔ **Property you own as a *joint tenant with the right of survivorship.*** This property often includes real estate, stocks, bonds, and bank accounts. When you own property as a joint tenant, your co-owners automatically get your share when you die even if you leave your share to someone else in your will. Married couples often decide to own property as joint tenants.
>
> Joint tenancy can be a useful estate planning tool for unmarried partners because it allows each unmarried partner to automatically gain full control of the property they own together when one partner dies.
>
> ✔ **Property you own as a *tenant by the entirety.*** Only husbands and wives can own property in this way. When one spouse dies, the other automatically gets the other's share. Only about half the states recognize tenancy by the entirety as a legal form of ownership, and of those that do, many limit the type of assets that can be owned in this way.
>
> ✔ **Proceeds from life insurance policies, IRAs, pensions, and so on.** If you own any of these assets, you've already designated the people who will receive these benefits when you die.
>
> ✔ **Your spouse's share of your community property.** If you live in a community property state, you only own 50 percent of the value of your marital property. You can find more information on this type of ownership in Chapter 4.
>
> ✔ **Property you've already given away as an *inter vivos* gift.** This refers to gifts you make while you're still alive.
>
> ✔ **Property placed in a trust.**

After you die, your will must be probated before your beneficiaries can receive the property you've given to them. The probate process is explained later in this chapter. Property that you don't give away in your will doesn't get probated and goes directly to your beneficiaries.

Thinking about who gets what

If there's anything fun about writing a will, it's choosing your beneficiaries and deciding what you want to give to each of them. Although an estate attorney can fill you in on all the technical details of gift giving with a will, this section explains a few of the basic things you should know.

Giving to your spouse

If you live in a community property state, you own half of your marital property, and your spouse owns the other half, unless you have a prenuptial contract that says otherwise. (See Chapter 4 for details on community property states.) You must say so in your will if you want your spouse to own your half after you die.

Shared or joint wills can create legal problems for the surviving spouse. If you're married, you each need your own will.

Separate property states have laws that prevent one spouse from disinheriting the other. These laws say that when you die, your spouse is entitled to a minimum share of your estate — the *elective share*. Although states can calculate this share differently, most allow a surviving spouse to take a fixed percentage of the dead spouse's property. Some include just the property in the deceased's will; others include everything the dead spouse owned. Regardless of the specifics, if you leave your spouse less than your state's minimum, your spouse can "take against your will" and opt for the elective share.

If you divorce after you've written a will, the provisions in your will relating to your spouse may be automatically canceled.

You can leave your surviving spouse as much property as you want, free of estate taxes because of the *unlimited marital tax deduction*. Consult with an estate attorney before using this deduction. Without adequate planning, it's possible to create future tax problems for your spouse.

To help your surviving spouse and minor children take care of their financial needs while your will is being probated, most states provide for a family allowance. The *family allowance* is essentially an advance on what your family will receive after the probate process has been completed. Each state has a different way of calculating the amount of this allowance.

All wills are not created equal

A typed or word-processed will that complies with the laws of your state is always your safest legal choice. Here are some other types of wills that may or may not be valid:

✔ **Hand-written will:** This type of will may not be legally valid in your state.

✔ **Fill-in-the-blanks will:** If you don't own very much and your estate planning goals are extremely simple, this kind of will may meet your needs. Before using one, however, be sure it meets your state's legal requirements. Fill-in-the-blanks wills can either be preprinted forms that you may purchase at an office supply store or produced using computer software.

✔ **Oral will:** If you're "on your death bed" and it occurs to you that you never wrote a will, your state may accept an oral rather than a written will. Your state may place limits on the dollar amount that you can transfer to others through an oral will, or it may require that your words be put in writing within a certain period of time.

✔ **Video will:** Although a video of you reading your will won't substitute for a written will, it may help prove that you were of sound mind when you prepared the written version. This kind of proof can be helpful if, after you die, one or more of your heirs or beneficiaries comes forward to contest the validity of your will.

Giving to young children

No matter what state you live in, if you give your minor child property worth more than a certain amount — in the $2,500 to $5,000 range in most states — you must designate in your will an adult to be legally responsible for managing the property until your child turns 18 or 21, depending on your state. This person is a *property guardian.*

Although leaving property to your minor children in your will is easy and inexpensive to do, it has some disadvantages. First, your minor child's property guardian has to prepare periodic reports for your state so that it can monitor exactly how the guardian is managing your child's property. Your state also expects the guardian to take an extremely conservative approach to managing your child's assets. These reporting requirements and limitations may be fine with you and even reassuring because you know that the guardian will be closely monitored. If, however, you want the value of your child's inheritance to be maximized after you die, including that property in your will is not the way to accomplish that goal. You may therefore want to consider another option like setting up a custodial account or a trust. These options are discussed later in this chapter in the section "Alternatives to a Will."

If you're leaving your minor child a substantial amount of property, another drawback of using your will is that when your child turns 18 — or 21 in some states — the property guardian's role ends, and your child automatically gains full control of his or her inheritance. The court doesn't care if your child is not a responsible money manager, and what kid is at 18? In the eyes of the law, your child becomes a legal adult at age 18 and is entitled to the inheritance.

Giving to charity

Making gifts to IRS–approved charities can help reduce the amount of taxes your estate may have to pay after you die because such gifts are exempt from federal estate taxes. Most states also exempt them from their estate taxes.

Giving to pets

Some people want to remember their pets in their wills; however, many states prohibit leaving property to pets. So, if you want to be sure that Spot or Whiskers will be cared for after you die, you should leave property to a friend or family member with the stipulation in your will that the property be used to pay for your pet's care.

Appointing an executor

The person you name as executor of your estate will serve as its legal representative during the probate process following your death. Depending on the skills and knowledge of the person you choose for the job and the complexity of your estate, your executor may need the help of an estate attorney during the probate process. Your estate pays the cost of this legal help unless you make other provisions.

If you're like most people, you will probably ask a trusted family member or close friend to be your executor. If you don't feel that anyone in your life is up to the job, or if your estate is especially complicated, a professional executor, usually an attorney or a bank, can be your best bet.

Executors are entitled to be paid a fee for their services, an expense that your estate covers. Most friends and family members who serve as executors waive this fee, but a professional won't be so generous. Be forewarned: The professional's services won't come cheap!

Be sure to specify in your will whether or not you want your executor to receive a fee; otherwise, most states automatically provide for payment, usually calculating the executor's fee as a percentage of your estate's value.

Most states require that an executor be bonded, the cost of which is charged to your estate. Usually however, you can waive the bonding requirement in your will. A bond is a financial guarantee that your executor manages the assets in your estate in a responsible, ethical manner. If your executor fails to do so and one or more of your beneficiaries are harmed as a result, the bonding company will compensate your beneficiaries up to a certain amount. The cost of a bond is paid by your estate.

After you die, at a minimum, your executor will do the following:

- Locate your will.
- Inventory your assets and determine their worth.
- Pay any outstanding debts your estate may owe. Unless you've made other provisions, your executor may have to sell assets in your estate to pay your bills.
- Manage the assets in your will until the court says that they can be distributed to your beneficiaries.
- Prepare tax returns and pay estate and income taxes if necessary.
- Prepare reports and budgets for the probate court.
- Distribute the assets in your will to your beneficiaries after the probate court gives its okay.

All states give executors specific powers. If you want your executor to have other powers, or if you don't want your executor to have the usual powers, say so in your will by specifically detailing the additional powers you're giving or the powers you're taking away.

After you've written your will, take the time to review it with your executor to make sure that he or she understands everything in your will. Explain anything unusual that may appear in your will — disinheritance of a child, for example — because you won't be there to do so when you're dead. Also, tell your executor where you plan to store your will; if you store your will in a home safe or safe deposit box, give your executor the key or combination.

Going through the probate process

After you die, your will must be *probated.* In a nutshell, this legal process begins by establishing the validity of your will and ends with the distribution of the property in your will to your designated beneficiaries. Any property in your will must go through probate.

The more assets that must be probated, the longer the process takes and the more it probably costs your estate. So, you may want to minimize your probate assets by using other estate planning tools besides a will to give your property away. See the following section, "Alternatives to a Will," for details.

A will is not forever

Your will is most useful when it accurately reflects the current realities of your life; therefore, when things in your life change, it's time to amend your will. Here are a few examples of changes that may affect the terms of your will:

✔ You start a family or add to your family.

✔ You get married or divorced or become widowed.

✔ You buy or sell your home or another significant asset.

✔ One of your beneficiaries dies.

✔ You move to a new state (your will may not be valid in your new state).

You can usually amend your will simply by writing a *codicil,* which is a written statement of the change. To make it legal, the codicil should be dated, witnessed, and notarized according to the law of your state. Store all codicils with your will.

To avoid confusion, it's best to limit your codicils to two. If you need more, revoke your current will and write a new one.

Whether or not you should be concerned about probate is a subject to discuss with your estate attorney. Depending on the value of your estate and its complexity, the cost of "avoiding" probate may not be worth it.

Some states allow relatively small estates to go through a type of probate process that is quicker and cheaper than the traditional process.

Alternatives to a Will

A will is not the only way to give your property away upon your death. Some of the alternatives in this section may even do a better job of meeting your estate planning goals. Understanding your alternatives is another good reason why working with an estate attorney can be really helpful. Without talking to an estate attorney, you may never know about all of your estate planning options unless reading books on estate planning is your idea of a good way to unwind after a hard day's work!

Although I can't begin to tell you all the ins and outs of using these other tools in this chapter, I can introduce you to some of them. If any sound interesting, talk to your attorney to learn more. Remember, none of the assets you give away using these alternatives will go through probate. Some of these tools also can help you reduce the size of your taxable estate.

Insurance policies, employee benefit plans, and IRAs

Although you may think of these things as wealth-building tools, they're also estate planning tools because after you die, each of them will provide either a direct payment of cash or a regular income for a period of time to whomever you named as your beneficiary.

Inter vivos gifts

You may not want to wait until you're dead to give away your money and other property. Consider making *inter vivos gifts,* a fancy name for gift giving while you're alive. With inter vivos gifts, you gain a number of important benefits. First, you get the pleasure of giving and of watching those you give to enjoy and benefit from your gift. Second, on a much more practical note, you can use inter vivos gifts to help reduce the size of your taxable estate. In fact, if you give enough away while you're alive, you may actually reduce the value of your estate by enough that your estate won't have to pay any estate taxes to Uncle Sam.

Federal law allows you to give away every year as much as $11,000 (in cash or other assets) each to an unlimited number of people without paying federal gift taxes. If you're married, you and your spouse combined can give away up to $22,000 each year to as many people as you want, tax-free.

There's a catch to inter vivos gift giving, however. In order for your gift to be considered an inter vivos gift, it must meet certain criteria; namely, it must be a completed and irrevocable gift. In plain language, when you make the gift, you can't retain any ownership rights to it, continue to benefit from it financially, or control it in any way, and you can't take it back after you make it. So, if you give your child a share of your vacation home and you own the rest, or if you give your partner a future interest in some stock you own, you're not making an inter vivos gift.

Custodial accounts

All states have adopted some form of the Uniform Gifts to Minors Act or the Uniform Transfers to Minors Act. Depending on what form of these acts your state has adopted, you may be able to give inter vivos gifts of money, securities, insurance policies, and annuities as well as real and tangible property to your minor child by placing the assets in a *custodial account* that you set up at a bank or brokerage house. This simple and inexpensive alternative to leaving property to your minor child in your will has a number of important advantages. First, the adult you designate as account custodian to manage the account assets for your child does not face the same restrictions and reporting obligations that property guardians face (see "Giving to young children"). He or she is therefore more free to maximize the value of the custodial account assets. Second, when you place property in one of these accounts, you gain the tax benefits of an inter vivos gift. Third, depending on your state, you may be able to stipulate that your child not receive the assets in the account until he or she is 25 and presumably more financially mature than he or she will be at 18 or even 21.

If you're leaving property to more than one minor child, you have to set up a separate custodial account for each child. However, you can name the same account custodian for each one.

Trusts

Depending on the value of your estate and your estate planning goals, a *trust* can be a great alternative to using your will to give away property. When you set up a trust, you create a new legal entity to hold assets for the trust's beneficiaries. To create the trust, you prepare a trust agreement. At a minimum, the agreement should indicate the following:

- ✔ The purpose of the trust
- ✔ The names of its beneficiary or beneficiaries
- ✔ The name of its trustee and substitute trustee
- ✔ The trustee's rights and responsibilities
- ✔ Your desires regarding how you want the trustee to invest the trust assets
- ✔ Whether the trustee can use the trust assets as loan collateral, sell the assets, give them to the trust beneficiaries, and so on
- ✔ When and under what conditions you want the trustee to disperse income from the trust to the trust's beneficiaries
- ✔ What the trust income can be used for
- ✔ When or if the trustee should give full control of the trust assets to its beneficiaries

A trust is a very complicated legal entity. Don't try to set one up without the help of an estate attorney! Two basic kinds of trusts are available: *testamentary* trusts and *living* trusts. Each has its own pros and cons, which are outlined in the sections that follow.

Why you still need a will if you have a trust

As wonderful a legal invention as a trust is, it does not substitute for a will. The following are four important reasons why you still need a will:

✔ To name a personal guardian for your minor child. In some states, writing a will is the only way you can do this.

✔ To designate a property guardian for your minor child.

✔ To convey property you may acquire after you set up a trust, assuming you don't amend the trust to include the new property.

✔ To transfer property that you may have forgotten to place in your trust.

If someone tries to sell you a living trust, check out the salesperson or company very carefully. Bogus salespeople and companies may try to scare you into purchasing a trust or claim that it's a panacea for all your estate planning needs. Also, steer clear of anyone who tries to sell you a fill-in-the-blanks living trust. If you want a living trust, your best bet is to work with a reputable estate attorney who will create a trust that meets your particular needs.

Trusts are popular for many good reasons, especially because they're the most flexible of all estate planning tools. You can set one up to do just about anything as long as it's legal. No other estate planning tool gives you as much control over the terms of your gifts. For example, you can decide if and when the beneficiaries of your trust will receive income from it and when — if ever — a beneficiary can take possession of the trust assets. You're the boss!

To help illustrate these advantages, here are some examples of why you may set up a trust:

✔ If you and your spouse were to die, your minor children will end up inheriting a considerable amount of property. You don't want them to automatically take possession of that property when they turn 18 or 21 as they would if you left them the same property in your will (or in a custodial account, depending on your state), nor do you want a property guardian to manage your children's inheritance.

✔ Your husband is a poor money manager, and you're concerned that if you were to die first, he would quickly squander the property he will inherit from you.

✔ Your child is profoundly handicapped and unable to earn a living. You want to ensure that after you die, your child's financial needs will be taken care of without jeopardizing any public assistance he or she may be receiving.

✔ You're seriously ill, and although death is not imminent, you know that at some point, you will no longer be able to manage your own financial affairs. You therefore establish a trust naming yourself both trustee and beneficiary and also designating a co-trustee. While you're still able, you will manage the trust assets, and when you become too ill, the co-trustee will take over management of the trust property according to the directions you spell out in the trust agreement.

✔ You've just remarried. Although you want to leave most of your property to your new wife, you want to be sure that when she dies, certain property goes to the children from your first marriage, not to the children from her former marriage.

✔ You own a closely held business and want to do what you can to ensure that when you die, your family won't experience an interruption in the income the business provides.

✔ You want to leave all your property to your spouse and, at the same time, minimize the federal estate taxes your estate has to pay after your death without creating a future estate tax liability for your surviving spouse.

With the help of an attorney who has a lot of experience with trusts, you can set up one or more trusts to address each of these and many, many more situations.

Testamentary trust

Easy and relatively inexpensive to set up, this kind of trust is actually part of your will. While you're alive, a testamentary trust exists only on paper. After you die, however, the trust is activated, and after the assets you've earmarked for it go through probate, they're placed in the trust. Because a testamentary trust does not come into existence until you die, it is always irrevocable after that point. But while you're alive, just as you can revoke or change your will, you can revoke or amend any testamentary trusts you include in your will.

Many parents use testamentary trusts to help provide for their young children. Also, people with substantial estates often use testamentary trusts to minimize their estate taxes and to help protect their property from creditor claims.

Living trust

This kind of trust takes effect while you're still alive — thus the name. Any assets you transfer to the living trust become the property of the trust. You no longer own them. However, because you can name yourself as the trust's trustee — the person who manages the assets — as well as the trust's beneficiary, while you're alive you can continue to control and benefit from the trust assets just as you did before you set up the trust and transferred the assets to it. When you die, the trust assets may be transferred into *subtrusts* — trusts that you set up for a special purpose within your living trust, like a children's trust, a marital trust, a family trust, a tax avoidance trust, and so on — or the assets may go directly to your beneficiaries. In your living trust document, you spell out exactly what you want to happen to each of the assets in your living trust upon your death.

Living trusts can be revocable or irrevocable. Most are revocable, which means that you can add or remove assets from the trust whenever you want, or you can even terminate the trust. A revocable living trust doesn't provide your estate with tax advantages or protect it from your creditors, but an irrevocable living trust does. Both kinds of living trusts avoid probate.

The cost of living trusts

Given the expenses associated with establishing a living trust, it's not a practical estate planning tool for everyone and certainly isn't appropriate if your estate is very small. For example, you have to pay an attorney at least $1,000 to help you set up a living trust, and you incur additional costs when transferring your assets into the trust. Also, the trustee of a living trust (and of a testamentary trust) is entitled to receive a fee for his or her services.

The federal estate tax: First you see it, then you don't

The *federal estate tax* is a graduated tax based on the fair market value of all of the assets in your estate at the time that you die, as well as on the cumulative value of any inter vivos gifts you may have given away.

In 2001, Congress passed the Economic Growth and Tax Relief Reconciliation Act of 2001, which mandated a series of gradual reductions in the federal estate tax as well as changes in the tax rate. For example, if you die in 2005, your estate won't be taxed unless it's worth more than $1.5 million. The tax rate on anything in excess of that amount is 47 percent. If you die between 2006 and 2008, your estate can be worth as much as $2 million before it has to pay federal estate taxes. The tax rate on any dollar in excess of that amount is 46 percent in 2006 and 45 percent in the next two years. In 2009, estates worth more than $3.5 million will be subject to the estate tax and will be taxed at a 45 percent rate, but in the following year, there will be no federal estate tax at all. Then, starting in 2011 and continuing on in subsequent years unless a new law is passed, the federal estate tax kicks in again. At that point, all estates worth more than $1 million will be subject to the tax and will be taxed at a whopping 55 percent. Leave it to Congress to make things confusing!

Assets you place in an irrevocable trust are treated as inter vivos gifts, so be sure that you don't exceed your annual $11,000-per-person gift maximum. If you do, your estate has to pay taxes on the excess amount.

Taxes (Of Course)

If your estate is worth too little to be subject to federal estate taxes, then you're lucky — your estate planning is a little simpler than if your estate is liable for those taxes. Without proper planning, federal estate taxes will take a big bite out of your estate, which means that there's less of it to go to your surviving spouse, children, your favorite charity, and any other beneficiaries you include in your estate plan. However, even if federal estate taxes are not an issue for you, you may still need to be concerned about other taxes, such as state estate taxes or income taxes for example.

If your estate doesn't pay all of the taxes it owes to Uncle Sam, the IRS will use all its tools to collect its due.

Planning for Your Incapacitation

Even if you're young and healthy, you may become temporarily or permanently incapacitated and unable to manage your own affairs, including your financial affairs and your medical care. If you don't plan for this possibility and you do become incapacitated, your family may have to petition the court to appoint a conservator to make health care decisions for you or a guardian to make financial decisions on your behalf. These legal actions can be tough on your family as well as expensive. And worst of all, the decisions of a conservator or guardian may not mirror what you would decide if you could speak on your own behalf.

Managing your financial affairs

Give a *durable power of attorney for your finances* (sometimes called a "poor man's trust") to someone you trust who also has sound financial management skills, to your attorney, or to a financial institution. You can create a durable power of attorney by completing a standard form that you can obtain at an office supply store or download off the Internet or by working with an attorney. If you use a standard form, be sure that it meets your state's requirements for a legally enforceable durable power of attorney document.

When you prepare your durable power of attorney document, you spell out exactly what powers you are or are not granting to this person. You can also specify how you want your incapacity to be determined — after consultation with your doctor or with two doctors, for example. You can cancel a durable power of attorney at any time. However, be sure you do it according to the cancellation requirements of your state.

To ensure that a power of attorney will be valid when you become incapacitated, you must set it up as a *durable* power of attorney.

To plan for the possibility of your incapacitation, you can also set up a living trust for your estate. Make yourself the beneficiary and the trustee of the trust, and name a successor trustee who can take over the management of the trust assets if you become incapacitated. In the trust agreement, specify when or under what conditions you want the successor to take over. The agreement should also spell out exactly what rights and responsibilities you are and are not giving to the trustee. For example, you may give the trustee the power to make bank deposits, pay bills, and buy and sell investments.

Making decisions about your health care

Prepare a *durable power of attorney for health care.* It works like a durable power of attorney but for health and medical care decisions when you're unable to make them for yourself due to physical or mental problems that are not life threatening. The person to whom you give a durable power of attorney for health care can also make health and medical care decisions for you when you're dying.

Don't just write down your desires for your health and medical care. Also talk about them with the person to whom you give your durable power of attorney for health care so that the person will feel comfortable carrying out this important and possibly emotionally difficult responsibility.

To cover all your health care bases, you should also write a living will. Use this legal document to spell out exactly what life-sustaining health and medical care you do and don't want when you're unable to speak for yourself. A living will not only helps you die with dignity but also helps control the costs of your care so that paying for the miracles of modern medicine and technology doesn't deplete your estate. I discuss living wills in detail in Chapter 16.

Chapter 16

Death and Dying: Doing It Gracefully

In This Chapter

▶ Living with a living will

▶ Creating a durable power of attorney

▶ Planning for your funeral expenses

▶ Euthanasia, or dying with dignity

*I*f you're like most people, death and dying are not things you enjoy talking about and certainly not things you want to plan for. Yet, as unpleasant a subject as it may be, death is something all of us will face sooner or later. Just as you should prepare for your death through proper estate planning (see Chapter 15), you should plan for your funeral, burial, or cremation and prepare health care directives such as a living will and a health care power of attorney. Tending to the details of what will happen if you become terminally ill and unable to speak for yourself is the ultimate act of love for your family and the others you care about. You can spare them from having to make difficult and possibly emotionally painful decisions in the midst of their sorrow. So even though it's hard, stop avoiding the subject and start preparing for the inevitable.

Laying It Out in a Living Will

As Chapter 15 emphasizes, if you have assets and care about who will receive them after you die, you must plan your estate, which may involve writing a will, or setting up a living trust, or doing both. Equally important are preparing health care directives such as a living will. A *living will* is a legal document that spells out the kinds of medical care and treatment you do or do not want if you become terminally ill and unable to communicate your wishes. Without such a document, your doctor may do whatever is necessary, often regardless of cost, to sustain your life for as long as possible.

The Patient Self-Determination Act

With passage of the Patient Self-Determination Act in 1990, Congress began encouraging the use of health care directives: living wills and durable powers of attorney for health care. The law says that patients admitted into any facility that receives Medicaid or Medicare funds must be given written information about health care directives upon admittance. If a patient prepares a directive, it must be stored with the patient's medical records.

You can prepare your own living will or you can hire an attorney to help you. If you write your own, be sure that it expresses your wishes clearly and without ambiguity. Also make certain that it meets the legal requirements of your state (perhaps by having an attorney review it); otherwise, it won't be enforceable when the time comes. Other ways to find out about the requirements include calling your state attorney general's office of consumer affairs, your local or state Agency on Aging, a hospital in your area, or your doctor's office. These same offices may be able to provide you with a living will form that is guaranteed to be legal in your state.

Partnership for Caring, Inc., a nonprofit organization, offers state-specific fill-in-the-blanks living wills. You can obtain a free one at www.partnershipfor caring.org, or you can purchase the form for a nominal fee by calling the organization at 1-800-989-9455. Partnership for Caring also publishes *Talking About Your Choices,* a booklet designed to help you think through the issues related to health care directives and clarify your desires. It also provides guidance for discussing your end-of-life decisions with your doctor and loved ones.

Always review your living will with your close family members, your spouse or partner, and your doctor to clarify any questions they may have so that they feel comfortable with your wishes and will respect them when the time comes. Also, be sure that a copy of your living will is a part of your doctor's medical records. And any nursing home into which you move or hospital to which you're admitted should have a copy of your living will, too.

Always review your living will with your doctor to make certain that he or she feels comfortable with your choices. If your doctor is not, find one who will support your wishes.

You can change or revoke your living will whenever you want, but you must do so according to the laws of your state and destroy all copies of the original living will to avoid confusion later. In fact, it's a good idea to review your living will on a regular basis to make certain that you continue to agree with its provisions. Also, if you move to another state, write a new living will that complies with your new state's requirements.

If you become terminally ill out of state, the state where you're being cared for may honor your living will as long as it doesn't conflict with any of the state's own laws. To be on the safe side, therefore, if you spend a lot of time in another state, prepare a living will and a durable power of attorney for health care for that state as well as your state where you legally reside. The section "Giving Someone a Durable Power of Attorney for Your Health Care," later in this chapter, explains how this document can help you.

It's easy to prepare a living will. Unfortunately, getting it activated can be more difficult sometimes. Officially, depending on the state, at least one doctor (sometimes two doctors) must certify in writing that you're terminally ill or permanently unconscious and therefore unable to make your own decisions before your living will can be activated. It won't be activated just because you're in a lot of pain or don't want to live anymore. You must be close to death.

Doctors are expected to comply with the directives in a living will if they're aware of the living will and if it is legally valid. However, they don't have to comply with a directive if it goes against their conscience, conflicts with the policy of the health care facility caring for their patient, or if following the directive would violate medically accepted standards for health care.

If, for one of these reasons, the doctor caring for you refuses to enforce your living will when the time comes, he or she must inform the person who has durable power of attorney for your health care — your health care agent. You designate this person by preparing a durable power of attorney for health care. (Health care agents are discussed in the next section of this chapter.) If this person requests that you be transferred to another doctor or to another health care facility that will abide by the wishes you expressed in your living will, the doctor who is currently caring for you must comply. If the doctor balks, your health care agent may need to consult with an attorney specializing in elder law.

Some of your family members may pressure your doctor to ignore your living will instructions. As a result, they may come into conflict with whoever has durable power of attorney for your health care and possibly with other members of your family. Sometimes a formal hearing must be scheduled to resolve such problems.

Giving Someone a Durable Power of Attorney for Your Health Care

The best way to help ensure that your living will gets enforced is to give someone you trust a *durable power of attorney for health care,* also called a *health care proxy.* This person has the power to push for activation of your living will and to make decisions about your medical care and treatment when you're unable to. You can also give this person the right to manage your health care if you're incapacitated temporarily because of an illness or accident. Obviously, the decision to give someone this power is a significant one; you should give it to someone you absolutely trust and who is strong and assertive, unlikely to back down or crumble when serious and difficult decisions must be made or if problems arise in activating your living will.

Prepare your living will and durable power of attorney for health care at the same time because the documents go hand in hand. In some states, these two legal documents are combined into one document called an *advance directive.*

To give someone a durable power of attorney for health care, you have to pre-pare a legal document that meets your state's requirements. You can find out what these requirements are by contacting the same resources that can tell you about the legal standards for living wills (jump back to the previous sec-tion, "Laying It Out in a Living Will"). In fact, many of them can provide you with a fill-in-the-blanks version of the durable power of attorney for health care form together with a sample living will. Again, if you write your own docu-ment, be sure to have an attorney review it to make certain that it meets the letter of the law in your state and is clearly worded. And again, discuss the details of the power of attorney with the person you're giving it to so that he or she feels completely comfortable with what you're asking.

Be very clear about what you do and don't want when writing your durable power of attorney for health care. If your proxy's power is challenged in court, he or she could lose some of those powers.

Make sure that the power of attorney you prepare is indeed durable. If you give someone a non-durable power of attorney, that person's right to act on your behalf ends as soon as you become incapacitated — at the very moment that you need their help the most.

If You Don't Have a Living Will or Durable Power of Attorney for Health Care

Without a living will or durable power of attorney for health care, you have no direct control over your medical care and treatment when you're close to death with no hope of recovery. Your doctor may work closely with your family to decide what to do, but their decision may or may not match your desires. Furthermore, your loved ones will probably experience considerable anguish when making their decision, and if they disagree with one another, your lack of planning could create a rift within your family.

If your family and your doctor disagree about how to handle your condition, your family may have to initiate a lawsuit to get its wishes enforced. As you can imagine, doing so takes time and money and puts your family in an emotionally difficult situation. Meanwhile, you're kept alive, possibly against your wishes, for weeks, months, years, or even indefinitely.

If you don't prepare a living will or give someone you trust a durable power of attorney of health care, your family can ask the court to appoint someone as your guardian. This person is responsible for making health care decisions on your behalf. Usually, the court appoints a family member as guardian. But if no one wants to assume the responsibility or the court believes that no family member is capable of handling the responsibilities of being a guardian, the court may appoint a complete stranger to make critical decisions for you. Although a family member seems like a better option than a stranger, even a family member may not be someone you want making life-and-death decisions on your behalf.

The case of Terri Schiavo

The story of Floridian Terri Schiavo, a brain damaged young woman who has been in a vegetative state for more than 13 years, is the most recent example of the kind of rift that can be triggered by failing to plan for the possibility that you may linger close to death. Schiavo's husband believes his wife would not want to be kept alive by artificial means given her current state, but Schiavo's parents maintain that Terri isn't brain dead and can recover with the appropriate medical care and treatment. They also argue that she would want to continue living no matter what her condition.

During six years of legal wrangling over whether or not Terri's husband could discontinue his wife's artificial feeding and hydration,

19 judges in six courts have ruled in his favor. Yet in 2003 when those life-support measures were stopped, the state of Florida intervened, and (on the request of the governor) the Florida legislature passed a new law that requires nutrition and hydration to continue even if a patient is in a persistent vegetative state, has not left a living will or advance directive, and has had feeding tubes removed. The law also applies even if the patient's spouse has asked that the feeding tubes be removed. The new law is being challenged and is expected to be overturned. However, the legal battles have caused years of anguish and heartbreak for everyone close to Terri Schiavo, not to mention major legal expenses.

Planning Your Funeral Without Getting Ripped Off

To ensure that the details of your funeral match your personal tastes and pocketbook, you may want to make the arrangements yourself. Put your desires in writing, arrange for payment, and discuss everything with your loved ones. This kind of planning has several important benefits.

- ✔ You have more time to shop for the best deal than your grieving relatives will have after you die.

- ✔ You spare your relatives from having to make what may be difficult decisions in the midst of their sorrow.

- ✔ Planning ahead can help protect your relatives from being victimized by the promises and offers of unscrupulous or greedy funeral home operators.

Paying for a funeral is not an insignificant undertaking. According to the Federal Trade Commission, the average cost of a funeral is $6,000, including a casket and vault. This cost does not include an obituary, limousine rentals, flowers, thank you cards, or burial. As a result, a typical funeral and burial can end up costing $10,000 or more. So, when planning your funeral, it pays to research your options, know the laws that govern the funeral industry, and compare prices and services.

If you're living in an unmarried relationship, and especially if you're living with someone of the same sex, make sure that when you write down your funeral plans you name your partner as the party responsible for carrying them out and then sign the document. You may also want to include your funeral instructions in your will, but sometimes a will isn't read until after the funeral.

Prepaying your funeral isn't necessarily a good idea because after you've paid, you may move to another area, marry, remarry, or change your burial desires and needs for another reason. If you do decide to prepay, be sure that you're working with a reputable funeral home. Before signing a contract, read it carefully and find out under what conditions you can get your money back. Also, be very clear regarding exactly what you're paying for. (Jump down to the section "Things to consider if you prepay your funeral," later in this chapter, for more information.)

The Funeral Rule

The federal Funeral Rule, which is enforced by the Federal Trade Commission (FTC), regulates the funeral industry and mandates that funeral homes provide consumers with certain information regarding the options they offer and the cost of those options. The Funeral Rule is intended to help consumers make funeral arrangements and to protect them from funeral scams.

According to the Funeral Rule, funeral homes are required to provide you with itemized funeral cost information in person or over the telephone if you request it. You're also entitled to written information about your legal rights and about what your state does and doesn't require for a burial or a cremation. For example, most states do not require embalming; however many funeral homes require it if a viewing is planned.

All states restrict the location of burial sites, so you're probably barred from burying your spouse under his or her favorite tree in the backyard!

If you visit a funeral home in person, an employee should give you printed cost information for all of the following:

- Basic services fee (for the services common to all funerals regardless of the type)
- Transfer of remains to the funeral site
- Preparation for embalming
- Use of ceremonial or viewing facility and cost of staff
- Equipment
- Hearse or limousine
- Caskets

If you intend to have a cremation and want a visitation and funeral, ask the funeral home if it has caskets to rent.

- Vaults, liners, and other burial containers
- Death certificates
- Music, flowers, and guest books
- Direct cremation and immediate burial
- Cash advances (fees charged by a funeral home for purchasing outside goods and services on your behalf, such as flowers, obituaries, organist, and so on)

    Although a funeral home is required to let you know if it will mark up the cost of any of the outside goods and services it purchases for you, the Funeral Rule doesn't require it to tell you how much the mark up will be.

Knowing your rights when arranging a funeral

Funerals can definitely be difficult affairs. Here are a few points to keep in mind if you find yourself in the unfortunate position of having to plan one:

✔ A funeral home cannot withhold information about the prices of its goods or services.

✔ You should be informed in writing of any special fees or upfront money you may have to pay.

✔ If you opt for direct cremation, the funeral home must make available to you an unfinished wood box or alternative container.

✔ After you've selected the items and services you want, the funeral home should give you a Statement of Funeral Goods and Services Selected, which lists the price of each item and your total cost.

✔ The funeral home cannot tell you that any type of embalming fluid, process, or type of casket can preserve a body forever. Nothing preserves a body forever.

✔ The funeral home cannot falsely claim that particular caskets can keep out water, dirt, or other materials.

✔ If the funeral home offers packages of commonly selected funeral-related goods and services, you have the right to purchase those goods and services individually.

✔ If your state requires that you purchase a specific good or service, that requirement must be disclosed on the funeral home's price list. The list must also reference the law that allows/mandates the funeral home to impose such a requirement.

✔ The funeral home cannot refuse to let you use a casket you purchased somewhere else or charge you a fee for letting you use it.

✔ A funeral home cannot provide embalming services without your upfront permission.

The Funeral Rule doesn't apply to mausoleums or cemeteries unless they sell funeral goods as well as funeral services.

If you're not sure how much something costs, ask. If the funeral home can't give you an exact price, it should still provide you with a good-faith estimate.

Never, ever buy a funeral-related item or service over the telephone. Get it in writing! Steer clear of funeral homes that require you to buy certain packages of services not required by your state's laws.

Things to consider if you prepay your funeral

Some people think that it's a good idea to prepay their funeral expenses. They may or may not be right, depending on their circumstances. To help you decide if prepaying is a wise option for you, here are some important questions to answer:

- ✔ Exactly what goods and services are you paying for and what will still have to be paid for?

- ✔ What happens to the money you pay in advance? Does your state have a law dictating how prepayments for funeral services must be handled?

- ✔ What happens to the interest that's earned on the money you prepay?

- ✔ What if you move out of town? Can your funeral plans be transferred to another location, and will this service cost extra?

- ✔ If you change your mind about the funeral arrangements you paid for, can you get out of the contract and get your money refunded? What if you just want to change some aspect of your arrangements?

- ✔ How are you protected if the funeral home you're doing business with shuts down?

Choosing caskets, burial vaults, cremations, and other options

Your religious beliefs, personal preferences, and/or your financial situation come into play in your decision on whether you want to be buried, cremated, donated to medical science, or preserved in liquid nitrogen (yes, you can do this).

If you want to be buried, your body will probably be placed in a casket or coffin. These items can be expensive — as much as $30,000 for a really extravagant one made of expensive materials and with a lot of features. At the other end of the spectrum, you may be able to buy a very basic casket for as little as $100, depending on where you live.

Save money on your funeral by building your own casket, or have a family member do it for you, just like in *As I Lay Dying* by William Faulkner! (Just kidding.)

Depending on the cemetery you will be buried in, you may be required to use a burial vault or a grave liner. Burial vaults are more expensive than grave liners and can cost anywhere from $100 to $5,000.

For financial and personal reasons, a growing number of people are opting for cremation rather than a traditional burial. If you choose cremation, you purchase a cremation urn, container, or wooden box instead of a casket. An urn is the more expensive option and when purchased from a funeral home costs between $100 and $1,500.

Burial societies

If you want a traditional funeral and burial but can't afford one, or if you just want to minimize your funeral costs, you can join a burial or memorial society. These nonprofit organizations are able to offer lower-priced funerals and burials because they buy and sell funeral services and goods in large quantities and, in turn, pass some of their savings on to their members. To join a burial or memorial society, you pay about $15 to $30 per year. In exchange, you may be able to save as much as 75 percent on your funeral costs. For more information about how burial societies work and a list of nonsectarian burial societies around the country, contact the Funeral Consumers Alliance at 1-800-765-0107 or visit www.funerals.org.

Express yourself with a creative container for your ashes. Check out your options at Casket Gallery, www.casketgallery.com/urns.phtml. The containers offered on this site include jewelry, bookends, angels, clocks, hand-crafted glass containers, and more.

If you decide to donate your body to medical science, your donation may be used to help train new doctors or to advance medical research. Also, you can donate your organs to patients who need them. Unless you expressly prohibit it, in most states, your family has the right to donate your body or body parts.

Not all bodies donated to medical science are accepted, so you should have backup arrangements in the event that yours is rejected.

If your body is refused by medical science and you still want to aid the medical field, try donating your gray matter to the Harvard Medical School. It is conducting research on Alzheimer's disease and other brain disorders.

Signing on for viatical settlements

If you have a terminal illness and need cash fairly quickly to pay your medical bills or finance your funeral, you may be able to sell your life insurance policy to a *viatical settlement company* for a lump sum of cash; the company continues making your premium payments until you die and then receives the policy proceeds. Usually, the company pays you a percentage of the face value of your policy, sometimes as much as 80 percent. This means that if you have a $100,000 policy, the viatical settlement can be as much as $80,000 in cash. And although it may sound pretty heartless, the shorter your life expectancy, the more the company pays you.

If you sell your life insurance policy to a viatical settlement company, the company becomes the sole beneficiary of that policy; the person you originally named as beneficiary no longer stands to benefit after your death. Therefore, before selling your policy, consider your beneficiary's financial needs.

Every viatical settlement company has its own rules for determining which policies it purchases. Most of them, however, only buy your policy if you're terminally ill and have just a few years to live — usually a maximum of two to four years. In addition, most companies require you to have owned your policy for at least two years and to give them written permission to review your medical records. The viatical settlement company you work with will probably want to make certain that the insurance company that sold you your policy is financially sound, and they will require the beneficiary or beneficiaries of your policy to sign a release giving up all rights to the policy proceeds.

If your life expectancy is two years or less, you can receive the viatical settlement proceeds free of federal taxes. However, you may have to pay state income taxes.

If your insurance policy is provided by your employer, the viatical company will not purchase the policy unless your group policy can be converted to an individual policy or some other arrangement can be guaranteed.

The following is a list of tips for getting the best deal from a viatical settlement company:

- **Comparison shop.** No matter how anxious you are for money, don't make a deal with the first viatical settlement company you contact. As with most things, you will get the best deal by shopping around.

- **Contact your state insurance commission.** Find out whether your state licenses these companies, and if it does, make sure that the company you deal with is licensed.

- **Check to see if you have to pay taxes on the settlement you receive.** In many states, it's tax-free money; however, you may have to pay federal capital gains tax on the difference between the amount of your settlement and what you paid into your policy.

- **Find out when you will receive your money.** Depending on the size of the viatical settlement company, you may get the money very quickly or it may take time. Also, some states mandate a 15-day cooling off period before you can finalize a contract with a company and receive your money.

✔ **Research company histories.** Check with your state attorney general's office of consumer affairs, your local Better Business Bureau, and the FTC to find out if the company you're considering doing business with has had any complaints filed against it. Even more important, find out if any of those complaints are unresolved.

✔ **Steer clear of any company that pressures you.** You need time to think about this important decision.

✔ **Don't sign anything from a viatical settlement company until it sets up an escrow account with a financial institution.** The settlement company should have no relationship to the financial institution holding the account. The funds the company pays to you should be transferred into this account.

✔ **Ask an attorney to review your agreement with a viatical settlement company before you sign it.** These agreements are quite complex, and an attorney can untangle the details and make sure that your rights are protected.

Don't expect to see cash from a deal with a viatical settlement company within days or even weeks. A reasonable time frame from signature to payment is three months.

Getting assistance from accelerated benefits

If you're terminally ill, another way to get money to pay for your medical care or funeral is through *accelerated life insurance benefits.* With this option, instead of selling your insurance policy, your insurance company pays you between 25 and 100 percent of your policy's proceeds.

Some companies will accelerate your benefits if you have a long-term catastrophic illness that isn't terminal.

Accelerated benefits may be a standard part of your insurance policy, or they may be offered as an extra or an attachment to the policy. If your policy doesn't include accelerated benefits, call your insurance company to find out if you can add this feature for an additional premium. If not, some insurance companies are willing to loan you money instead, depending on the kind of policy you have.

Collecting accelerated benefits or a viatical settlement can affect your eligibility for financial assistance from need-based public programs such as Medicaid.

Euthanasia, Doctor-Assisted Suicide, and Your Right to Die

Among some segments of American society, there's a growing belief that extremely ill people should have the right to a "good death" — in other words, the opportunity to determine when their lives will end so they don't have to go through a painfully protracted death. Good death proponents generally advocate euthanasia and doctor-assisted suicide.

Euthanasia occurs when a doctor administers a specific medication or amount of a medication known to cause death to a patient or provides a certain treatment that is known to result in death. Euthanasia is not legal in any state.

Doctor-assisted suicide occurs when a doctor provides a patient with information and/or the means to end his or her life but does not actually administer the life-ending drugs or dose of drugs. For example, a doctor gives the patient a prescription for medication that will end the patient's life, but the patient, not the doctor, administers the lethal dose. Presently, only one state (Oregon) allows doctor-assisted suicides under certain circumstances set out in its Death with Dignity law. The law also includes rules to ensure that persons who want a doctor-assisted suicide are mentally competent, in great pain, and truly want to end their lives. Thirty-eight states have specifically outlawed doctor-assisted suicides, and most others prohibit it either through case law or their general homicide laws.

Part V

Crime and Punishment

In this part . . .

The chapters in this part deal with legal issues that you or your juvenile child may face if either of you is accused of a crime. Specifically, I provide an overview of the criminal justice system, and I delve into the details regarding juveniles and crime.

Chapter 17

Do the Crime, Do the Time

*M*ost of you will never see the inside of a jail, so you'll be spared the considerable anxiety and expense that comes with being arrested. Bad things do happen, however, and sometimes they have legal consequences that involve the criminal justice system. So, if you or someone you know is arrested, or if you're the victim of a crime, it's helpful to have a basic knowledge of how the criminal justice system works and an understanding of the rights of criminal defendants and victims. This knowledge can help you cope with what may be a frightening and overwhelming experience.

What Is a Crime?

Although you probably think you know a crime when you see one, in reality, the definition of a crime is not always straightforward. Officially, a *crime* is a wrongful act that violates the laws of your community, state, or country. But in plain English, a crime is an act that breaks the law and that causes injury or harm to people or to society in general.

Sometimes, *not* doing something is considered a crime. For example, if you're a pediatrician and believe that one of your young patients is being abused, if you don't report your suspicions, you can be accused of a crime, depending on the state in which you practice medicine.

Criminal lawsuits are brought by a state government or by the federal government — they're actually initiated by a prosecuting attorney acting on the government's behalf — and are tried in a criminal court. A criminal defendant can be an individual or an organization. Among other punishments, those convicted of committing a criminal act may be given probation, fined, sentenced to jail or prison, required to perform community service, or a combination. In some states, they can even be sentenced to death if they're convicted of murder.

Types of Crimes

State governments, not the federal government, have jurisdiction over most types of crimes. Each state has its own penal code, which places crimes in particular categories. Although states can differ in how they categorize crimes, in general, the categories are as follows:

- **Petty offenses or citations** are relatively minor crimes like littering, running a stop sign, speeding, illegally parking, jaywalking, and so on. Usually, when you commit a petty offense, you're ticketed, not arrested. In fact, many states have decriminalized certain types of petty offenses.

- **Misdemeanors** are more serious crimes such as assault, battery, shoplifting inexpensive items, vandalism, writing a bad check for a small amount, and so on. Depending on the seriousness of the misdemeanor you're convicted of, you may be fined, ordered to do community service, sentenced to jail (usually for a year or less), or given some other type of relatively light punishment.

- **Felonies** include kidnapping, rape, spousal abuse, arson, burglary, drug dealing, murder, and manslaughter. A felony is the most serious type of crime, and if you're convicted of committing one, you can be punished with a year or more in prison. Some felonies, like capital murder, are punishable by death in some states. You can also lose some of your civil rights — your right to vote, to possess a firearm, and to serve on a jury, for example, if you're convicted of a felony.

In some states, certain kinds of crimes may be treated as misdemeanors *or* felonies, depending on the circumstances. For example, if you're arrested for drunk driving and you've been arrested and convicted for the same crime before, you may be accused of committing a felony instead of a misdemeanor. Just how many previous arrests and convictions would cause you to be charged with a felony rather than a misdemeanor depends on your state.

If you're charged with a crime and you're not sure of how it's categorized by your state, ask your attorney.

To be convicted of committing a serious crime, a judge or jury must decide that you're guilty *beyond a reasonable doubt.* However, depending on the specific type of crime you're accused of, a jury may also have to find *specific intent* — in other words, you had a specific motive or reason to commit the crime.

An increasing number of crimes have been *federalized*. Rather than allowing individual states to adjudicate particular crimes according to their own penal codes, the federal government has made those crimes federal crimes, which means that anyone accused of committing one is tried in federal, not state, court.

The federal government mandates minimum sentences for drug-related crimes. Basically, if you're convicted of such a crime, the judge who hears your case can't sentence you to less time in jail than the mandatory minimum associated with that particular crime. Also, you can't get parole. The mandatory sentencing guidelines have been severely criticized by many judges, attorneys, criminal justice experts, and citizen groups. They argue that the guidelines restrict a judge's ability to take into account during sentencing the circumstances surrounding a crime, the defendant's prior criminal history, his or her likely chance of being rehabilitated, and so on. Many states have adopted their own mandatory sentences as a result.

Getting Arrested

A single chapter could never contain a comprehensive discussion of the various roads down which a criminal case may travel. Which road a case goes down depends among other things on the state where the crime occurs, whether it's a federal or state crime, the type of crime, and whether the person accused of the crime pleads guilty or agrees to a plea bargain. This section, therefore, presents a very general overview of what is most likely to happen if you're arrested for committing a misdemeanor or felony. It doesn't address what will happen when you're charged with a petty violation, because the court system treats these minor crimes much differently than more serious ones.

Being arrested means that you're suspected of having committed a crime, but it doesn't mean that you're necessarily guilty. In fact, the American legal system is based on the assumption that you're innocent until proven guilty. And to be found guilty, you either have to admit your guilt or go through the trial process.

You can be arrested in a couple of ways. If you commit a crime in front of a police officer, you can be arrested on the spot. But if you're suspected of committing a crime or assisting with a crime, ordinarily a judge must issue a warrant giving the police or another law enforcement agency the right to arrest you.

Federal cases vs. state cases

Although states prosecute most crimes, the Constitution gives the federal government jurisdiction over certain types of crimes, which are ordinarily tried in federal court.

If your case is heard in federal court, a federal magistrate (not a judge) sets your bail, assuming bail is an option, and a judge (instead of attorneys for the defense and prosecution) performs the *voir dire* (French for "to speak the truth"), which involves interviewing prospective jurors. Also in federal cases, a judge can comment to the jury about the evidence, and when it's time for sentencing, the federal judge must normally adhere to strict guidelines that don't apply in state courts.

Although it doesn't happen often, sometimes the jurisdictions of the state and federal courts overlap in regard to a crime. When this situation occurs, the federal and state prosecutors have to decide which jurisdiction will hear the case.

You can also be arrested without a warrant if the police believe that they have *probable cause;* although there's no single definition of probable cause and when it exists varies from case to case, in general it means that the police have objective evidence that you've committed a crime or are about to. For example, if a police officer sees you wearing a mask, holding a flashlight, and prying open the window of a home in your neighborhood, the police officer most likely has probable cause to arrest you. Some states also permit warrantless arrests if the police have *reasonable suspicion.* Like *probable cause,* there's no set definition of reasonable suspicion and it also varies from case to case. (In fact, reasonable suspicion is an even more vague term than probably cause!) Basically, to arrest you on reasonable suspicion, the police need something more than a gut feeling that you have or are about to commit a crime, but something less than *probable cause.* Warrantless arrests most often occur when the police need to make an arrest on the spot, and the delay involved in getting a warrant could prevent the arrest from taking place.

If you're arrested without a warrant, you're entitled to a prompt hearing to determine whether sufficient probable or sufficient reasonable cause exists to formally charge you with a crime. If you're released, however, you can later be rearrested for the same crime.

Ordinarily, to arrest you in your home, the police need either a warrant or your consent. The same rule applies if the police want to search your home.

If you're arrested, you will be taken into police custody, which means that you're under their control. Most likely, the arresting officer will tell you why you're being arrested (if you don't already know!). But you don't have a legal right to be told. It's a courtesy.

Can't my case be dismissed if the police forget to read me the Miranda warning?

Contrary to popular belief, when you're arrested for a crime, the police don't have to read you the Miranda warning unless they intend to interrogate you. The Miranda warning says that you have the right to remain silent and that anything you say can be used against you in a court of law; that you have the right to speak with an attorney and to have your attorney present when you're questioned by the police; and that if you can't afford to pay an attorney, the government will provide one for you. The Miranda warning helps protect your Fifth Amendment right not to incriminate yourself. Whether you're read your Miranda rights or not before you have an attorney, don't volunteer any information to the police, and after you have an attorney, always exercise your right to remain silent unless your attorney tells you to do otherwise. If you're arrested and the police don't read you your Miranda rights, any confession you may have made cannot be used as evidence against you in court.

In states that use grand juries, you can also be arrested if a grand jury indicts you for a crime, which means that it formally accuses you of committing a crime based on a review of the evidence.

Search warrants and search and seizure

If you're arrested, the police can search you for evidence related to your alleged crime. They can also search the area immediately surrounding you — essentially the area that is at your arms' length. The police can take anything they find that they think may be evidence of your crime.

The Flex Your Rights Foundation educates citizens about their legal rights when they encounter the police. For information about those rights, go to www.flexyourrights.org or call 202-986-0861.

Usually, if the police don't have a warrant and you consent to a search, you waive your Fourth Amendment rights, the search becomes legal, and any evidence found during the search can be used against you. However, the law presumes that a warrantless search you don't consent to is invalid in most instances, because it violates your Fourth Amendment rights, which protect you from unreasonable searches and seizures. Therefore, such a search can be challenged in court. However, there are circumstances when a warrantless search can be conducted legally against your will. For example, a judge will probably uphold a warrantless search of your home if the police believe that someone inside is in imminent danger, that a suspect in your home is about to escape, or that you're about to destroy evidence.

Legal help

Yes, lawyers are expensive, but when you're charged with a crime, not hiring one is penny-wise and pound-foolish. You can represent yourself in court, but (usually) you'll be doing yourself a serious disservice. Here are some reasons why:

- The prosecuting attorney you'll be up against has completed law school and passed the bar. In other words, he or she knows more about the law and legal procedures than you do.

- The prosecuting attorney has tried criminal cases before and is more comfortable in the courtroom than you will be.

- The judge or jury can't consider the fact that you're representing yourself when deciding your case, which means that trying to play on their sympathies by acting as your own attorney doesn't work as a defense strategy.

Even if you're an attorney, representing yourself is not advisable because it will be tough for you to separate the facts from your emotions and perform well in court.

If you don't have enough money to pay an attorney, you can ask for a *court-appointed lawyer* (a private attorney who the court pays a very small amount of money to represent you) or a *public defender* (a lawyer who works for you but is paid by the county or state), but only if conviction for the crime you're accused of can result in a jail sentence. To prove your financial situation, you may have to provide the court with copies of your tax returns, bank statements, or other financial documents.

The downside of asking the court to give you an attorney is that you have to take what you get, and the skills and experience level of the lawyer you end up with may not be what you need to win your case; however, if you're dissatisfied with your attorney and can convince the court that you should have a different one, the court may agree to appoint someone else to your case.

After the court provides you with a court-appointed attorney or public defender, he or she can petition the court to have a private investigator or expert assigned to help with your case. This additional assistance is typically requested to help level the playing field for an indigent defendant. The court is most apt to okay such a request if you've been accused of a very serious felony.

Honesty is the best policy when you're working with your lawyer — even if you're guilty of the crime you're charged with committing. To provide the best defense possible, your lawyer needs to know all the facts. Think of your attorney as a doctor trying to cure your legal problem. In order to have a fighting chance of doing so, your attorney must know all of your "symptoms." If you withhold information from your doctor, he or she may not have all the facts necessary to determine the best way to cure your health problem. The same is true of your attorney. And remember, what you tell your lawyer is confidential information. It can't be used against you in court.

In most cases, if a judge believes that there is probable cause or a reasonable belief that a crime has been committed or that someone is about to commit a crime, the judge will issue a search warrant that states exactly what the police are looking for. The police must conduct their search soon after the warrant is issued. They must also conduct the search in a reasonable manner, which means, for example, that if the warrant says that the police are looking for a shotgun because they believe you used it to murder someone, they should not search through your jewelry box because a shotgun doesn't fit in most jewelry boxes.

If the police want to search you and/or your property without a warrant, don't consent to it, even if you're innocent and anxious to vindicate yourself. Don't expect the police to inform you that you have a right to withhold consent. If you do consent, the police can take what they consider to be evidence and use it to build a case against you.

Getting booked

After you're arrested, the police will take you to the local police station to be booked. You will probably be put in jail until you're booked. At the booking, you're photographed and fingerprinted, and you may also have to provide a sample of your handwriting, your voice, your blood, or your urine, depending on the crime you're accused of committing.

You're entitled to be booked within a "reasonable" period of time — a couple of hours or overnight — after you've been put in jail at the police station. If your booking is considerably delayed, your attorney (assuming you have one at this point) can ask a judge for a *writ of habeas corpus,* which requires the police to bring you before a judge who decides if you're being legally held in jail.

After you're booked, information about you and the crime or crimes you've been accused of is sent to the prosecutor's office so that the prosecutor can decide whether you should be formally charged with one or more crimes.

The law views your blood, urine, breath, handwriting, and the sound of your voice as physical traits — parts of your identity; therefore, your Fifth Amendment rights are not violated when you're asked to provide samples of these physical traits, and you're not incriminating yourself when you do. You should always, however, speak to an attorney before providing such samples.

After you're arrested, the arresting officer will write up a report detailing the circumstances surrounding your arrest and why you were arrested. He or she may write a longer report later or supplement the original report with new or additional information. The officer will also fill out a property report listing everything you had in your possession at the time you were booked, including your personal effects and anything the police take as evidence.

When you go to jail, you have to turn over to the police all of your personal effects, such as your watch, jewelry, wallet, and so on. Make certain that the police create a written inventory of the items you turn over or you may have trouble getting them back later. You may be required to sign the inventory.

Depending on the nature of the crime you've been accused of, a state or federal detective or investigator may be assigned to your case. He or she will begin searching for additional evidence and talking to witnesses in an effort to build a solid case against you.

Going to jail (Do not pass go; do not collect $200)

If going to jail were as inconsequential as it is in the game of Monopoly, being arrested would be taken a lot less seriously. After you're booked, unless you're immediately released on bail because you've been arrested for a relatively minor crime such as a misdemeanor, you will spend some time in jail waiting to be arraigned or formally charged with a crime. Usually this period is quite brief — just a day or two or maybe less, depending on your crime — but when you're in a crowded, smelly jail with a lot of strangers, a brief time may feel like an eternity.

You may also be released from jail *on your own recognizance,* which means that you don't have to post bail. Instead, the court trusts you to show up in court on the appointed date. You must sign paperwork promising to do so.

Here are a few things to remember about going to jail.

✔ You don't have a Constitutional right to make a phone call from jail, but you may be allowed to make one call. Don't forget that the call has to be collect, because any money you had in your pocket was taken from you and put with your personal effects when you were booked. Because your calls from jail are limited, make yours count. For example, if bail is an option, call a relative or a friend who can help you arrange for it. (Bail is discussed later in this chapter.)

✔ Don't assume that your phone conversations from jail are confidential; yours may be recorded, and anything you say can be used against you! The only exceptions are any phone conversations you have with your attorney. Even so, don't discuss your case in detail — your guilt or innocence especially — whenever you're on the phone. Do it in person.

✔ You may be videotaped while you're being arrested and from the minute you go to jail. So watch what you say and how you behave!

✔ Some states void the privileged nature of conversations with people like doctors, therapists, religious advisers, and spouses. In those states, anything you say to anyone can be used against you if your case goes to trial. So hold your tongue!

If you're incarcerated in a county or municipal facility, you're in a jail. If you're in a state facility, you may be in a jail, prison, restitution center, or rehabilitation center, and if you're in a federal facility, you're in a prison. You may stay in jail until you're tried for the crime you're alleged to have committed, and then if you're convicted, you may be sent to prison.

Being formally charged

After you're booked, you must be formally charged with a crime in order for your case to move forward. Formal charging must happen within a certain period of time — within 72 hours in most states. How you're charged depends on whether you've been arrested for a misdemeanor or a felony and on the particular criminal process in your state. Also, you may be charged with one crime initially, but later the prosecuting attorney may decide to charge you with new or additional charges if new evidence surfaces.

Arraignments

Regardless of the crime you're accused of, you must appear in court at an *arraignment* or *initial appearance*. At the arraignment, the judge formally tells you what you're being charged with and reads you your rights. At the arraignment you enter your plea — guilty, not guilty, or *nolo contendere* (no contest). If you refuse to enter a plea, the judge enters a not guilty plea for you, unless you have an attorney already. If you do, the attorney answers for you. Flip to the section "Making your plea" later in this chapter for additional information regarding the various ways you can plead.

At the arraignment, the judge also tells you that you have the right to an attorney if the crime you're alleged to have committed could result in you serving time in jail if you're convicted. If you can't afford to hire an attorney, the judge will arrange for you to have legal representation.

Arrangements for your release on bail or on personal recognizance may be initiated at your arraignment if these arrangements haven't already been made. However, if you're accused of committing an extremely serious crime, your bail may be set so high that you aren't able to post it, which means that you remain in jail until your trial date.

Preliminary hearings and grand juries

If you've been arrested for committing a felony, shortly after you've been arraigned, a preliminary hearing related to your case may be held to determine if there's sufficient evidence to take your case to trial. The hearing functions much like a mini-trial, with both the prosecuting attorney and your defense attorney making arguments before a judge about why you should or should not be tried. Witnesses may be called, and physical evidence can be introduced. You attend the hearing, but you're not allowed to say anything.

If the judge believes that there's sufficient probable cause, your case moves forward; otherwise, the case against you is dropped. However, some states allow a prosecuting attorney to try to get a grand jury indictment even when a judge dismisses a case.

It's possible that the prosecuting attorney may decide to take your case to a *grand jury* — a group of so-called everyday people. (If you've been charged with a federal crime, a grand jury is always involved.) The grand jury reviews the evidence in your case as presented by the prosecuting attorney to decide if you should be indicted. If it believes that you should be indicted, it also decides what crime or crimes you should be indicted for. When a grand jury issues an indictment, the indictment is referred to as a *true bill,* and the case against you moves forward. Otherwise, the grand jury returns with a *no bill,* which means that the grand jury has decided that there's not enough evidence to pursue a case against you.

You may breathe a sigh of relief if you get a *no bill* from a grand jury. However, you may not really be off the hook because it's possible that the prosecutor could return to the same grand jury with new or additional evidence or could present evidence against you to a new grand jury in order to get an indictment against you.

In some states, you have limited rights to have your side of the story explained to a grand jury, and the process can be pretty much a one-sided affair. In fact, typically, you can't even sit in on the grand jury's deliberations. You may, however, be called as a witness to answer questions. If this happens, you aren't entitled to have your lawyer represent you, but your lawyer may be able to watch and listen. Also, depending on your state, you may be able to testify in person before a grand jury or submit your testimony in a letter. But you should be aware that anything you say or write to the grand jury can be used against you later.

Making your plea

How to plead can be a strategically critical decision and is something you and your lawyer should discuss. In many instances, your attorney may be able to help you avoid the cost and stress of a trial by negotiating a plea bargain for you, which means that in exchange for pleading guilty to a lesser charge, you get a more lenient sentence. Also, other charges against you may be dropped. (The section of this chapter called "The days or months leading up to your trial" tells you more about plea bargains.)

The several ways that you may plead are explained in the following sections.

Pleading guilty

This plea is an admission of guilt. You're saying, "Yep, I did it," and you're giving up your right to a defense. If you plead guilty, usually there's no going back; you can't change your mind later. And depending on what you've admitted to, you may be sent to prison immediately.

The only time you should plead guilty is when your attorney tells you to and when you understand why it's a good idea. For example, you may plead guilty as part of a plea bargain agreement.

Pleading nolo contendere

Depending on your state, you may have the right to enter a plea of *nolo contendere,* or no contest. If you do, you're not saying that you're innocent or guilty, but simply that you're not contesting the charge.

Many states view a plea of no contest as an admission of guilt, and if you plead it, you're sentenced as though you're guilty of the crime you've been charged with. Therefore, it's essential that you consult with your attorney before you plead no contest. If you're not being represented by an attorney, the judge should explain the implications of a no contest plea to you directly.

Pleading not guilty

If you state that you did not commit the crime you're being accused of, a trial date is set so that your guilt or innocence can be determined.

Planning your defense

If you plead not guilty to the crime you're charged with, you and your lawyer have to determine what the basis of your defense will be now that your case is going to trial. You have several defense possibilities, the most common of which are alibi, entrapment, self-defense, or insanity. You and your lawyer should discuss your defense early in your case.

Alibi

If you can prove that you were someplace else or with someone else when the crime you've been accused of was committed, or if you can prove that some other reason explains why you could not have committed the crime, you have an *alibi.* In most states, if you want to use an alibi defense, you have to do so at the start of your trial; in other words, you can't introduce an alibi midway through the proceedings.

Entrapment

When you claim *entrapment,* you're not denying that you committed a crime; instead, you're claiming that you were induced or lured into the crime by a police officer or another agent of the law. Entrapment is a common defense in drug cases involving undercover cops; in some states it's also used in prostitution cases. To make the defense work, however, your attorney must be able to show that the crime probably would not have occurred if you had not been entrapped.

Self-defense

To use self-defense successfully, your attorney must convince the judge or jury that you committed a crime because you believed that your life was in danger and that you had to protect yourself and/or your property. For example, if you're arrested for killing someone who broke into your home, self-defense may be an effective argument.

Insanity

Pleading insanity works if your attorney is able to convince the court that at the time you committed the crime, you were unable to discern between right and wrong because of your mental state. The insanity defense is usually reserved for very serious crimes, and at least one medical expert has to testify about your mental state. In some states, you must let the court know ahead of time of your intent to use the insanity defense. If you're found *not guilty by reason of insanity,* you will receive treatment for your mental problems at a psychiatric facility, and then assuming you are cured eventually, you will be released back into society. Most but not all states have this kind of defense.

In many states you can be found *guilty but insane.* This is an option when a defendant is found to be mentally ill but not too ill to be found criminally responsible. When a defendant is found to be guilty but insane, the court decides whether or not the defendant needs treatment for his or her mental illness, and if it decides that treatment is necessary, the defendant receives medication, talk therapy, and so on in a psychiatric facility, which may be part of a prison. Assuming the defendant subsequently becomes mentally healthy, he or she serves out the rest of his or her sentence in a prison.

What is bail?

At the time of your arraignment, if not before, the judge usually gives you the opportunity to post bail, which means that you pay a certain amount of money to get out of jail. (You may be able to put up property instead of cash.) Bail is something you're legally entitled to for certain types of offenses, but not all, depending on your state and the circumstances. For example, if you've committed a particularly violent crime, there will probably be no bail or the amount of the bail is set so high that it's impossible for you to come up with the money.

The amount of your bail is intended to help ensure the court that you will show up for subsequent court dates. If you show up, you'll eventually get back the amount of your bail minus any fees and fines you may owe; but if you don't show up, you lose that money. A warrant for your arrest will probably be issued as well.

According to the Eighth Amendment, the amount of bail you have to pay can't be unreasonably high given the crime you are charged with. For example, if the police charge you with shoplifting $100 worth of clothing from a department store, your bail should not be set at some outrageous amount like $250,000. Both your attorney and the prosecuting attorney can suggest an amount they think is fair, but the judge has the final say.

In some states, if you can't afford to pay your bail, you can borrow it from a *bail bondsman*. Working with a bondsman is expensive, however, because you have to pay the bondsman a non-refundable premium of about 10 percent to 15 percent of the total bail bond, and you may also have to use your house, car, or bank account as loan collateral.

If you work with a bondsman and you don't show up in court when you're supposed to, the bondsman may hire a bounty hunter to track you down and bring you to court or jail. Sometimes in such a situation, a bondsman will ask the court to *go off* your bond, which essentially means that the bondsman wants to be released from being financially responsible for your showing up. If the court grants the bondsman's request, a warrant is issued for your arrest.

Instead of posting bail to get out of jail, the judge may decide to release you on your own recognizance, and you have to sign a written promise to appear at the next scheduled court date. This situation is most likely if the crime you've been accused of is not extremely serious and you have no criminal record.

If you're out on bail or on personal recognizance and you don't show up for your court date, a warrant is issued for your arrest. After you've been arrested and are back in jail again, it's unlikely that you will get released on your own recognizance for a second time because you've shown that you can't be trusted; also, your original bail amount may be raised. In addition, you may lose all the money you paid for your bail.

If you're convicted of a crime by reason of insanity, you're likely to be sentenced to a psychiatric facility, which isn't much better than being in prison. Furthermore, studies show that the average stay in a mental institution for someone who is sentenced to such a place is longer than the average stay in a prison for someone who is convicted of a crime.

At any time during your trial, you may be found *mentally incompetent,* which means that you're unable to understand the court proceedings and assist your attorney with your defense. If this happens, you're sent to a mental institution until you're deemed mentally competent. At that point, a new trial is held to determine your guilt or innocence.

The days or months leading up to your trial

As soon as your attorney knows that your case is going to trial, he or she begins planning the pretrial motions that he or she will introduce as part of the strategy for helping win your case. These motions can include motions to suppress evidence, to change the location of your trial, or to learn the names of the witnesses that the prosecution plans to call. The prosecuting attorney can also introduce pretrial motions. Both attorneys present arguments for or against each motion, and the judge rules on the motions.

In most states, the discovery process, including interrogatories, depositions, and other tools of discovery, isn't used a lot in criminal cases. However, the defense is more apt to use it than the prosecution because a criminal defendant has a constitutional right to be protected from self-incrimination, and being required to respond to a deposition, an interrogatory, and so on can lead to self-incrimination.

Prior to your trial date, the attorneys may discuss the possibility of a plea bargain and begin working one out. In fact, most criminal cases never go to trial. A plea bargain involves your agreeing to plead guilty to a crime that is less severe than the one you've been charged with in order to get a lighter sentence and/or so that other charges against you will get dropped. However, if you're offered a plea bargain, you don't have to accept it. If you do however, the judge hearing your case must approve it.

Why are plea bargains so common? One reason is that mounting a criminal defense costs a lot of money, and most defendants want to minimize their legal costs. Also, prosecuting attorneys often have very heavy caseloads, so frequently, they're amenable to a plea bargain as a way to lighten their loads. A third reason for the number of plea bargains is that defendants typically want to pay as small a price as possible for their crimes. So if being exonerated of the crime they've been accused of doesn't appear to be a realistic possibility, they're apt to go with a plea bargain instead.

The Trial

If your criminal case goes to trial, it may be heard by a judge (a *bench trial*) or a jury. (Most criminal cases are heard by a jury.) If you've been charged with committing a felony, you have the right to choose who you want to decide your fate. But if you're accused of a misdemeanor, your state may not give you that option, and your case is automatically heard by a judge.

The Sixth Amendment entitles you to a speedy trial, meaning that you can't be detained in jail for a long time due to "unreasonable delays." But in reality, some court schedules are so crowded that you can literally spend a year or longer in jail for a serious offense, if you're not out on bail, waiting for your trial date.

If a judge hears your case, he or she listens to all the evidence and decides whether you're guilty or innocent. A bench trial is almost always cheaper and faster than a jury trial. Also, if your crime has received a lot of negative publicity, a bench trial may be preferable because the jurors hearing your case may be prejudiced against you by the media. However, in a jury trial, your attorney will try to avoid having individuals who have seen the negative media coverage seated on your jury. In fact, your attorney may ask for a change of venue so that your trial can be moved to a community where members of the jury pool have not been exposed to a lot of information about you and your crime.

Jury selection

If you're going to be tried by a jury, when your day in court arrives, the first thing on the agenda is selecting the people who make up your jury. They're chosen from a list called a *venire*. The names on that list come from lists of registered voters, lists of people with driver's licenses, and/or tax assessment rolls.

The individuals on the venire are screened during the *voir dire* process, which is essentially an interview process. Either your attorney or the prosecuting attorney can oppose or reject some of the jurors. To do that, they can use two different types of challenges: *for cause* and *peremptory.*

- ✔ **For cause:** Both attorneys have an unlimited number of *for cause* challenges. They can use them to reject potential jurors whom they believe may be potentially prejudiced, unsympathetic, or biased against their side of the case, but the attorneys have to provide a basis for that opinion.

- ✔ **Peremptory challenge:** Neither attorney has to provide any reason or justification when they dismiss a juror using a peremptory challenge. (A juror's race or gender can't be the basis for a dismissal.) The number of peremptory challenges the attorneys can use is limited, however; different states set different limits.

The right to testify . . . or to not

If you're a defendant, the Fifth Amendment of the Constitution protects you from self-incrimination; therefore, you don't have to take the stand in your trial and testify, but you can if you want to, even if your attorney feels that it's a bad idea or is unnecessary because the prosecution's case is weak. Although the final decision regarding whether or not to testify is yours to make, you should take your attorney's advice about what to do very seriously.

Although you may be able to help your case by testifying, there have been many instances when a defendant's testimony and ability to hold up under the prosecution's cross-examination have had disastrous results, especially when the defendant said things damaging to his or her case that the jurors might not have heard otherwise.

If you testify in your trial, you're expected to answer all questions truthfully even if your answers will harm your case. Otherwise, you risk being charged with the crime of perjury. If you decide not to testify, your decision can't be considered an admission of guilt and can't be used against you in the courtroom. The jury is told that, during their deliberations, they should not take into account the fact that you did not testify on your own behalf.

Alternate jurors are selected in case a jury member needs to be replaced during the trial. The alternates hear the case but do not participate in the jury's deliberations.

Opening statements

Your trial typically begins with the prosecuting attorney's opening statement. The attorney presents the facts and the evidence of the case to the jury but does not argue points or draw conclusions. Your attorney (the defense attorney) can also make an opening statement at this point or can wait until the prosecution has rested its case and it's time for the defense to present its case.

After opening statements, the prosecution presents its case using physical evidence, direct testimony, and sometimes circumstantial evidence. Your attorney has the right to cross-examine any witnesses that the prosecution puts on the stand and to object to statements that the prosecution makes in the courtroom.

After the prosecution calls all of its witnesses, the defense takes center stage. Although your attorney is not obligated to call witnesses, he or she probably will, and the prosecuting attorney has the right to cross-examine them.

Closing arguments

After both sides argue their cases and examine witnesses, closing arguments begin. First, the prosecution sums up its case, argues the facts, and comments again on the evidence. Then your attorney presents his or her closing arguments and also responds to the prosecution's statements. Because the state (the prosecution) bears the burden of proof, it's allowed to make one last closing statement, a *rebuttal* — it's a final chance to convince the jury of your guilt.

Jury deliberations

After both sides have their says and close their cases, your fate is in the hands of the jury. The judge gives the jury instructions regarding what they are and are not allowed to consider in their deliberations and the laws that should apply during those deliberations, among other instructions. Jury members then retire to the jury room to consider your guilt or innocence. But first, they select a foreperson or presiding juror to act as their spokesperson. The jury members may or may not be sequestered. If they are, they're required to live in a hotel during the trial, their access to the media is limited, and their ability to speak with non–jury members is strictly limited as well. Juries are most often sequestered in highly publicized trials.

While the jury is deliberating, no one can make contact with them. If they have a question for the judge or want to reexamine evidence, they must give a note to this effect to the court bailiff who then delivers it to the judge.

Typically, the jury in a criminal case must reach a unanimous decision about a case, although in Louisiana and Oregon, the decision can be 10–2. If the jury can't reach a decision, the jury is *hung,* and the trial ends in a *mistrial.* When this happens, the state can try you again for the same crime.

The decision

If the jury comes to a decision, it informs the bailiff who in turn notifies the judge. Anyone who has ever watched *Perry Mason* knows that the jury usually reaches one of two decisions — *guilty* or *not guilty.* Sometimes, however, the jury's unable to decide on a defendant's guilt or innocence because it's deadlocked. If this happens, the jury's work is over, and a new trial is held at a later date.

Depending on your state, if you're on trial and the court believes that you're mentally incapacitated, you may be found *not guilty by reason of insanity* or *guilty but insane.* For a refresher on what each term means, return to the "Making your plea" section of this chapter.

If you're found not guilty, you're released, and in most cases, you can't be charged for that same crime again because you're protected by the double jeopardy rule. But if the jury decides that you're guilty, either attorney (but usually the lawyer for the losing side) can ask that the jury be polled, which means that each juror is asked to state his or her verdict aloud. Polling gives the attorneys for both sides the opportunity to hear from each jurors' mouth how he or she decided and also provides each juror one last time to change his or her mind. Then the judge sets a sentencing date, although in some jurisdictions, sentencing happens almost immediately after the jury's decision is announced.

The Fifth Amendment protects you from being prosecuted twice for the same offense — the *double jeopardy* rule. But there are exceptions. For example, although it rarely happens, you can be tried twice for the same crime — once in your state court system and once in the federal system. And you can be tried again for the same crime if your case results in a mistrial or if you appeal your case and your conviction is overturned.

The sentence

Generally, a judge determines your sentence, but in some states, jurors play a role. Regardless, during the sentencing process, your attorney can present evidence of mitigating factors that may help lessen your sentence. The prosecuting attorney can object to your attorney's arguments and present evidence of his or her own.

As an outgrowth of the victim's rights movement, it's also become quite common for victims to play a role in the sentencing process. They may be allowed to make statements regarding what they feel is fair punishment for your crime, and the judge may take those recommendations into consideration. If, however, your state has *mandatory sentences* (minimums or maximums) for certain crimes and you're convicted of one of those crimes, the judge's decision-making powers regarding the most appropriate sentence are limited no matter what anyone has to say.

Although mandatory sentences limit a judge's sentencing power, they ensure that criminals committing the same crime receive equal punishment.

Penalties in a criminal trial can include fines, restitution, community service, a suspended sentence, probation, jail time, and sometimes even death. The particular penalty you receive depends on whether you're a first offender, the severity and circumstances of your crime, whether or not you seem to be truly contrite, and your age, among other considerations. You may receive more than one penalty.

Fines, restitution, and community service

The judge may order you to pay a fine to the state. If the crime you're convicted of is relatively minor, your only penalty may be a fine or a fine combined with some other form of relatively light punishment such as restitution. *Restitution* is money you pay to the victim of your crime or to the victim's loved ones. For example, if you're convicted of burglary, you might be required to compensate your victim for the cost of what you stole; or if you physically injured someone, you may be ordered to pay his or her medical bills. *Community service* — volunteering with a nonprofit organization, for example — is another example of a penalty often combined with fines, restitution, and/or probation.

Suspended sentence

Rather than require you to do time in jail, the judge may decide to suspend your sentence assuming you comply with certain requirements, such as go into treatment for substance abuse. However, if you fail to meet the requirements, the judge has the right to send you to jail immediately to serve your sentence.

Probation

If your sentence is probation, you avoid jail time as long as you comply with the terms of your probation. In addition, you have to live under the supervision of a probation officer for a certain period of time. You're most likely to receive probation if you're a first-time offender and have committed a nonviolent crime. While you're on probation, you have to report to your probation officer on a regular basis so that he or she can make sure that you're meeting the conditions of your sentence. Those conditions can include such requirements as finding steady employment, performing a certain number of hours of community service, quitting drinking, supplying urine samples for drug testing, staying away from people with criminal records, or attending meetings that can help you address the root cause of your crime — Alcoholics Anonymous or Gamblers Anonymous, for example. You may also be subject to random searches and seizures if you've been convicted of a drug offense. Some states limit the circumstances under which judges can give someone probation.

Prison time

If you're convicted of a crime, you may be sentenced to prison. Your time in prison could range from a relatively short time to life in prison with no hope of parole. If you're eligible for *parole,* which means that you may be able to get out of prison before your term is up, a parole board decides whether or not you can be paroled when the time comes. The board's decision depends in part on your behavior in prison, but it can also be influenced by the severity and nature of your crime. For example, the infamous Charles Manson has been eligible for parole many times, but the parole board in California has turned him down time after time. If you're denied parole, you can go back to the parole board after a certain amount of time has passed.

The death penalty

Presently, the death penalty exists in 38 states, although 6 states have not used it since 1976 and New York State's death penalty was declared unconstitutional in the summer of 2004. Texas far exceeds all other death penalty states in the number of executions it has carried out since 1976. Each death penalty state has its own rules regarding the age that someone can be sentenced to death, what crimes qualify for death, and how executions can be carried out. Most of these states provide for lethal injection, but others permit electrocution, the gas chamber, and even hanging or a firing squad in some states. Federal death penalty laws permit capital punishment for certain federal offenses, including running a large-scale drug operation, treason, killing a government official, and kidnapping that results in death. In recent years, scrutiny and criticism of the death penalty have been renewed because the use of DNA in some states has exonerated people who were on death row.

Pardons

Pardons are rare occurrences. Usually, governors can pardon people whose cases were tried in state court, and the president can pardon federal cases. If you're granted a pardon, all of the legal consequences of your conviction are wiped out. Your punishment is set aside, and any civil rights you lost as a result of your conviction are restored.

Appeals

Although the Constitution doesn't include the right to an appeal, if you're unhappy with the outcome of your trial, you may be able to appeal to a higher court if the appeal has a legal basis. When you appeal, you ask the higher court to overturn or throw out the lower court's decision. Most appeals are based on technical error; that is, a procedure wasn't followed properly, and it affected the trial's outcome. After your attorney files your appeal and prepares a legal brief, the prosecuting attorney responds with an answering brief, and your attorney may respond with yet another brief. Sometime later, the court can make its decision regarding your appeal, and you're notified of the decision in writing.

If you're found guilty and your case is under appeal, you may be able to stay out of jail during the appeals process if the court allows you to post an appeals bond.

Your Rights as a Prisoner

Being incarcerated means you lose many of the things you normally take for granted — your right to drive a car, to take a walk in the park, to go out to dinner with your family or friends, and so on. That's why being in jail or prison is such difficult punishment for most people; however, as a prisoner, you still have legal rights. For example, you're legally entitled to be treated fairly and not be subjected to brutality or cruelty. Also, you're entitled to food, water, medical attention, and access to the legal system, including access to a law library where you can research the law and prepare motions in order to end your imprisonment.

Depending on your sentence, you may not have the right to parole. If you're eligible for parole, after serving a certain amount of your sentence, you can apply for an early but supervised release from prison. A parole board reviews your case and listens to you explain why you should be released. If your request is rejected, you have the right to know why and the right to be heard by the parole board. If you're approved for parole, you have to meet certain conditions after you're free, including regular meetings with your parole officer.

Due to prison overcrowding, some prisoners are being released early, not paroled.

If You're the Victim of a Crime

Being the victim of a crime, especially a violent crime, can be frightening and emotionally scarring. Over the years, therefore, victims' rights advocates have pressured states and the federal government to enact laws that better define and protect the rights of crime victims.

If you're a crime victim, the police must make a reasonable effort to find the person who committed the crime. If they find that person, you have the right to press charges. In some state cases and in all federal cases, you have the right to be paid for damaged or stolen items and any medical expenses you may have incurred as a result of the crime. If the person who harmed you or your property is found and convicted, the judge may make restitution or reimbursement part of the convicted person's probation. You can also file a civil lawsuit against that person for reimbursement, and in some states, you can apply for compensation from a Victim's Compensation Fund. You may also want to get in touch with a victim's organization in your state or The National Center for Victims of Crime, which offers many services to crime victims and their families. The center's Web site, www.ncvc.org, features many resources for victims, and if you call the center at 1-800-211-7996, you can get referrals to service providers in your areas that can help you rebuild your life after you've been victimized.

Many courts have assistance programs that counsel victims.

You also have the right to testify in court against the person accused of the crime, and ordinarily, you can be present throughout the criminal proceedings. At sentencing, you may even be allowed to deliver a victim's impact statement before the judge about how the crime has affected your life and what kind of punishment you would like for the criminal. Although the judge doesn't have to consider your statement, many judges do listen to victims.

It's almost always a good idea to become actively involved in the criminal process when you're the victim of a crime. At the very least, you should stay in touch with the prosecuting attorney and ask the attorney any questions you may have about the proceedings or the status of the case. Sometimes, becoming involved in the criminal process can help you work through the emotions you may be feeling as a victim.

If a suspect accused of committing a crime against you gets out of jail on bail, you have the right to be protected by the police if that person threatens you. For example, a restraining order may be issued ordering that person to stay away from you, but realistically, these measures are of limited value. Also, depending on your state, you may be notified if the person who committed a crime against you is being considered for parole, and you can participate in parole hearings. Also, about half the states let a crime victim know if the person who committed the crime has escaped from prison.

Chapter 18

Juvenile Law: The Times Are Changing

In This Chapter

▶ Understanding the rationale for a juvenile justice system

▶ Knowing how the juvenile justice system works

▶ Trying kids as adults

▶ Accepting parental responsibility

*W*hether it's from reading the daily paper, watching the local nightly news, or from personal experience, most of us are aware of the fact that children commit crimes, some of which are extremely violent. It's sad to say it, but some kids today make the "juvenile delinquents" of the 1950s look downright innocent.

Although your child will probably stay on the straight and narrow, it's in your best interest to prepare for the worst by getting educated about how juveniles who end up on the wrong side of the law are treated by the courts. This chapter helps you do that by filling you in on the juvenile justice system, including how a juvenile hearing works and what may happen if your child is found guilty. It also highlights the changing ways that our courts are treating juvenile defendants, including transferring children who commit very violent crimes into adult courts and even sending them to adult prisons.

Juveniles and the Law

The courts' treatment of juveniles who commit crimes is a matter of state law, and those laws vary considerably. However, most state laws recognize that children under a certain age, usually 10 and under, don't have the mental capacity to commit a crime. For example, at one time or another when you were still quite young, you may have taken a piece of candy without paying for it even though you knew it was wrong. But as a second or third grader, did you really think, "I'm committing a crime against the laws of the state by taking this candy?" Probably not. Most likely, you were more worried about getting "busted" by your parents! In other words, even though you may have known that stealing the candy was wrong, it's doubtful that you understood the potential legal consequences of your behavior at such a young age. However, if your very young child participates in any delinquent behavior and the judge believes that he or she is not only capable of telling right from wrong but also understands the consequences of his or her actions, then your child will probably be accused of a crime and will become part of the juvenile justice system.

In most states, a juvenile, or *minor*, is legally defined as a child under the age of 18 who still lives with or is supported by his or her parents. In maintaining a justice system just for juveniles, the courts acknowledge that most minors haven't yet developed the reasoning ability and judgment of an adult; therefore, when they get into legal trouble, juveniles shouldn't be subject to the same rules, procedures, and punishments that apply to adult offenders. Traditionally, the juvenile court system has worked quite differently from the criminal justice system, with an emphasis on rehabilitation instead of punishment. However, as this chapter makes clear, there's a general trend among states to take away many of the special protections afforded juveniles, particularly when they're repeat offenders or have committed violent crimes, and to even move certain juvenile offenders into the adult criminal justice system.

The legal term for a child charged with a crime is an *adjudicated delinquent* or an *adjudicated minor*.

If Your Child Gets Arrested

As a parent, you no doubt pray that your child will never get into legal trouble by committing a crime. Technically, most states call a crime committed by a juvenile an *act of delinquency*. If the worst happens, you need to know that your child has most of the same basic rights as any adult who is arrested. (If you're not sure how the criminal justice system works, flip back to Chapter 17.) For example, your child can't be exposed to an unreasonable search or seizure, and when arrested, your child should be read his or her Miranda rights, including the right to remain silent and to obtain a state-appointed lawyer.

Don't assume that you can do a good job of representing your child in juvenile court. Even if the crime your child is accused of is relatively minor, you should hire an attorney familiar with the juvenile justice system in your area.

For your child to be charged with a crime or act of delinquency, a prosecutor must convince the juvenile court judge that your child knew or had the ability to know that he or she was committing a crime. Obviously, your child's age and mental capacity play significant roles in making this determination. If the judge believes that your child can discern right from wrong, legal from illegal, a juvenile hearing will take place, assuming your child will not be tried in criminal court. And, like an adult charged with a crime, if your child is charged in juvenile court, he or she has the right to be released on bail until the date of the hearing.

If your child is accused of a nonviolent crime or a first offense, you won't have to post bail to get him or her released.

The Changing Road to Justice in Juvenile Hearings

Some important distinctions separate a juvenile criminal case from a regular criminal case. For example, in the juvenile justice system, the proceeding related to a child's alleged crime is called a *hearing,* not a trial (although just like trials, evidence is presented, witnesses are called, and so on), and at the end of the hearing, a judge who is specially trained to deal with juvenile matters decides the child's guilt or innocence and determines what will happen to the child assuming he or she is found guilty. A jury is never involved in a juvenile hearing.

However, many of the other traditional distinctions between juvenile and regular criminal cases are becoming blurred; one especially important changing distinction relates to confidentiality. It used to be that all juvenile hearings were closed to the public and to the media and that the names of juvenile defendants were kept confidential. Now, however, a majority of states allow most juvenile hearings to be open to the public, and even more states permit the names of juvenile defendants to be released, especially when they have committed particularly serious crimes.

It used to be that if you had a juvenile record and later were tried for a crime as an adult, your juvenile record could not be used against you. Now however, all states allow an adult defendant's juvenile record to be taken into consideration, and if the adult is found guilty, that record can be used to justify an increase in his or her length of sentence or to make the sentence more severe in some other way. A few states even allow an adult's juvenile crimes to count as the first one or two "strikes" against him or her. In other words, in these states, as a result of that juvenile record, someone can end up being sentenced to life in prison the first time he or she is convicted of a crime as an adult because that adult crime is counted as the third "strike."

Another very significant trend in how juvenile defendants are being treated is that in most states, depending on the crime your child is alleged to have committed, after an initial hearing in juvenile court, the judge may decide that your child will be tried as an adult. If that happens, the case will be transferred out of the juvenile justice system and into the criminal justice system. In some states, older juveniles and even younger ones who have committed especially serious crimes such as rape or murder go directly to an adult court. I discuss child defendants in the adult justice system in a later section in this chapter, "Harsher Treatment for Some Juveniles."

What May Happen If Your Child Is Found Guilty in Juvenile Court

Unlike the role of the judge in a regular criminal trial, the traditional task of a judge in a juvenile hearing is to decide what's in "the best interest of the child," not to punish the child. Or, at least that's the way it used to be. However, in a growing number of courts, the emphasis is increasingly on punishment. In fact, especially in urban areas, juvenile courts increasingly function much like criminal courts.

In juvenile courts where rehabilitation is still the focus, a youth may be sentenced to probation instead of having to spend time in a juvenile detention center, which is the equivalent of a juvenile prison. Other juvenile offenders may be required to get alcohol or drug treatment, to get mental health counseling, perform community service, provide restitution to his or her victim or victims, participate in a wilderness program, or they may receive a combination of punishments.

A judge is much more likely to give your child probation if you show up at the hearing and are obviously involved in your child's life. Other factors the judge will consider are the seriousness of your child's crime and whether your child has been in legal trouble before.

If your child is sentenced to probation, he or she must visit a juvenile probation officer on a regular basis. (The officer is trained to work with children.) In some ways, the role of a juvenile probation officer is much like that of a guidance counselor — helping children stay out of trouble, teaching them about acceptable behavior, and sometimes even becoming a role model for troubled juveniles.

While your child is on probation, he or she must follow certain rules such as attending school, obeying a curfew, and working a steady job if your child is old enough — the kinds of things ordinarily expected of most kids. No big deal. But if your child violates probation, he or she may end up in a juvenile detention facility. A much bigger deal!

It's also possible that the judge will send your child to a juvenile detention facility right away without putting him or her on probation first. The judge is most likely to do this if your child has been in trouble with the law before or if the judge feels that your child's offense is especially serious.

Although the age varies from state to state, generally children as young as 12 and as old as 18 can be sent to a juvenile detention facility. However, some states have begun sending even younger children there.

A Boston shoemaker began the use of juvenile probation in the early 1840s. The practice was funded by philanthropic organizations until the end of the 1890s, when the states began to hire probation officers. About this same time, the Illinois Juvenile Court Act was passed, marking the beginning of a separate juvenile justice in the United States and triggering the establishment of juvenile courts in most states over the next 25 years.

No two juvenile detention facilities are exactly alike; they vary in strictness and security. Therefore, courts try to place juveniles found guilty of crimes in the facility most appropriate to their crimes and past behaviors. If your child is a repeat or a violent offender, like the two boys from Chicago mentioned in the sidebar "Age limits changing for juvenile detention," he or she is more likely to end up in a strict, maximum-security, juvenile detention facility.

Age limits changing for juvenile detention

On January 29, 1996, two boys, ages 12 and 13, were sentenced to juvenile prisons for dropping Eric Morse, a 5-year-old boy, out of a 14th floor window at a Chicago public housing project because he refused to steal candy for them.

At the time the crime was committed, Illinois law stated that children under the age of 13 could not be sent to a juvenile prison. But the law was changed as a result of Eric's death. The 12-year-old who actually dropped Morse out the window became the youngest child in the country to

be sentenced to a maximum-security juvenile prison. Because the 13-year-old only aided in the crime, he received a lighter sentence. The new law allowed both boys to be released and legally free of their crime on their 21st birthdays.

Although many adults and juvenile justice advocates were appalled at the Illinois court's decision, since the decision other states have allowed children as young as 10 to be sent to a juvenile detention facility, although the younger children are usually kept apart from the older kids.

You can find lots of national statistics and trend information regarding all aspects of the juvenile justice system at the Web site for the U.S. Department of Justice's Office of Juvenile Justice and Delinquency Prevention, www. ojjdp.ncjrs.org.

Harsher Treatment for Some Juveniles

States have begun taking increasingly harsh approaches toward some juvenile offenders. Now, for example, nearly every state allows juveniles to be tried as adults in criminal courts when they're accused of committing heinous crimes such as murder or rape or when they have histories of criminal behavior. (In fact, some states have had laws on the books since the early 1920s permitting children to be tried as adults. However, for decades, these laws were used rarely if ever.) Often, the sentences these juveniles receive are quite harsh. For example, a few years ago in Florida, a 14-year-old boy was tried as an adult and sentenced to 28 years in prison for shooting his teacher. When they're placed in adult prisons, children are often treated just like adult prisoners and get lost in this country's overcrowded prisons.

Furthermore, at the time this book was revised, 19 states and the federal government allowed juveniles to be executed for capital crimes — crimes of murder in most instances, although in reality children are rarely put to death. More than half of these states only allow juveniles to be sentenced to death if they were 18 years old at the time of their crimes, but the remainder have set age 17 or 16 as the minimum age that a juvenile can be sentenced to death. Recently, several states legislatures have taken steps to raise this minimum.

In the past, the U.S. Supreme Court has ruled that subjecting children to capital punishment doesn't violate the Eighth Amendment, which prohibits the infliction of "cruel or unusual punishment." However, at the time this book was revised, the court was revisiting this issue by considering *Roper vs. Simmons,* a case that involves the conviction and death sentence of Christopher Simmons, a boy who committed murder when he was 17 years old.

There are three basic ways that a juvenile case can end up in criminal court, although the exact methods tend to vary from state to state:

- ✔ **Judicial waiver:** With this method, whether or not a juvenile's case is transferred to criminal court depends on the child's age and offense. Most of the time, such transfers are ordered by a juvenile court judge in response to the request of a prosecuting attorney. The defense attorney can argue why trying the child in criminal court is not appropriate, but in the end, the decision lies with the judge.

✔ **Prosecutorial discretion:** In many states prosecutors have the freedom to charge certain crimes committed by juveniles in criminal court rather than juvenile court. However, the prosecuting attorneys must show that the child understood that he or she was breaking the law when the crime was committed.

✔ **Statutory exclusion:** A growing number of states now have laws requiring juveniles who commit particular types of crimes — particular types of violent crimes — to be tried in criminal court.

When a juvenile is tried as an adult, he or she is subject to the same trial process that an adult defendant would face, including the possibility of a trial by jury. If a jury decides your child's case, they may not be particularly sensitive to the problems in your child's life that may have caused him or her to commit the crime your child is on trial for. Also, if a judge decides your child's fate, he may or may not have much experience with juvenile offenders.

If your child is found guilty, he or she may be sentenced to an adult prison, which will probably be a lot more crowded and dangerous than a juvenile facility. Also, it's unlikely that your child will get much rehabilitation there. Alternatively, your child may be sent to a juvenile detention facility until he or she turns 18, at which time your child would be transferred to an adult prison to serve out any time remaining on his or her sentence.

Since the 1980s, upwards of 200,000 children a year have been tried as adults!

Parents Beware: The Laws May Hold You Accountable!

Starting in the 1990s as a strategy for reducing juvenile crime, many states and some cities as well passed *responsibility laws.* These laws try to force parents to exert more control over their children's behavior by holding the parents at least partially liable — civilly or criminally — for their children's crimes. Some individuals and organizations believe that parental responsibility laws are unfair. After all, they argue, single-parent homes and the added stresses they create are commonplace, and even when two parents are in the home, both are usually trying to juggle the demands of full-time careers with their parental responsibilities. But proponents of these laws point to the following: Most juvenile delinquents don't receive the emotional support and nurturing they need from their parents, which puts them at risk for criminality. (Chapter 5 has more information on parents' rights and responsibilities.) For example, the two boys from Chicago who murdered Eric Morse (see the sidebar "Age limits changing for juvenile detention") had continually run away from home, slept in abandoned buildings, and failed school subjects including gym class. One boy's father was serving time in prison. Obviously, these children's lives lacked something — maybe supervision, maybe support, maybe love, and maybe all three.

Parents who are found liable for their child's criminal behavior are subject to a variety of punishments depending on the state; punishments range from fines and even imprisonment to the requirement that they pay the costs of their child's institutionalization and/or treatment, provide restitution to their child's victim or victims, or get counseling.

Punishing parents

Did you know that in some states...

✔ Parents can be fined when their children vandalize public buildings.

✔ Courts can send parents to counseling or classes when their children commit crimes.

✔ Parents can be jailed if their child skips school.

✔ Parents who are found guilty of "improper supervision" can be fined and imprisoned.

Part VI
The Part of Tens

The 5th Wave   By Rich Tennant

"I just think we need to make provisions in our Will
for disposition of our property. Who'll get Park
Place? Who'll get Boardwalk? Who'll get the thimble
and all the tiny green houses...?"

In this part . . .

This part is a staple of every *For Dummies* book. I give you a couple of top-ten lists, including easy ways to avoid legal problems and common mistakes when hiring an attorney.

Chapter 19

More Than Ten Ways to Avoid Legal Problems

. . . .

In This Chapter
▶ Being smart
▶ Keeping out of trouble

. . . .

*Y*ou can never completely avoid legal problems, but you *can* keep them to a minimum, especially if you follow the advice in this chapter.

Increase Your Legal IQ

When it comes to the law, ignorance is no excuse if you end up on the wrong side of it. So, bone up on the basic laws that affect your life; know your rights and responsibilities; and one last thing, be sure to obey the law!

You can take advantage of several low-cost and even free ways to get a legal education. You're already on your way if you're reading this book. Other ways to expand your understanding of all things legal include visiting the Web sites highlighted throughout the book, ordering free brochures from the Federal Trade Commission (FTC) on subjects of concern or interest to you, and contacting your state attorney general's office to obtain publications explaining your state's laws.

Think Before You Act

A good offense is always the best defense; therefore, before you take an important action in your business or personal life, be aware of the potential legal risks and what you can do to minimize them.

In addition to consulting the resources I mention in the previous section to help you understand potential risks and how to deal with them, you also may want to talk with an attorney. For example, if you're going into business for yourself, you can save both money and heartache, not to mention improve your chances for success, if you consult an attorney at the outset about such things as different legal structures, employment law basics, and your state and federal tax obligations as a business owner.

Although estimates vary, some studies show that as many as 85 percent of all new businesses fail within three years. Some of these businesses would no doubt have survived if their owners had sought legal advice at the start and not at the end, when it was time to file for bankruptcy.

Use Common Sense

Some people seem to attract trouble like honey attracts flies! Their proclivity for legal problems is not because they walk around with a dark cloud hovering over them or because a black cat crossed their paths. It's usually because they apply little or no common sense to the way they live their lives.

I'm sure you know at least a few people like this. They regularly exceed the speed limit and then bemoan the fact that they've lost their license. They're a sucker for every get-rich scheme they hear about and then wonder why they have no money. They do little or nothing to check out a used car before they buy it and inevitably end up with a clunker. They get involved in important business deals without written contracts and then rant and rave about being taken. And if their lives aren't complicated enough already, these people are always quick to sue, to right the so-called wrongs that have been done to them! If they spent even half as much time and energy evaluating their actions and transactions with at least a modicum of common sense and skepticism, then their legal hassles would be fewer, their lives would be happier, and I bet they'd have more money in their bank accounts, too.

Commit Important Agreements to Writing

I can't say it enough: Get all your important agreements in writing, especially those that involve money. A handshake is *not* enough, even if you're dealing with a friend or relative. If problems develop later, it's a lot easier to resolve them when your agreement is spelled out on paper than if you and whoever else is party to the agreement have to reconcile what may be dramatically different memories of what you agreed to.

Writing things down in a contract can help you think through and address many if not most of the issues and problems that may arise during the duration of your agreement. It also helps minimize the likelihood that legal problems will develop down the road and can provide mechanisms for resolving them outside of the courtroom.

Never sign anything without reading it first (yes, even the finest of fine print). If you don't understand a provision in a contract you're being asked to sign, get an explanation or have your attorney review it.

Purchase Adequate Insurance

Although having adequate insurance won't insulate you from legal problems no matter how honest and cautious you are, insurance does provide you with a financial safety net should things go wrong. Without appropriate liability insurance for your home, your business, and your car, if you're sued, you could lose everything you've worked hard to accumulate.

Keep Your Debt to a Minimum and Save Regularly

Now that long-term job security appears to be a thing of the past, if you want to avoid trouble with creditors and even bankruptcy, keep your debt to a minimum and save as much money as you can. That way, if you do lose your job or if you're forced to take a cut in pay, you'll have a shot at keeping your credit record trouble free.

In the past, staying with a single employer and working one's way up the corporate ladder was often the safest way to maximize your earnings. Now, however, it's generally accepted that you must be ready and willing to move from employer to employer, to change careers, and to accept periods of unemployment along the way, if necessary, in order to maximize your career opportunities and earning power. In such an employment environment, the less debt you have, the easier it will be for you to cope successfully with such changes in your job situation.

Use credit only when you absolutely have to, and only use it to purchase the things that you really need or that are extremely important to you, such as a home, a car, or a college education for your child.

Be Forgiving in Your Dealings with Others

Not every social or business exchange with an unsatisfactory outcome merits a lawsuit. In fact, most don't. And most things that end badly are not the result of malfeasance or deception.

Although many problems do merit legal action, before you hire an attorney, give yourself time to get over your initial anger, hurt, disappointment, or frustration about what went wrong. Talk about the situation with a dispassionate friend. You may be surprised to find how just a few days or weeks can put something in a whole new light!

Don't Argue with Law Enforcement Officials

An infraction that may have resulted in little more than a warning or a slap on the wrist can become a much more serious legal problem if you make a law enforcement officer angry. And on a more serious note, there's an old saying in the legal world that "you can beat the rap but you can't beat the ride." In other words, although the courts may find you innocent of whatever you're charged with (the rap), if you do something to anger the arresting officer during the arrest process, you may find yourself the victim of police brutality (the ride). Videotapes in recent years have provided dramatic documentation of these sorts of consequences.

Don't Thumb Your Nose at the IRS

You're asking for legal trouble if you ignore your tax obligations to the IRS. It doesn't matter whether you're an individual or a business, the IRS *will* get what's coming to it sooner or later, even if the agency has to force you or your business into bankruptcy to collect its due.

Don't Mix Flirtation with Business

If you tell off-color jokes on the job, flirt, or make sexual advances to a fellow worker, you not only risk losing your job but you can also be sued for sexual harassment. What you may view as innocent fun may be seen as offensive and disrespectful behavior to others.

Even if the person you flirt with doesn't object to your behavior at the time or laughs at your jokes, your actions may legally be viewed as sexual harassment.

Meet Your Child Support Obligations

Not meeting your legal obligations to your children not only speaks volumes about you as an individual but also is almost certain to get you in legal trouble sooner or later. Federal and state governments are very serious about tracking down deadbeat dads and moms to make them pay what they owe and have developed new and more effective means of doing so. Furthermore, private child support collection firms are even more effective at collecting past due child support because they're not encumbered by the bureaucratic red tape of government.

If you have a child with a man that you're no longer living with, most states expect the child's father to assume all the legal responsibilities of paternity, whether you were married to the man or not.

If you have failed to meet your child support obligations, depending on where you live, your state may have posted your photo as a deadbeat parent on a special Web site. Many states use these Web sites to track down parents who are seriously behind on their child support payments.

Don't Set Up Your Business as a Partnership

There ought to be a warning against partnership agreements like the one on cigarette packages. Only this warning would say *WARNING: Partnerships can be hazardous to your business.*

Based on my work as an attorney and on my own experience in two different partnerships, I've come to the conclusion that when you're involved in a partnership, you're almost always asking for legal trouble. Sure, some partnerships work well and make money for everyone involved, but most, sooner or later, become legal quagmires, even if you've got the best agreement money can buy. For example, one of you may begin feeling as though the other isn't working hard enough or is taking too much out of the business. Or you may discover that your partner lied about his or her professional abilities or resources or that your partner is stealing from the business. Even if your partnership provides you with a legal means of dealing with these and other potential problems, doing so isn't easy. When you're joined at the pocketbook (as you are in a mutually-dependent relationship like a partnership), breaking up is always hard to do.

The actions of one partner legally obligate all other partners, which means that if your partner incurs a financial obligation on behalf of the business against your wishes or without your knowledge, it's your debt as much as it is your partner's in the eyes of the law; and if your business can't make good on the debt, the creditor can try to collect directly from you or from your partner — whoever has the money.

Plan Your Estate

No, *you* won't have to deal with the repercussions that you may create for your loved ones if you don't plan your estate. But if you own property and other assets and you die without a will, or if your will isn't legally valid, then your bequest to those you leave behind may be legal and financial headaches and expenses. The greatest gift you can leave your loved ones is good estate planning.

Depending on the size of your estate and the needs of your spouse or unmarried partner and any children you have, you may need to do more estate planning than just writing a will. See Chapter 15 for details.

Chapter 20

Ten Common Mistakes Consumers Make When Hiring an Attorney

In This Chapter

▶ Doing your homework

▶ Avoiding all the wrong moves

*H*iring an attorney can be intimidating, especially if you've never used one before and your legal problem is serious. What should you expect from an attorney? How can you tell a good one from one who's not so good? Will you be able to afford the legal help you need? You may have these questions (and many others) swimming around in your head. But the best way to know what to do is to first know what *not* to do. Knowing the kinds of mistakes consumers most often make when hiring an attorney can make you an extra-confident consumer of legal help.

Not Asking an Attorney to Come Down in Price

With law schools sending about 50,000 new lawyers into the world every year and thousands of them already in practice, there's obviously no shortage of attorneys in the marketplace. In fact, when it comes to getting legal help, it's a buyer's market and not a seller's. You're the one in the driver's seat. Believe it or not, you may find that attorneys are actually eager for your business and are willing to negotiate on price to get it!

When an attorney proposes charging you on an hourly basis, suggest that he or she bill you on a flat-fee basis instead. Or if an attorney is willing to take your case on a contingency fee basis, find out if he or she will accept a lower percentage of the settlement you're awarded if you win your case. When an attorney takes your case on contingency, you don't have to pay any money up-front, and if you lose the lawsuit, the most you owe the attorney is reimbursement for his or her expenses related to your lawsuit.

If an attorney refuses to negotiate on price, don't automatically scratch him or her off your list. You may be making a penny-wise and pound-foolish decision if the attorney has unique skills or abilities that can increase the chances of resolving your legal problem in your favor.

Thinking That Lawyers Who Advertise Should Be Avoided

Some people think that attorneys who advertise should be avoided because they're desperate for business or somehow inferior. Don't be so shortsighted! Many good attorneys advertise, and some bad ones don't. Highly qualified attorneys who specialize in certain areas of the law, including consumer bankruptcy, wills, and personal injury, often use advertising to market their legal services.

Attorneys who advertise often provide their services for a lower than usual cost.

Hiring an Attorney You Don't Feel Comfortable With

Have you ever sat across from someone whose manner intimidated you? Or how about someone who seems bored with what you're saying? Have your instincts ever told you that someone isn't trustworthy? If your answer to any of these questions is "Yes," then you probably had a tough time talking honestly with that person and felt uncomfortable with him or her. Maybe you even felt a little angry that you weren't being taken seriously.

If an attorney triggers any of these feelings in you, even if the attorney comes highly recommended, follow your instincts and look elsewhere for legal help. When the legal issue you're dealing with is serious and you've got a lot at stake, you need an attorney you can trust, an attorney you can talk to, and one who listens with sympathy, not boredom. Although money-hungry attorneys who view clients as little more than contributions to their bottom lines have certainly helped give the legal profession a bad name, many lawyers are truly interested in helping others.

Steer clear of attorneys who don't give you their full attention when you're explaining your legal problem, who don't ask questions, or who spend a lot of time bragging about themselves.

Not Avoiding Attorneys Who Win by Intimidation

Attorneys who try to intimidate the other side or try to grind people down until they yell "Uncle!" rarely serve their client's best interests. More often than not, such tactics make the other side so angry that he digs in his heels and swears off compromising. Worse yet, lawyers who think they're Rambo in a suit have a habit of turning a relatively minor legal problem into a more serious, not to mention more expensive, one. Ordinarily, you want your attorney to be a problem solver, not a pit bull!

To find a problem-solving attorney, consider asking other attorneys you may know about the reputation of the attorney you're considering. Rambo attorneys usually have well-known reputations in their legal communities for playing hardball. Also, pay attention to how the attorney describes the likely progress of your case. If he or she never raises the possibility of compromise and never suggests that you think about what you'd be willing to settle for, the attorney is giving you some pretty strong clues that legal problem solving is not his or her strong suit.

If you hire an attorney and subsequently become unhappy with his or her approach to your legal problem, you can always fire that person and hire someone else.

Hiring an Attorney Because You're Angry and Want to Get Even

Using the legal system to get revenge or to assuage your hurt feelings is an awfully expensive way to deal with problems! Far better responses involve using mediation or arbitration, talking to a therapist, or simply forgetting about what got you upset in the first place. Using the courts to pursue grudges, to hurt others because you think that they hurt you, or to pursue claims for minimal actual damages is little more than a waste of your time and money and of the legal system's already overtaxed resources. Furthermore, such tactics reinforce America's image as a country full of lawsuit-crazed people. But if you insist on using the courts to make yourself feel better, I can guarantee that you'll find an attorney who will be perfectly willing to take your case — as long as you've got the money!

Not Telling Your Attorney Everything about Your Case

Attorneys *hate* to hear the phrase, "By the way, I forgot to tell you. . . ." Those words make us want to tear our hair out! Not to mention that when you fail to tell your attorney the whole story, warts and all, right from the start, you do yourself a serious disservice. The information you keep to yourself can derail your attorney's entire legal strategy. So tell the truth, the whole truth, and nothing but the truth, not only on the witness stand but in your attorney's office, too!

Information you withhold from your attorney is likely to come to light sooner or later. Your attorney may discover it in the course of working on your case, or the other side may unearth it. When the information is revealed, your attorney may not be able to do anything to minimize its negative impact, and you may even lose what would otherwise have been a winnable case.

Hiring Someone You Know to Represent You

Hiring a relative, a friend, or an attorney you're dating to represent you is a prescription for disaster, and you risk destroying the relationship by hiring someone you know. For one thing, you may find it difficult, if not impossible, to tell an attorney with whom you have a personal relationship the whole truth about your legal problem. Also, because attorneys often have to tell their clients sobering and serious things — things clients may not want to hear — you may put your attorney friend or loved one in an unfair position if you ask him or her to represent you. And if you're unhappy with something that your attorney does or doesn't do, you're likely to find it difficult to express your displeasure if that attorney's relationship with you is based on more than just business.

Keep in mind, too, that losing your case can create a rift in your family, put a damper on a wonderful friendship, and squelch a relationship that may have developed into a beautiful thing.

Not Checking Your Attorney's Courtroom Track Record

Contrary to what you may think, many attorneys rarely (if ever) step foot into a courtroom. Some are just great at negotiating solutions to legal problems and are at their best when dealing with legal problems that can be resolved in the calm and comfort of their offices — and most legal problems can be. Often, these lawyers studiously avoid cases likely to end up in the courtroom because they don't like the stress and aren't cut out for courtroom drama.

So, if you're facing a legal problem that may very well end up in court, you need someone who enjoys courtroom action and who has a successful track record trying cases like yours; otherwise, if it looks like your case may be headed for a trial, your lawyer may pressure you to settle for something that may not be in your best interest simply because he or she wants to avoid going to court.

Not Getting a Written Contract or Agreement of Representation

Doing business with an attorney is no different from doing business with anyone else. You need a written agreement. It should spell out in specific terms the services that the lawyer will provide you and all financial arrangements, and it should also state what will happen if you or your lawyer want to get out of the agreement.

Not Making Certain That Your Attorney Doesn't Have a Conflict of Interest

Always avoid working with an attorney who has represented the individual, business, or organization that you're having a legal problem with; otherwise, given your attorney's past relationship with the defendant in your case, you may find yourself in the uncomfortable position of wondering whether or not your attorney is really trying to settle your problem in a manner that represents your best interests.

Although it's the duty of an attorney to check for potential conflict of interest, an attorney who really wants your business may rationalize away such a conflict; therefore, be sure to do your research and bring up the issue at your initial meeting and certainly before you sign an agreement of representation.

Not Interviewing More Than One Attorney

As the saying goes, "There's more than one way to skin a cat," and the same holds true for resolving legal problems. You may be surprised by the number of different approaches to the same legal issue you'll hear when you talk to more than one attorney, not to mention the differences in their costs! So, shop around to find an attorney who's willing to work with you on price and whose approach to your problem makes you feel the most comfortable.

Index

• G •

• H •